CW00515209

The
Degeneracy Crisis
and
Victorian Youth

The
Degeneracy Crisis
and
Victorian Youth

THOMAS E. JORDAN

State University of New York Press

Published by
State University of New York Press, Albany

© 1993 State University of New York

For information, address State University of New York Press,
State University Plaza, Albany, N.Y., 12246

Production by Marilyn P. Semerad
Marketing by Dana E. Yanulavich

Library of Congress Cataloging-in-Publication Data

Jordan, Thomas E.
    The degeneracy crisis and Victorian youth / Thomas E. Jordan.
        p.   cm.   .
    Includes bibliographical references and index.
    ISBN 0-7914-1245-8. — ISBN 0-7914-1246-6 (pbk.)
    1. Children—Great Britain—Social conditions. 2. Children—
-Health and hygiene—Great Britain. 3. Great Britain—Social
conditions—19th century. 4. Stress in children—Great Britain.
I. Title.
HQ792.G7J665   1992
305.23'0942—dc20   91-39941
                                                            CIP

10 9 8 7 6 5 4 3 2 1

Contents

Chapter One. The Degeneracy Question

Chapter Two. Towns, Housing, and Work

Chapter Three. Circumstances of Life

Chapter Four. Height and Body Mass of Children

Chapter Five. Mars and Hygeia

Chapter Six. Social-Economic Circumstances and Height

Chapter Seven. Public Policy and Reform

Chapter Eight. Discussion

List of Illustrations

List of Tables

Preface

$\mathcal{S}$ tudy of *stress* in the lives of children takes several forms. There is the impact of health-centered vectors such as mental retardation (Jordan, 1976), communicable diseases such as the nearly forgotten poliomyelitis, and the all-too-frequent tragedy of abuse within the family. These and similar instances are generally approached within a contemporary, brief span of time. We look to instances in current or recent experience for data and derive our observations. Occasionally, large spans of time, in decades, are engaged and, as in the work of Werner and colleagues (Werner, Bierman and French, 1971; Werner and Smith, 1971; and Jordan, 1980) we learn about stress-bound children and the positive and negative outcomes of their lives (Werner and Bierman, 1982).

A more ambitious if less manageable approach is to extend the span of decades. The most obvious form is to draw on longitudinal archives and to take data from the probands. A drawback is that the questions which structured the original data taking may not lend themselves to the current inquiry. Further, the idiosyncrasies of data sets may not be extant, having been interred with the departure of those who grasp the strengths and weaknesses of the original and accrued data. Even so, such inquiry, as in Elder's (1974) study of Depression children, can be informative.

In this study, the diachronic examination of stress required an independent, or predictor, variable diffused over a long period of time. Stress is broadened as a vector of influence to be an index of society enduring a profound change. Pandemics express the breadth

xi

and intensity of radical change, for example, the Black Death, but defy micro analysis. War is equally acute and has been the subject of many inquiries. But war and disease come and go, and two world wars seem to have wrought little permanent change on the evolution on some aspects of society (Gillingham, 1985). Economic forces are not teleological, but their effects are far reaching. For that reason, I have chosen to include economic change as a source of stress in children's lives.

The Victorian age continues to be appealing to the curious. Ending the sequence of Georges the period runs to the age of dreadnought battleships and the beginnings of the welfare state. It suggests, as Walvin (1987) has demonstrated, a set of values thought to be relics of a golden age whose certainty, if not validity, is an object of longing in some quarters. On close inspection, the traits of the Victorian era were the values of some people, but not of others. The range of Victorians was broad, and only the privileged minority espoused the values we think of as Victorian and propagated in their day around the world by Dr. Samuel Smiles. In fact, most people were not Victorian in their values, in the sense that most were poor and aspired to, if not actually reached, the Smilesian virtues of Thrift, Ambition, and Longanimity. Being poor, though less desperately so as the century progressed, their horizons were payday and sickness, leavened with the promise of the Nonconformist churches. Thus, there were several Victorian societies, in the sense that the range of wealth separating rich and poor, the "standard of comfort" as the commentators of the Social Science Association phrased it, was very broad. Today, Britons are rarely as wealthy or as poor, comparatively speaking, as their Victorian ancestors. The origins of that comparative leveling within a higher standard of living lay in the radical changes wrought in people's lives by a tumultuous century.

Social discontinuity is a useful construct for understanding how major changes affect parts of society at different rates and produce social change in some but not all segments of society. For the last two centuries the complex of processes called the *Industrial Revolution* has been the major influence on Western society and, subsequently, on the entire world. Ideologically, it set the stage for the major intellectual movement of the twentieth century, Marxism.

A major social discontinuity in the nineteenth century was change precipitated by the rise of factories and factory towns. There, the rise of industrialism created places—one hesitates to call them communities—in which some people became rich and the rest remained poor. For the latter, the majority, life began as a crisis of survival in infancy, and the lucky ones led brief lives always at risk for fatal diseases and factory accidents. In the aggregate, it was the working class, the ordinary people dwelling for the most part in British factory towns, on whom the Industrial Revolution left its deepest scars. Polluted rivers run clean in our lifetime, and civic buildings of pale limestone have recovered a beauty unglimpsed by a century of workers hurrying to and fro, attuned to the whistle "at t'mill." For the population, a similar cleansing or rejuvenation was much slower to come; social class differences in heights can still be discerned in the child population of Great Britain, as in many countries. The scourge of communicable diseases such as cholera and tuberculosis is gone, and most of the back-to-back houses which deterred circulation of fresh air have disappeared. However, the return of health to the population was not automatic.

This work addresses the early phase of the phenomenon, looking at the state of health, and habitus, of the British population in the period roughly from Trafalgar to the Great War. In so doing, it extends the consideration of stress in the lives of children set forth in *Victorian Childhood* (Jordan, 1987). Such consideration requires a broad span of time, and longitudinal studies such as the British birth cohorts of 1946, 1958, and 1970, the New Zealand studies of Silva, and the St. Louis Baby Study (Jordan, 1991) can take us only so far. This study takes an extended period of time, approximately a century, and examines stress due to health and work and social circumstances. It focuses on the young and examines height as an empirical variable in their growth. This work is set in a historical period and, like *Victorian Childhood*, is not intended primarily as a work in the history of childhood, but in the ecology of child development across a period of social change. The two works are connected since this second volume focuses on a problem raised in the first.

Chapter One presents an overview of the nineteenth century noting the changes in population, urbanization, the reform movement, and the rise of Darwinism. In Chapter Two we consider the social circumstances within which human development took place. Growth does not occur in a vacuum and may be distorted and even arrested when living conditions are poor (Bielicki and Charzewski, 1982; Tanner, 1986). For nineteenth and early twentieth century British society the growth of towns and correlated problems of living were a major challenge. The overall impression of a society growing richer merits closer examination to see if all participated in the enormous accretion of wealth started by the Industrial Revolution and nurtured by the

Long Peace. In Chapter Three we address the circumstances of health considering genetics, nutrition, health, mortality, and climate.

Chapters Four, Five, and Six introduce data from the corpus of studies of height in the period 1805 to 1914. There, I address empirically the nature of growth in Victorian children and young adults. Chapter Four presents height data for both genders and two social classes across the nineteenth century. Chapter Five deals mostly with the height and health of young males conveyed in army records. Chapter Six introduces the Victorian economy as the major topic, using height data as the dependent measure for descriptive and multivariate analysis. Chapter Seven discusses the degeneracy question as a topic in evolving public policy. Chapter Eight discusses the problems of Victorian data and evaluates the merits of the degeneracy question.

For information about the illustrations used in this work, which are by John Leech (1817–1864) readers are referred to my essay, "Children of the Mobility: A Street-Level View of Early Victorian Childhood." *Journal of the Royal Society of Health.* 1992, *112,* 25–30.

I wish to express my thanks to Mary Ellen Heckel for typing the manuscript with her usual skill, to Michael Nitzsche and Amanda Taylor of the Bush Center for Policy Research; Karen Hopkins reproduced the figures.

For assistance with the text I wish to express my thanks to Eugene Meehan, K. Peter Etzkorn, Sidney Rosenbaum, and to several anonymous readers.

Acknowledgments

I express my thanks to the following for permission to quote materials:

Nutrition Abstracts and Reviews. (1957) Boyne, A. W. Aitken, F. C. Leitch, C. Secular Change in height and weight of British children, Including and Analysis of Measurements of English Children in Primary Schools: 1911–1953. *27,* 1–18.

Journal of the Royal Society of Health. (1988) Jordan, T. E. and Silva, P. A. Height and Weight Comparison of Children in New Zealand and America. *108,* 166–172.

Routledge, Ltd. Neale, R. S. (1972) *Class and Ideology in the Nineteenth Century.*

Historical Methods. (1983) *16,* 1, 1–7. Reprinted with permission of the Helen Dwight Reid Educational Foundation. Published by Heldref Publications, 1319 18th Street, N.W. Washington, D.C. 200 36–1802. Copyright 1983.

The Lancet (1880) Granville, J. M. A Note on Intention in the Determination of Sex, and the Mental and Physical Inheritance of Children. *2,* 524–536.

Bobbs Merrill Publishers (1964). Bolitho, H. *Albert, Prince Consort.*

The Royal Statistical Society. Journal of the Royal Statistical Society (1841). Comparative Statement of the Income and Expenditure of Certain Families of the Working classes in Manchester and Dukinfield, in the years 1836 and 1841. 4:320–324.

Pergamon Press. Reprinted with permission from the *Journal of Clinical Epidemiology.* *31,* Killeen, J., Vandenberg, Harlan, W. R.

Application of Weight-Height Ratios and Body Indexes to Juvenile Populations–the National Health Examination Survey Data. Copyright 1978. Pergamon Press, Plc.

The Royal Meteorological Society. Lewis, L. F. (1949). Secular Trend of Temperature at Oxford. *Quarterly Journal of the Royal Meteorological Society.* 68, 61–62.

Leeds University. Beresford, M. W. Jones, G. J. R. (1971). *Leeds and its Region.*

Paediatric and Perinatal Epidemiology. Campbell, M. J., Rodrigues, C., MarFarlane, A. J. and Murphy, M. F. G. (1991) Sudden Infant Deaths and Cold Weather: Was the Rise in Infant Mortality in 1986 in England and Wales Due to the Weather?

Longman Group UK. Cook, C. and Stevenson, J., (1983) *The Longman Handbook of Modern British History. 1714–1980.*

State University of New York Press. Jordan, T. E. (1982). *Victorian Childhood: Themes and Variations.*

Population Studies (U.K.) Logan, W. P. (1956). Mortality in England and Wales from 1848 to 1947. 4:132–178.

Journal of Historical Geography. Ward, D. (1980) Environs and Neighbours in the "Two Nations": Residential Differentiation in Mid-Nineteenth Century Leeds." 6:133–162.

History Today. Floud, R. (1983). Tall Story: The Standard of Living Debate. 33:36–40.

Croom Helm, Ltd. Skelly, A. R. (1977) *The Victorian Army at Home: The Recruitment and Terms of Conditions of the British Regulars 1855–1899.*

Rostow, W. W. (1948). *British Economy in Nineteenth Century.* By permission of Oxford University Press.

Methuen, Ltd. Silver, H. (1977). *The Concept of Popular Education.*

Constable, Ltd. Slater, G. (1930). *Poverty and the State.*

Robert Woods and P. R. Andrew Hinde, "Mortality in Victorian England: Models and Patterns, reprinted from *The Journal of Interdisciplinary History,* XVIII (1987), 40, with the permission of the editors of *The Journal of Interdisciplinary History* and the MIT Press, Cambridge, Massachusetts. C 1987 by the Massachusetts Institute of Technology and the editors of *The Journal of Interdisciplinary History.*

Also, I wish to express my thanks to:

Basil Blackwell, Publishers, for permission to quote from Fussell, G. E. (1929). The change in Farm Labourer's Diets During Two Centuries. *Economic History.* 1:268–274; McKeown, T. (1979). *The Rule of Medicine: Dreams, Mirage or Nemesis?* Hoppitt, J. (1970). Counting the Industrial Revolution. 43:173–195; Hammond, B. (1928). Urban Deaths in the Early Nineteenth Century. *Economic History.* 1:419–428.

To Octopus Publishing Group Library and Lord Asa Briggs for permission to quote from Briggs, A. (1968) *Victorian Cities.*

To Cambridge Press, for permission to quote from Armstrong, A. (1974) *Stability and Change in an English Country Town;* Floud, R., Wachter, K., Gregory, A. (1990) *Height, Health and History: The Nutritional Status of the British, 1750–1980;* Mitchell, B. (1967) *Abstract of British Historical Statistics.*

The Degeneracy Question

Circumstances of Life

*I*n the period after Waterloo the major characteristic of British society was the stress of the transition from a wartime economy to one of peace. A depression took place and with it came social tensions leading to the Six Acts of 1819, designed to suppress disorder without attending to the underlying causes. At the time, the causes were ill grasped, and solutions were less evident in an era of laissez-faire economics and minuscule government. The hero of the age was the Duke of Wellington and the villain was the Corn Law, which kept out cheap, imported grain.

Although it is true that there was a substantial degree of unrest it is clear that upheavals on the scale of the French experience in 1789 were improbable. However, there were calls for reform of government and extension of the vote. Such steps came slowly, starting with the Benthamite agenda of describing by numbers the scope of problems; the first example was the examination of the Poor Laws and their amendment in 1834 by a quite different philosophy, which emphasized low costs and moral entitlement to public relief, although at the price of immurement and derogation. This stream of thought ran for several decades and set precedents for the welfare state of the mid-twentieth century.

Politically, stability was the rule, and Princess Victoria began her long reign in 1837. A series of prime ministers served her well across the decades to 1901. In the House of Commons and within the

1

Whitehall bureaucracy it was slowly becoming apparent that the population as a whole was as much the victim as the beneficiary of the factory system. By the 1840s reform was in the air, and a series of acts led to reduced hours for child and adult workers; for example, Fielden's Ten Hours Act (1847). Such reform came none too soon because long hours and dangerous conditions made factory work stressful. There emerged in the period a series of reform-minded bureaucrats and factory commissioners and inspectors. In concert with like-minded physicians the "condition of England" was examined in detail. However, reform came slowly because the privileged yielded control slowly. However, galvanized by the oratory of, for example, Lord Shaftesbury, hearts and minds softened toward the working class and also toward those of the poor who seemed deserving—as opposed to the disorganized, nasty, and so undeserving. Equally slow to evolve was public education, due to conservatism and squabbling between Anglicans and Nonconformists.

In the last half of the century, Britain's internal evolution into the workshop of the world reached its zenith. With wealth came relaxation of social tensions and enjoyment of the Long Peace begun at Waterloo. There were military escapades in the Crimea and later in Africa, followed by quiet until the fiasco of the Boer War, which demonstrated the poor health of the nation's young men. Ireland came close to Home Rule, but did not quite achieve it. Two other countries, Germany and the United States, evolved into successful industrial competitors, while Canada and Australia became targets for placing a surplus population.

In the same period, the public philosophy continued to accept more responsibility for children and the poor. By 1880, public discourse had reached a level of debate fairly recognizable to present-day thinkers; for example, immorality and disorganization were construed as consequences of poverty, rather than its cause. Journalists and orators saw that alcoholism, disease, and bad housing were all heads of the same hydra. Acts bringing government into peoples' lives were passed; for example, education and housing bills. There were a few advances in medicine, such as anaesthesia and antisepsis, but therapy remained palliative for most conditions. Hospitals grew in number, and health generally improved as a consequence of the rising standard of living. Oddy (1982) noted that the late Victorian concept of health consisted of the absence of ill-health; in the 1880s emerged the idea of good health as a normal state, with a decline in the romantic notion of suffering associated with infection by the tuberculosis bacillus.

With the advent of the Edwardian era, social philosophy became more obviously German, and Lloyd George put a social net under the elderly and unemployed. Ameliorism rather than revolution distinguished public philosophy even when Fabian and capitalist collided. Although not a golden age, the years immediately before Sarajevo were not without enviable aspects. Respectability (Thompson, 1988) replaced survival as the leitmotif. Reform was in the air benefitting young and old, although the motives ranged from altruism to imperialism. However, fiscal conservatism prevailed, as the twentieth century opened. The Speech from the Throne in 1900 set forth on behalf of the government the axiom that, "the time is not propitious for any domestic reforms which involve large expenditures" (Masterman, 1901).

The nineteenth century had opened with the British nation engaging two elements of social change. The first was the war with the French in a period of struggle which saw maritime supremacy at Trafalgar in 1805 yield to the ferocity of the Peninsular War. The second was the maturing stage of incorporating the urban population into the emerging factory economy. The social change set afoot sent agricultural workers migrating to nearby factories and, in the case of the Clark family, migrating from Norfolk to Leeds concluding that, on the whole, they were much better off (Springall, 1936). Also migrating, but involuntarily, were orphans "apprenticed" to small manufacturers in the industrial cities of the Midlands and the North, but constituting so much cheap labor (Emmison, 1944). At the mill operated by the enlightened Belfast family, the Gregs, at Styal in Cheshire, the cost of maintaining apprentices was carefully recorded. Costs per week per apprentice were as follows: 1822 = 5 shillings; 1830 = 5 shillings and a halfpenny; 1835 = 4s. 2d; 1840 = 4 s. 5d; 1846 = 9s. 2d; and 1847 (when the last apprenticeship ended) = 13s. 4d. Clearly, it was the 1840s, the Hungry Forties, when the cost of maintaining apprentices soared. In London, according to *The Times* of January 9, 1847, a Mr. Drouet was paid by the Board of Guardians of St. Luke's, Chelsea, to board orphans at a fee. He put some of the boys out to work at five shillings profit per boy per week. Also subject to change were the handloom weavers of various fabrics. Woolens, cottons, and linens were woven in the North, and Spitalfields had its exile Hugenot community of silk weavers. They are noteworthy because there are contemporary references to them as a group reduced in stature since former times and frequently the object of popular philanthropy (Reports from the Assistant Hand-Loom Weavers' Commissioners, 1839).

TABLE 1.1 POPULATION GROWTH IN SCOTLAND, ENGLAND AND WALES, 1801–1911[1]

Year	Scotland Population in Millions	England & Wales Population in Millions	Persons/ Sq. Miles U.K.	Percent of Population Urban	Percent of Population Rural	Percent of London Increase	Percent of[2] Manchester Increase
1801		8.89					
1811		10.16					
1821	2.09	12.00	173			10	20
1831	2.36	13.89	199			21	35
1841	2.62	15.91	221			20	41
1851	2.88	17.92	227	50.20	49.80	18	29
1861	3.06	20.06	240	54.60	45.40	21	30
1871	3.36	22.71	261	61.80	38.20	19	18
1881	3.73	25.97	289	67.90	32.10	16	16
1891	4.02	29.00	313	72.00	28.00	17	22
1901	4.47	32.52	343	77.00	23.00		
1911	4.76	36.07	375	78.10	21.90		

[1] Aggregated from tables in, *Census of England and Wales 1911* (1917)
[2] Baker (1882)

For Great Britain as a whole, the stresses experienced by the population were enormous. The population of England and Wales in 1801 was 8.89 million and it increased four-fold in the course of the century, reaching 36.07 million in 1901; see Table 1.1. The acreage of an island does not alter however great the intensity of social change. The density of population rose from 173 persons per square mile in ninety years. It had doubled by the turn of the century, 1901, and then rose once more from 343 persons to the end of our period, approximately, in the census year of 1911. From the rural context of "Sweet Auburn" framed by Oliver Goldsmith the population balance shifted to the "Dark Satanic Mills" of William Blake. At mid-century, the period sometimes known as High Victorian, the population was almost in balance at 50.20 percent urban and 49.80 rural. By 1881 the ratio was 2:1 urban to rural, and by 1910 four out of every five Britons (78.10 percent) were city dwellers. According to Williamson's (1990) analysis of census data for major cities in the decade beginning in 1841 just over one-half of the growth in population was due to immigration from the country; natural increase accounted for the remainder. In the two decades beginning in 1851 the proportion of the increases in population created by country folk was much smaller, and occurred within smaller overall rates of growth in population. For major northern cities population increases in the three decades beginning in 1841 were 2.44, 1.75, and 1.62 percent. For major cities in the south of England, comparable figures were 1.92, 1.73, and 1.45 percent. By age, the peak for young adults becoming a major segment of town populations was in the period 1821–1841. Radical shifts in a population previously undisturbed, demographically speaking, since the Norman Conquest wrought devastation on the health and welfare of the population.

The Degeneracy Problem

Pick (1989) has pointed out that the term *degeneration* pervaded the lexicon of British and continental thought, arising in conjunction with social problems such as crime and mental health; in France and Italy it acquired the trappings of intellectualism with prime movers such as Benedict Morel and Cesare Lombroso. In contrast, British usage was less conceptually broad, although the term was applied at a practical level to a variety of problems. In this work, the term is pursued in the context of biosocial problems, especially those involving the young.

In 1875 F. Ferguson had been "certifying surgeon" for the factory children of Bolton in Lancashire for fourteen years. He was empowered to authorize thirteen-year-old boys and girls to work in factories and mills when they presented "ordinary strength and appearance." Dr. Ferguson reported that, "for nine years I have closely observed, and am certain that each year the proportion of physically feeble children presented to me has gone on increasing. . . . I am constantly meeting with young persons, aged from fifteen to nineteen years, of not more than the average weight of a healthy factory child of thirteen" (1987, p. 211).

The dismay recorded by Dr. Ferguson was an echo in a provincial factory town of a theme that had dismayed thoughtful observers throughout Britain for a number of years. Floud and Wachter (1982) analyzed the height records of Marine Society Boys in the period 1770–1870. They concluded that those London street children who were thirteen years old in the years 1753–1780 averaged 51.4 inches (130.55 cm.) in height, 10 inches below the height of thirteen-year-old London boys in the 1960s. That height is also approximately that of today's eight-year-old boy (see Table 1.2). In 1835, an Edinburgh physician, J. Harrison, had cautioned that a child had to be 47 inches tall (119.38 cm.) to be judged at a twelve-year-level of maturity, and 48 inches tall (121.92 cm.) to be judged at least thirteen years old, and so eligible for factory work. These minimum heights describe average six and a half and seven year olds today (see Table 1.2). In 1870, the great anthropologist, John Beddoe reported a mean height of 64.90 inches (164.85 cm.) for thirty Bristol shoemakers. He ended his treatise by concluding that "the facts are best explained by the theory of a hereditary and progressive physical degeneration in certain classes of the inhabitants of towns." The concern about shrunken bodies would reach a crescendo of alarm when the Boer War, at the end of the century, documented the poor physical condition of young volunteers. By that time, the problem had several aspects ranging from high infant mortality to poor teeth (Pickering, 1901) and represented the cumulative stress of urbanization and the factory system on the population in their years of growth and development. The process was complex and consisted of several historical processes occurring simultaneously, frequently interacting, and usually operating at different velocities. In this chapter we examine the events of the nineteenth century which created the "degeneracy crisis," a problem not fully addressed until the twentieth century.

With the opening of the nineteenth century thoughtful men had achieved the insight that the developing centers of population were

TABLE 1.2   MEDIAN (P_{50}) VALUES OF HEIGHT AND WEIGHT IN THREE POPULATIONS[1]

	Weight (kg.)						Age	Height (mm.)					
	Boys			Girls				Boys			Girls		
	Holland	United States	New Zealand	Holland	United States	New Zealand		Holland	United States	New Zealand	Holland	United States	New Zealand
Birth	3.5	3.5	3.4	3.4	3.2	3.4	Birth	518	533	524	518	490	516
	15.6	14.8	15.0	14.9	13.5	14.5	Three Years[2]	975	973	952	965	914	944
							Four Years[2]		1044				
	20.9	18.9	18.6	18.9	18.0	18.3	Five Years	1114	1115	1085	1109	1053	1080
							Six Years[2]		1173				
	25.6	22.7	23.2	23.2	22.2	22.9	Seven Years	1238	1231	1215	1233	1232	1207
							Eight Years[2]		1288				
	31.5	29.3	28.4	28.5	29.2	28.2	Nine Years	1348	1346	1330	1342	1298	1317

[1]Jordan and Silva (1988)
[2]Interpolated
(Late twentieth century)

places "where wealth accumulates and men decay." The elder Robert ("Parsley") Peel addressed the House of Commons on the problem in support of the 1802 bill to protect the health and welfare of apprentices. Child workers were already showing the effects of industrialization which placed long and heavy strains on them. Mortality among the young was high, as much as one child in two dying between birth and age five, and those who made the transition from child to adult were frequently in poor health. Specific occupations had particular risks; for example, cutlers in Sheffield developed lung diseases, and young Irish workers in Bradford woolen mills died at an appalling rate when engaged in the early, rough stages of manufacture in which dust filled the air.

To thoughtful observers it was clear, by the 1830s, that there were two Englands. In that regard we cite a work of considerable interest from that decade. Peter Gaskell of Manchester wrote *The Manufacturing Population of England*, published in 1833, one year after Dr. James P. Kay's (-Shuttleworth) book *The Moral and Physical Condition of the Working Class Employed in the Cotton Manufacture in Manchester* (1832) was published. What is distinctive about Gaskell's work is the lack of reticence in discussing morality and sexuality. Equally candid is his description of the habitus, the general appearance of workers (pp. 161–162).

> Any man who has stood at twelve o'clock at the single narrow door-way, which serves as the place of exit for the hands employed in the great cotton-mills, must acknowledge, that an uglier set of men and women, of boys and girls, taken them in the mass, it would be impossible to congregate in a smaller compass. Their complexion is sallow and pallid— with a peculiar flatness of feature, caused by the want of a proper quantity of adipose substance to cushion out the cheeks.[1] Their stature low -the average height of four hundred men, measured at different times, and different places, being five feet six inches. Their limbs slender, and playing badly and ungracefully. A very general bowing of the legs. Great numbers of girls and women walking lamely or awkwardly, with raised chests and spinal flexures. Nearly all have flat feet . .

In 1845, Benjamin Disraeli, wrote his novel *Sybil*, in which he expressed in fictional form the tensions of life experienced by

---

[1]In 1859, the American Frederick L. Olmsted recorded the same observation in Liverpool, as did a second American twenty years later (Beard, 1879).

working-class people. In that quite bad novel Disraeli appears to have drawn on Edwin Chadwick's great report of 1842, "Report on the Sanitary Condition of the Labouring Population of Great Britain." Relevant to the degeneracy question is Chadwick's evaluation of a condition, "which causes the children to grow up an enfeebled and diminutive race of men." This is an interesting expression for several reasons. It addresses children, but notes that the health of children determines the health of the next generation of adults. The scope is evident in his reference to the race of men, and *diminutive* acknowledges that heights appeared to be dropping. Of course, the sentence quoted is a generalization; we know that rural workers who lived in areas such as Cumberland, Westmoreland, and in Scotland where oatmeal was a part of the diet remained strong. Indeed, Beddoe (1870) reported that the average Scottish farmer in the county of Berwickshire stood 71.3 inches (181.10 cm.) and weighed nearly 200 lbs (90.91 kg.).

In the 1839 report to Parliament is a commentary on the silk weavers of Spitalfields. It should be noted that handloom weaving was perhaps the best instance of an occupation threatened at all times by competition from people laid-off from other occupations. The "out of collar" carpenter could always rent a loom and use his children as helpers. When the temporary but repeated threat of intrusion from other occupations passed, it was replaced by the irreversible trend to machine-powered weaving. Under the circumstances, weavers became marginally competitive at best. Dr. Mitchell reported on the health of weavers in Spitalfields and Bethnal Green that, "the whole race of them is rapidly descending to the size of Liliputians"; he took those words from a Mr. Redfern, himself a weaver, noting that, "you could not raise a grenadier company amongst them all." Thirty years later, Beddoe (1870) reported the Bronte's fellow townsmen, the worsted weavers of Haworth, as "stunted." He thought facts "*proved* that the stature of man in the large towns of Britain is lowered considerably below the standard of the nation, and as *probable* that such degradation is hereditary and progressive." Beddoe was always impressed by the stature of the people of Galloway (Beddoe, 1870; 1911); he is probably the un-named person quoted by Beard (1879) as the author of the view that only Highland immigration provided the cities with replenishment without which, "there would be constant degeneracy." Scotland was not spared industrialization in the lowlands, but Robert Owen's mill at New Lanark near Glasgow showed that profits and health were not always incompatible. The matter of stature in Scotland had arisen many years before when Sir John Gordon introduced tall men into the

Parish of Ordiquhill to marry local girls in order to raise the stature of the population (Plackett, 1986). It did not work, and today, we use Galton's (1886) concept of "regression towards the mediocre" to explain the matter.

In Chadwick's (1842) report is the formulation of a problem which would get worse. The enfeebled people Chadwick cited had a high rate of sickness, drank excessively, and suffered the ravages of "phthisis" or tuberculosis. In our day, cancer is probably the closest we come to the pervasive threat of a fatal disease not yet understood; in contrast to cancer, syphilis, and tuberculosis turned out to be both preventable and curable in the twentieth century. As the decades passed, the statistics of enfeeblement piled up and the scope of the health problem evolved beyond challenge for urban populations. Tuberculosis appeared to run in families, a concept paralleled to a degree by our recent formulations of alcohol dependence as a genetically linked susceptibility. Since syphilis and tuberculosis were transmitted, and small adults were having small children, thoughtful people worried that a process had begun which was irreversible (Lomax, 1979). Chadwick, in the Health of Towns report (1844), addressed children. In a passage on the effects of bad drains on health he wrote of children who "have the appearance of persons not having half sufficient food—they are exceedingly pale." Many of them probably had rickets, a condition the French called *the English disease*. Addressing the National Association for the Promotion of Social Science. Henry Rumsey (1871) cited the *Pall Mall Gazette*'s report that, "Broad chests and powerful limbs are no longer the rule among labourers and artizans." Perhaps the nadir of pessimism was expressed in *Macmillan's Magazine* in 1862 with an essay reporting, "the weak state of health into which, in this age, all classes seem to be sinking" ("The History of a Hospital," 1862). The condition of pottery workers in Staffordshire, was cited by Karl Marx in *Capital*. From the third medical report of the Privy Council he quoted the words of Dr. J. T. Arlidge:

> The Potters as a class, both men and women, represent a degenerated population, both physically and morally. They are, as a rule, stunted in growth, ill-shaped, and frequently ill-formed in the chest; they become prematurely old, and are certainly short-lived . . . of all diseases they are especially prone to chest disease, to pneumonia, pthisis, bronchitis, and asthma.

In 1842, S. S. Scriven had reported the condition of boy pottery workers. Table 1.3 is extracted from data in his report to the Children's

TABLE 1.3 INFORMATION ABSTRACTED FROM SCRIVEN (REPORT, 1842) ON THE CONDITION OF BOY POTTERY WORKERS, WITH TWENTIETH CENTURY NORMS

Name	Age in Years	Height in Cm.	1966[1] Normative Height	Discrepancy	Physical Condition	Can Read	Can Write	Job	Years Worked
Samuel Lovatt	11.25	129.54	141.9	12.36	"Below par"	No	No	Mould-Runner	2.9
Wm. Pickerill	12.83	129.54	153.4	23.86	"Below par"	No	No	Mould-Runner	6.0
Emmanuel Tatler	11.16	135.89	141.9	6.08	"At par"	No	No	Jigger-Turner	2.5
Wm. Bradshaw	10.58	117.47	141.9	24.43	"At par"	No	No	Jigger-Turner	2.0
Henry Emery	12.66	130.17	153.4	23.32	"At par"	Yes	Yes	Mould-Runner	4.5
Richard Burnett	9.66	123.36	136.8	13.44	"Below par"	Yes	Yes	Mould-Runner	1.8

[1]Tanner, Whitehouse and Takaishi (1966)

Employment Commission. Additional information in the table is the mid-twentieth century norm (P_{50}) for British boys gathered by Tanner, Whitehouse, and Takaishi (1966). From those heights I have calculated how far below the 1966 averages were six boy pottery workers in 1842. The height discrepancies in Table 1.3 are in centimeters; expressed in inches they are from top to bottom, 4.86, 9.39, 2.39, 9.61, 9.18, and 5.29 inches. For three of the six boys, health is described as "Below Par," compounding low stature with poor health; also four were illiterate and innumerate. In the case of the six boys reported in Table 1.3, most had worked about two years, after starting at about nine years of age. However, William Pickarell and Henry Emery, who were the smallest, had started working in the pottery at six and eight years of age. Both were mould runners in 1842, a job constantly drawing on their strength.

Balance requires that we note that not every child was subjected to the stress of premature and excessive work. Nardinelli (1980) observed that the trend to replace child workers had begun earlier than is generally appreciated. He used the factory act of 1835 as a benchmark for a serious decline. On the other hand, part-time work in the pre-adolescent years was a fact into the twentieth century.

The state of health of the urban population apparently grew steadily worse. It appeared that urban life itself constituted a disease; in 1885, Dr. Cantlie lectured at the Parker Museum of Hygiene and introduced the term *urbomorbus* to describe the condition. The mechanism leading to ill health "is the presence of non-ozonized air, air that has been pre-breathed." To that Cantlie added the observation that few Londoners had London-bred grandparents, noting that twenty-seven of the last thirty lord mayors had been born in the country. To the notion that cities bred unhealthy people was added the worse possibility of no people at all, in his view; the race of city dwellers was losing the capability to reproduce themselves in a few generations. Cantlie marshalled his clinical observations beginning with

> the man with the Somersetshire grandfather, but whose folks had lived in London, commencing from the grand-parents. Height 5 feet 1 inch; age 21; chest measurement 28 inches. His head measure around above the eyebrows is 19 inches (nearly 3 inches below the average); measured across from tip of ear to tip of ear, 11 inches (1½ below the average). His aspect is pale waxy; he is very narrow between the eyes, and with a decided squint. Solemnity intense.

> I shall now describe the man with the Irish grandmother, but the others of whose predecessors have lived rigidly in London from the grand-parents downwards. Height 5 feet 3 inches. Age 19. Chest measurements 29 inches. His head measures 20 inches round (2 inches below the average). His face is mottled, pale, and pimpled. He squints rather badly. His jaws are misshapen; he cannot bring his front teeth within half an inch of each other; his upper jaw is pointed, and falls within the arch of the lower; his teeth spiculated, and must be well nigh useless to him. Solemnity great.

Three years later, addressing the British Association meeting at Bath in 1888, Dr. G. B. Barron moved to a more generalized level of analysis. He pointed to the origins of "Degeneracy of Race" in "bad air" and "bad habits of life." The former encompassed "bad sanitation and overcrowding," and the latter included "imperfect feeding and consequent malnutrition." In one rhetorical sweep, Barron set straight the course of regeneration:

> The remedies are Imperial legislation to improve the social conditions of the town dwellers. Insanitary surroundings, overcrowding, uncleanliness, impurity, intemperance, must all be swept away. The children must be educated in the pure air of the country. Make the parents sober and moral; give them pure air and plenty of it, and away fly pale faces, dyspepsia, crooked backs (generally resulting from tuberculosis), lowered vitality, stunted development, muscular attenuation, and the imperfect elimination of functional products.

The zeitgeist, or sensibility, of the last third of the nineteenth century was neither troubled by the thought of Karl Marx and Sigmund Freud nor enlightened by the contribution of Gregor Mendel. The Victorians had enough to contend with in Charles Darwin's picture of Nature: red of fang and claw, relentlessly casting aside those "unfit" to compete, let alone survive. What could be the future if the race of Britons was shrinking before one's eyes, if Londoners did not beget Londoners? How could an expanding empire, already spanning the globe, be run for the benefit of "the lesser breeds without the law," in Kipling's phrase, when the Anglo-Saxons were wilting under the heat of industrial stress and apparently implacable laws of heredity transmitted acquired defects? In 1889, Major Barrington Foote described Newcastle men seeking to enter the army after working in the mines as, "a little weedy and pale-faced" (Don, 1889). At the opening of the new century, Rippon-Seymour (1903) noted that, "in the course of a walk through the poorer quarters of any large town in Scotland (or England) . . . may be seen the white, pinched faces, the ill-developed bodies, the all-too-prevalent and apparent signs of disease in skin and eye." In 1902, C. R. Ashbee noted "the bent shoulders, the broken lungs . . . the poor sight, the slouching gait, the slovenliness and vulgar truculence of the undergrown ill-bred mass of East London" (Rose, 1986). Four years later, in 1906, Sydney Webb emphasized the culture of the poor and proliferation of their non-middle class values: "The decline in the birthrate appears to be much greater in those sections of the population which give proofs of thrift and foresight than among the population at large."

In 1904, A. A. Mumford presented a theory of degeneracy in which the terms *nature* and *nurture* were used in apposition, and the terms *civic worth* and *energy* were emphasized. Mumford set forth in a quasi-scientific idiom the view that "energy" could be deficient and become abnormal as well as subnormal. The key concept, energy, was not presented analytically and appears analogous to George Bernard Shaw's "life force," if only in its vagueness. Mumford saw three stages of defective energy:

- deterioration, which was remediable;
- degeneration, from which normality could not be regained;
- decadence, which led to extinction.

The essential difficulty with these ideas is that they are mere verbalisms and lack a foundation or origin in empirical data. Such terms can be applied retroactively, but fail to meet the scientific requirement of predicting. That is, these and similar terms are not rooted in data that they can analyze and explain. Mumford's speculations led him to conclude that social and sanitary conditions were the true causes, to use his terminology, for the state of people's health in towns. In the same year, an unnamed London journalist (Lindsay, 1906) reported that "There has evolved in London a race distinct, unlike any other race in the British Isles, with strongly marked characteristics, with alien features and habits. It is a race stunted in size, sallow complexioned, dark-haired. Its moral sense is blunted, its mentality low. It has even evolved a speech of its own."

Not all analysts were pessimistic about the health of the laboring classes. Professor Leone Levi, addressed one of the last meetings of the Social Science Association in 1884. Reviewing the social condition of the working class Levi examined changes since 1857, a period of a quarter-century. Drawing especially on the British association's recent anthropometric study Levi asserted that, "the physical condition of the labouring classes is better now than it ever was." However, it was not until the new century began that social commentators generally began to refute the postulate of inevitability in the decline of health. Bernard Bosanquet (1904) thought the problem of degeneration over-estimated; but he thought and spoke in an era of constructive social policy, one in which Joseph Chamberlain of Birmingham would find an audience for his radical formulations of the public good, of the social order, and of mutual obligations within the community. Social Darwinism had evolved into socio-industrial "efficiency," fanned by the rising flames of European rivalries. The Physical Training Committee of 1902 and the Physical Deterioration Committee of 1904 saw that proper nourishment and exercise (Hawkins, 1895; Roberts, 1895) could do wonders for poor children. Bosanquet introduced the quality of parenting into the picture, an element which stressed what we would call the nurture side of the question. The other side of the question, heredity, was still in the shadows of pre-Mendelian genetics. A year after Bosanquet's enlightened commentary, Arthur Newsholme (1905), the conservative public health doctor at the Local Government Board, from Brighton, also resisted the proposition that degeneration was progressive. Newsholme asserted that the problem was in fact "morale," as he termed it. That is, he believed that environmental circumstances were the point of leverage for improvement. Progressive governments of the first decade were attentive, and stability of income through unemployment insurance, free school meals, and physical training did much to improve things. Progress, however, was slow; after 1916, according to Birch (1974), four of each nine conscripts to fight the Great War were wholly unfit, and only three of each nine were healthy enough for active service in the army or navy. In the case of Scotland's urban areas the problems persisted long after the Great War.

Despite Bosanquet's moderate statements the degeneracy question persisted in the twentieth century. It is epitomized in Dugdale's 1877 study of the eponymous Juke family and in Goddard's study of a family fictionalized as the Kallikaks, a term derived from Greek adjectives meaning the beautiful and the bad. To thoughtful, if less than fully informed, analysts, a major aspect of degeneration was regression of homo sapiens. Through that process, the latest and highest traits acquired phylogenetically would be the first given up when regression occurred (Gelb, 1989). By inference, moral sensibilities would be among the first traits lost, and evidence would be the prevalence of criminal behavior. This last criterion was not distinguished from middle-class conventionality in behavior, so that there was no shortage of degenerates, prima facie. The Kallikaks had their *kalloi* (beautiful) and *kakoi* (bad) branches, and the self-evident nature of evolutionary regression was trumpeted by Goddard. Unfortunately the conclusion soared beyond the facts, as the disreputable and tipsy were attributed to the degenerate lineage because they were unconventional and disreputable; the reasoning fell in the error of begging the question.

The mischief of that social complex persisted far into the twentieth century and was summarized in Rafter (1988). Eugenics led to involuntary sterilization of the retarded (Jordan, 1976), and to development of the managerial philosophy of isolation in rural institutions. Views on the hereditability and progressive nature of physical deterioration across the nineteenth century reached their nadir in the eugenics movement. An over-reductionism in reasoning reflected the absence of information on the vectors of change within family trees (Chatterton-Hill, 1907). Lest this seem an unnecessary denseness on the part of analysts it is helpful to recall the naiveté of the 1960s that expressed itself in unrealistic expectations for programs of preschool education as a way to break up the cycle of poverty and social problems.

We can reach back to Gaskell in 1833 for a commonsense view of how to improve a population living nasty, brutish, and short lives. Gaskell noted that many successful businessmen in the early 1830s had sprung from humble origins—"the very humblest ranks of labourers."

> The force of external circumstances in modifying bodily form, is seen equally forcibly, in another and more pleasing point of view, in the manufacturing districts. Many of the masters have raised themselves from the very humblest rank of labourers—in many instances after a family had been born to them in their humility. These individuals with their families, at this period, of course, possessed all the traits distinguishing their grade, both moral and physical. Change of condition, better food, better clothing, better housing, constant cleanliness, mental cultivation, the force of example in the higher order of society in which they are now placed, have gradually converted them into respectable and even handsome families. The first remove places them still more favourably, and ceteris paribus, they become elegant and intelligent

females, and well formed and robust men. They now resemble but slightly, in their general aspect and deportment, the class from which they have risen.

Degeneracy as Theory

It is noteworthy that the concept of degeneration arose in more than the limited sphere of health and the reports of factory inspectors. Criminology, psychiatry, and ethnology, for instance, found the concept central to understanding discoveries about people and the world. Beliefs and styles of living inconsistent with a traditional view of the nineteenth century world imposed themselves on insular sensibilities (Livingstone, 1991). Such deviations from the familiar could be grasped most readily as evidence of inferiority and, in an age of optimism, reversion to a less mature stage. Thus, chronic violations of law were reversions to barbarism or, at worst, to near-simian tendencies; from angel back to ape was a demonstrable risk. For groups of people, primitivism and atavism were demonstrable and were evident in the decorations or absence of clothing demonstrated in the tropics, for example; at the same time, British women wore elaborate bustles and men cultivated mutton-chop whiskers. Racial inferiority justified slavery (Drescher, 1990) and colonialism, and in selected instances, degeneracy seemed to explain the seething urban plebs whose irruptions had shaken western Europe since 1789. Literature was not immune, and the popularity of Dorian Gray and Dr. Jekyll expressed popular acceptance of degeneracy as a hazard to human development. The most sophisticated formulations were those of Lombroso, who asserted that degeneracy existed in visible ways written in the physiognomy.

Britons generally avoided the all-embracing concepts of degeneracy prevalent on the Continent. There, degeneracy acquired theoretical proportions and became the topic for books by Benedict Morel (1857) and Cesare Lombroso (1891). As set forth in, *Traité des Dégenéréscences . . .* (1857), Morel saw a large number of conditions including crime, cretinism, and mental retardation as phenotypic reversions to primitive states of humankind. Implicitly, Europeans were held to be near the top of the Great Chain of Being, in relation to other groups (Lorimer, 1978). This presumption led New England missionaries to segregate their children from Hawaiians lest they, by association, revert to a phylogenetically primitve condition (Grimshaw, 1989). Recalling his missionary experiences, in 1836, A. Chaplin recoiled from the Hawaiians' proclivity, "to eat when they were happy, to recline in sluggish inactivity under the shadow of trees."

Morel believed that his views, based on his observations, enjoyed, "la triple sanction de la vérité révélée, dé la philosophie, et de l'histoire naturelle" (Morel, 1857, p. 2). His concept of degeneracy embraced a wide range of causes, from alcoholism to geology. Morel was quite familiar with the British situation and cited studies of towns (e.g., Wolverhampton) with attention to their juvenile populations. Morel ended his treatise on an optimistic note asserting that *traitement moral*, a term we tend to associate with Edouard Séguin (Jordan, 1976) should prevail, culminating in *la moralisation des masses* and in their regeneration (p. 693). Morel's treatise was an attempt to combine clinical observation with a larger view of the natural order in a grand exposition of human nature within the kingdom of nature.

In contrast, the problem-centered sensibility of the Victorians avoided intellectual excesses, but at the price of a fragmentary view of human development. This fragmentation has been documented by Desmond (1991), who set forth the social-political-biological context of competing agendas. The clash of scholarly armies on a darkling plain was discernable to sociomedical reformers struggling with the problems of urbanization, public health, child welfare, factory reform, and other matters in a practical manner.

Only at the beginning of the twentieth century did the Interdepartmental Committee on Physical Deterioration (1904) provide a view of the condition of the disadvantaged reviewing (e.g.) odd-job data on child health from the Johanna Street School in Southwark. Given the extent of health problems among poor children (Warner, 1893; 1896) it is perhaps as well that there had been no mass data on the growing young; had there been, a comprehensive theory of degeneracy might have plagued the human race. The Interdepartmental Committee heard testimony from distinguished to odd people and might have generalized from situational factors into the form of an unmanageable degenerate class produced by social Darwinism. The popular mind, as conveyed by the literature it absorbed, seems to have been fertile soil for such a development. Happily, the reality is that the Interdepartmental Committee (1904) chose to highlight the connection between social circumstances and health problems.

Fiction and Fact

Across the nineteenth century commentators consistently observe that the development of towns had a deleterious effect on life. In documents ranging from literature to the local statistical society's journals thoughtful people saw that town life was hard, impersonal, and unhealthy. The novels of Frances Trolloppe (*The Life and Adventures of Michael Armstrong, the Factory Boy*); of Benjamin Disraeli (*Coningsby* and *Sybil*); of Dickens (*David Copperfield* and *Hard Times*); and of Elizabeth Gaskell (*Mary Barton* and *North and South*) gave middle-class readers insights into the life of the poor. Liardet (1839) conducted one of the few studies of the rural poor, in Kent. Leech (1841) combined sketches and essays in his *Portraits of Children of the Mobility* (in contrast to the nobility). Combining humor with pathos Leech sought to convey the situation of poor children to the higher orders of society (Jordan, 1991c).

Eventually, a genre emerged in which journalists such as Henry Mayhew, George Sala and Hugh Shimmin (Walton and Wilcox, 1991) and others of the same style reported the exotic and possibly dangerous way of life of the working class and the poor. Examples are "Medical Gentleman's" *An Enquiry into Destitution, Prostitution and Crime in Edinburgh* (1851), John Hollingshead's (1861) *Ragged London in 1861*, and "Journeyman Engineer's" (Thomas Wright) (1867) *Some Habits and Customs of the Working Class*. At a more technical level were the statists' analyses of town life. They were exemplified in Peter Gaskell's study of the working poor (1833), Dr. James Kay's study of Manchester life (1832), Dr. H. Baker's (1839) report on Leeds, Edwin Chadwick's Health of Towns report (1844), and Friedrich Engels's study of British workers (1842). Later, came the *Morning Chronicle*'s 1851 series of articles from, inter alia, Angus Reach and Henry Mayhew.

Beginning in 1889, Charles Booth, originally of Liverpool, reported on his series of studies of London's poor (Fried and Elman, 1969). In 1890 Salvation Army General William Booth wrote *In Darkest England, and the Way Out*, and at the turn of the century, 1901, Seebohm Rowntree provided his studies of poverty in York seven years earlier. A key work in 1901 was C. F. C. Masterman's book *The Heart of the Empire*. In nine separately authored chapters, including one by George M. Trevelyan, Masterman and his close friends analyzed urban life in London, the heart of the empire.

The Problem

From the point of view of today, questions arise about which problems commentators were addressing. At the risk of Whiggism we need to discern the nature of the questions that appear in the literature of the nineteenth century and appear to the current mind as salient. In addition, we need to discern the questions that are answerable at our present viewpoint in time, as they were not during the period of the degeneracy crisis. From this second challenge we can formulate ways to answer the first.

The prime problem faced by the Victorians was the dawning, demoralizing realization that the age of steam and manufacturing represented progress at a high price (Heywood, 1988). While wealth was evidently being created the working people were equally evident as an unhealthy, urban mob. Given to drink and religious indifference they lived from day to day and pursued aimless pleasure in their few leisure hours. Their children were wretched, unhealthy, and singularly suceptible to political and social radicalism. In 1859, Mary Bayly described problem families she had encountered in, *Ragged Homes and How to Mend Them*. In her forays down Cut-Throat Lane and other streets in the Kensington potteries she encountered pigs and people in great numbers. Bayly organized mothers meeting that met weekly to discuss domestic problems and read the Bible. The phenomena of mothers meetings and missionaries to the poor have been described by Prochaska (1988, 1990). Balance requires that we note that poor nurturing occurred among the wealthy and was noteworthy a half-century after Mrs. Bayly's account. In 1902, Dr. James Crichton-Browne (1902) pointed out to an international conference that neglect of children was common among "a smart set, rich and luxurious . . . who rely on . . . feeding bottles, nurses, governesses, French maids and Lady-helps relieve them of them . . . their children grow up bereft of mothering, and may be damaged in health by their deprivation."

Thus, even sensitive, perceptive observers realized that there were disorganized families and individuals, always had been, and probably always would be, as we, their descendants can attest. The life of the nation was a series of acute crises such as wars, epidemics, and economic depressions, relieved by periods of comparative quiet. The prevalence of ill-health and disorganized families in the early decades of the nineteenth century was not, at first glance, anything new. There was, apparently, no new problem, and Dr. Andrew Ure (1835) testified that factories were healthy, indeed downright salutary, places even for the young. A decade later, Dr. Daniel Noble (1843) concluded that there might be sickly workers in Manchester, but it was not the factory system, merely their self-selected domestic arrangements that created their problems. Thus, there was no crisis in the form of a societal evil or problem, merely a continuation of the poor personal choices the lower classes invariably and historically made. To say there was a crisis was to misread personal calamities that were unfortunate but quite familiar. Salient for our discussion is the ill health of poor children. Although the population grew, the rate of infant mortality among the under fives was appalling; those who survived, especially urban dwellers, were unhealthy, having pinched cheeks, sunken chests, and other stigmata of a degenerated constitution or habitus. From this we adduce the degree, nature, and scope of poor people's development, ex utero, into a "weeny, weedy, weaky" population. In 1887, George H. Sargant described the physical condition of Birmingham children for whom he provided meals:

> The children to whom they were given get little or no food at home; they are insufficiently clothed, usually in rags. Their home life is miserable, and though in most cases the influences are not altogether for evil, in many they are hopelessly bad. Reduced by privation, they cannot resist disease; they cannot eat, many are quite unfit for school work.

The course of physical development is particularly salient because growing people are especially susceptible to deleterious influences. A variety of noxious influences register themselves on growing children by arresting or distorting the normal processes of growth.

So far, we have attended to urban dwellers, but country folk were not immune to problems (Horn, 1974, 1989). Poor sanitation and housing created a setting for communicable diseases. Rural slums seemed picturesque only to those who did not cope with leaky thatch, damp floors, and overcrowding. The life of most agricultural workers was long and hard. In one of his essays in the 1870s Heath (1893) recounted a Norfolk surgeon's description of farm laborers' poor muscular development, which was compounded by tuberculosis and rheumatism. In Oxfordshire, Heath encountered the ill-health of men who had walked ploughed fields at an early age. By age fifty, their knees were damaged, and they were bent from overexertion. Heath and other observers believed that Northumbrian farm workers and servants were exceptionally healthy. As we shall see in Chapter Three, oats played a large part in their diet, and their way of life was quite orderly.

Among the aspects of growth amenable to distortion growth in height is sensitive. Today, we expect children in the developed world to meet the norms expressed in Table 1.2. There we see that youngsters in three countries—the Netherlands, the United States, and New Zealand—uniformly reach substantial heights. However, their Victorian ancestors from the bulk of the population fell far behind. Accordingly, a purpose of this work is to discuss in detail the course of growth in height from 1805 to 1914, an epoch we label for convenience, *Victorian,* acknowledging the years of George III and William IV, in the early period, and the years of Edward VII and George V in the last period. It may be useful to consult Table 1.2 when reading Chapters Four and Six.

A second topic was the probability that once started on the downward slope of ill-health a child would fall further behind as the chronological age progressed. It appeared that an infant growing in poor circumstances would fall behind height and weight norms to a greater degree, so that a discrepancy of a fraction of an inch in young children had widened to several inches by adolescence.

A third matter the Victorians pursued was the disturbing probability that the existing degeneracy was progressive. That is, by some unknown mechanism—a topic to which we shall turn later—the physique of the average working-class man, woman, or child seemed to grow worse in each successive generation. To some, for example, Dr. James Kay (-Shuttleworth) of Manchester, it was clear in 1832 that the working classes were prone to unseemly behavior and religious infidelity and could not be trusted to raise literate, responsible children. A decade later, Friedrich Engels (1845) would draw on Kay's work to point to the crisis in economic teleology known as *capitalism,* as would his master, Karl Marx, in *Capital.* At the end of the century, the Boer War would present the crisis of Kipling's mentors for "the lesser breeds without the law" falling short of the standard needed to run an empire. Some were known to have fallen far short of that standard. Akin to the Jukes of eugenical notoriety was the case of Ada York who died early in the nineteenth century, "a victim of vice." Of 700 descendents 569 (81 percent) were adjudged to be pathological. With murderers were placed illegitimate babies in a typical muddle of morality and poverty. An observer in 1909 estimated their charge had cost the state a quarter of a million pounds over the years.

A fourth, more fundamental question which was unanswerable at the time was the matter of how traits passed from one generation to another. To us it is relatively self-evident that environment plus the biochemistry of the DNA molecule interact, if only in opaque ways. In Victorian times people were prone to think that acquired traits were readily transmitted to the next generation (Whetham and Whetham, 1909). To understand that outlook toward the world we need recall that, today, heredity tends to be dismissed in favor of environmentalism, even by those who use both words by way of explanation. The problem for the Victorians was that things were bad, and the downward spiral of human stock seemed irreversible. To William Farr, degeneration of the race was most likely in unhealthy climates and in towns. Victorian Britain was increasingly urban, and the volatile climate was not improved by air pollution caused by soft coal and industry. Eugenics entered Farr's thinking and Eyler (1979) ascribes an interest in hereditary insanity as an explanation of degeneration to him; in particular, he viewed the aristocracy as at risk due to the incidence of consanguinous marriages. Criminality was also susceptible to heredity and so led to degeneration in a moral and social sense. Eventually, he adopted a Darwinian view of the eugenics competition, as did many of his era, and saw Europeans as the winners in the race for survival, compared to peoples indigenous to other regions.

The haunting question of progressive degeneration across the generations persisted, mutatis mutandis, into the twentieth century in the form of the eugenics movement, whose abuses showed twentieth century people at their worst. The evidence from the nineteenth century to pursue that line of inquiry consisted of genealogical studies and formulations of the environment surrounding the growing human organism. The growth of towns, the nature of housing, and the state of medical knowledge are topics through which the circumstances of life may be glimpsed. With regard to exploration of the Victorian consideration of degenerated health as transmitted from one generation to the next, it helps to recall that the period of interest, 1807–1914, was pre-Mendelian in its formulations. Neither Darwin nor his predecessor, Lamarck, addressed intergenerational mechanisms with the focus of Gregor Mendel, but his work did not suffuse biology until 1900 (Bennett, 1983). Indeed, the word *genetics* appears to have been coined only in 1910 by Bateson.

In summary, we have shown in this first chapter that the degeneracy question arose within the enormous span of social and industrial changes that constituted the dynamic nineteenth century in Britain. Sensibilities evolved from those of the eighteenth century when life for most people followed the cycle of nature to a degree of modernism in outlook which, a century later, is quite recognizable. Across that vast range of urbanization and population growth, within a stable polity, thoughtful men saw a degenerating population, one afflicted with appalling rates of infant mortality and tuberculosis across succeeding generations. We now turn to a closer look at specific aspects of the complex.

Towns, Housing, and Work

A major phenomenon of nineteenth century Britain was the rise of towns and the accretion of population in an urban culture. Attuned to the rhythms of factory and mill, workers refined the preindustrial cycles of work and preurban life into a homogeneous working-class culture with a political arm, the Labour Party, and when religiously inclined, a preference for non-Anglican celebration. Today, we regard cities as machines which perform functions. Historically, the city has been many things from fortress to utopia. British towns evolved from armed, defensive structures into marketing and travel centers. In the case of the cathedral cities it appeared, sometimes, as if they had slept through the turmoil of the Industrial Revolution. Their inhabitants lived in the Barchester of Trollope untouched by the major phenomena of the age. Others were less fortunate; based on proximity to coal and water, populations expanded and the infrastructure of systems for sewage, housing, and health were overloaded.

The Reform Law of 1832 recognized that Old Sarum in Wiltshire was a rotten borough, and that mound of earth was deprived of its Member of Parliament. Barely touched were the expanding and underrepresented towns of the Midlands and the North which continued to lack a voice in Parliament. In the early decades specific pieces of legislation modernized cities one by one. However, in small towns and the cathedral cities tranquility prevailed and Barchester's population remained as it had been in the eighteenth century. In contrast were the port cities, with London growing eastward toward the North Sea, Liverpool growing both in emigrant traffic and cargo, and Bristol yielding

25

its situationally improbable, if historic, eminence. The major change affecting health lay in the immiseration of populations.

To nineteenth century aesthetes the Victorian factory town was a terrible place. Thomas Carlisle, a Scot of conservative bent, saw change in a historical perspective. John Ruskin reacted more emotionally, recalling in 1875 that he had just,

> driven leisurely through the midland manufacturing districts, which I have not traversed, except by rail, for the last ten years. The two most frightful things I have ever yet seen in my life are the south-eastern suburb of Bradford, (six miles long,) and the scene from Wakefield bridge, by the chapel; yet I cannot but more and more reverence the fierce courage and industry, the gloomy endurance, and the infinite mechanical ingenuity of the great centres, as one reverences the fervid labours of a wasp's nest, though the end of all is only a noxious lump of clay. (Ruskin, 1896)

People lived in those ugly, dirty areas of Wakefield and Bradford (Koditschek, 1990), and they died early if they were poor. The factory towns were inimical to life and health, and the physical degeneracy evident in child workers grown old before their time was obvious to all.

Health in Towns

Quite early in the nineteenth century it became apparent to observers that the health and appearance of town dwellers was poor. In France, Benoiton de Chateauneuf (1830) studied sickness and mortality by age group and geographical dispersion among the arrondisements and faubourgs of Paris. In Britain young factory workers dragged themselves to and from the workplace at an age when they should have been in school or at play. That phenomenon was the first stage of a reduced life span replete with bouts of sickness. It seems likely that people got sick more frequently than we experience and stayed sick longer. They probably had relatively briefer spans of sound health before the next bout of dysentery or droplet-borne disease struck again. City dwellers were exposed to both vectors of disease, and medicine could do little to effect cures. Given the doubtful benefits of active therapy—hospitals were dangerous places at best—the populace did not share our relative confidence in physicians. Frequently, the neighborhood's dispensing pharmacist was the source of aid, and he probably sold vast quantities of alcohol- and opium-based palliatives (Jordan, 1987a).

The major point at which urban life and health came together was in Edwin Chadwick's report of 1842, "Report on the Sanitary Condition of the Labouring Population of Great Britain." In that work a superb propagandist defined problems, and in the case of sewage promoted a cheap and effective solution. A testy person, Chadwick was succeeded by John Simon (Lambert, 1963), and the machinery of the Privy Council became the bureaucratic bastion from which the medical-social reformers pushed their plans for two decades. The efficacy of those plans may be seen in Table 2.1, which is taken from Simon's Ninth Report to the Privy Council in 1866. There, we see data from ten of twenty-four towns, only one of which, Bristol, was large; several had populations of under 8,000. In the table Simon presented data on the incidence of diseases before and after introduction of sanitary works and clean water. Death rates fell in twenty-two towns but rose fractionally in Penzance and Merthyr Tydfil; of the two, Penzance seemed the more refractory. The data on cholera are impressive with towns such as Carlisle, Salisbury, and Brynmawr showing elimination of mortality.

The classic example of the health problem of town life was the contamination of drinking water by sewage. The investigation of Dr. John Snow in 1849 led to the conclusion that cholera was being transmitted in water from the public pump in Broad Street, Golden Square. By removing the handle from the pump the outbreak of cholera was arrested and the epidemic died out. (We will return to this anecdote to illustrate the vagaries of public policy in Chapter Seven.) It should be pointed out that Snow's demonstration was not convincing to all. Dr. John Simon was not persuaded and referred in his 1858 report to the Privy Council to Snow's "peculiar doctrine" of etiology; subsequently, Simon accepted Snow's findings. In provincial towns, sanitary reform came slowly, and Hamlin (1988) has described how Leamington, for example, coped with the anxiety provoked by legal compulsion to inaugurate public works.

In the work of Chadwick, and the simpler, elegant work of Snow, there is demonstration that social evils can be analyzed within the capacities of people to follow and comprehend. Change becomes something manageable through familiar objects and procedures. In particular, Chadwick persuaded his readers that pure water would lead to better health and then persuaded them that it could be done cheaply. His analyses of materials to carry water and his specification of the cost in pennies reduced illness and death from a malignant inevitability which induced passivity and mute acceptance to a series of

TABLE 2.1 "IMPROVEMENTS OF PUBLIC HEALTH THAT RESULT FROM PROPER WORKS OF DRAINAGE AND WATER SUPPLY"

| Population in 1861 | Towns in Order of Population | Comparison Periods for Death Rates | | Death Rate per 100,000 | | | | | | | | | | |
| | | Before | After | General Death Rates | | Typhoid Fever | | Diarrhea Excluding Cholera | | Cholera | | | Mortality of Infants Under One Year | |
				Before	After	Before	After	Before	After	1848–49	1854	1866	Before	After
160,714	Bristol	1845–47	1851–62	215	206	10	6	10.5	9.5	82	11	1.5	54	52
68,056	Leicester	1845–51	1862–64	236.3	225.3	14.6	7.6	16	19.3	1	10	0	84.2	81
39,693	Cheltenham	1845–57	1860–65	194	185	8	4.75	8.5	7	0	0	0	40.5	37
29,417	Carlisle	1845–53	1858–64	284	261	10	9.75	11.3	12.5	22	6	—	71	65.5
24,756	Newport	1845–49	1860–65	318	216.5	16.3	10.3	11	6.5	112	1.5	12	67.25	53.25
9,414	Penzance	1843–50	1856–65	221	222	7.5	8	5.3	9.3	0	0	0	-	-
8,664	Chelmsford	1843–52	1855–65	196.3	215	12	8	7	8	4	0	0	44	42.75
6,823	Stratford	1845–53	1860–64	217	202	12.5	4	11.25	5.75	0	0	0	46	48
5,805	Worthington	1843–52	1857–65	139	136.5	7.5	9.5	4.75	5.5	0	0	0	56	57.5
3,840	Ashby	1845–51	1855–64	216	202	13.5	6	4	8	0	0	0	48	31

Source: Adapted from J. Simon (1866), *Ninth Report to the Privy Council.*

concrete steps that even the reactionary could see as cheap and cost effective. But the essence of Chadwick's cheap, pure water, like Snow's identification of the handle on the Broad street pump, lay in its empowerment of people to control a major threat in their lives. Social ills were brought within the capacity of the public to comprehend and to solve by collective local action. Table 2.1 demonstrates what communities did in the face of their historic health problems to alleviate suffering. Personal convenience and the common good merged to generate public policy whose components were comprehensible to ordinary folk.

Towns

Nineteenth century British society grew haphazardly, structured—if that is not an overstatement—by the form of local government centered on the parish as the civic unit. So inefficient was the system of local government that Disraeli (1845) used the Marylebone Vestry of the 1830s for one of the characters in *Sybil* to cite for corruption, "if I had a taste for business." Efficient management in local government increased after the 1834 amendment of the Poor Laws; Harling (1992) reported that employment of former sergeants and corporals increased the efficiency of work houses. The inefficiency of the vestry in the matter of crime is explained by James and Critchley (1971) in their semi-fictional account of a series of murders in the East End. The City of London was particularly anomalous; although a center of population by day, the resident population declined from a peak of 129,128 people in 1851. The City Corporation managed affairs on behalf of a tiny minority of freemen-householders. Revenues were high, and expenditures were lavish for salaries and perquisites of holders of ancient offices. Lambert (1963) pointed out that administration of the City cost £140,000 while larger cities were spending one-seventh of that amount. The possibilities for corruption were considerable. On the positive side is the fact that the city provided the first public health position occupied by Dr. John Simon. In his subsequent career at the Privy Council Simon established national government as a major and positive influence on public health. In his earliest annual reports for the city he addressed the problem of bad housing and overcrowding.

In the nineteenth century the welfare of the population of the London metropolitan area was caught up in the dynamics of growth. In one place were the political, bureaucratic, financial, and social centers of the entire country. Profit from the coal mines of Wales and the mills and factories of the Midlands and the North flowed to the southeast. London steadily lost its manufacturing components, for example, ship building, to be replaced by an economy of services and of international hegemony in money and banking. The rich got richer and the poor competed for places to live. Wages were compromised by rising rents, and overcrowding set the stage for communication of diseases by propinquity and the absence of sanitation. Of course, there were efforts to provide model lodgings and apartments, but in the slums of St. Giles families competed for one room in decaying buildings. There were instances of a single room rented corner by corner to the poor (Sykes, Guy, and Neison, 1848; Mearns, 1889). In, "How the Poor Live," in 1889, George Sims described,

> E. Williams, costermonger, two rooms in a court which is a hotbed of vice and disease. Has eight children. Total earnings, 17s. Rent, 5s. 6d.
>
> T. Briggs, labourer, one room, four children. Rent, 4s. No furniture; all sleep on floor. Daughter answered knock, absolutely naked; ran in and covered herself with a sack.
>
> Mrs. Johnson, widow, one room, three children. Earnings, 6s. Rent, 3s. 6d.
>
> W. Leigh, fancy boxmaker, two awful rooms, four children. Earnings, 14s. Rent, 6s.
>
> H. Walker, hawker, two rooms, seven children. Earnings, 10s. Rent, 5s. 6d.
>
> R. Thompson, out of work, five children. Living by pawning goods and clothes. Wife drinks. Rent, 4s.
>
> G. Garrard, labourer, out looking for work, eight children. No income. Rent, 5s. 6d. Pawning last rags. No parish relief. Starving. Declines to go into workhouse.

While clearly extreme situations existed, London was always an expensive place to live and to die. The literature of the period is replete with accounts of unburied children around whose biers other children played. In such circumstances disease spread quickly, and the sanitary diseases had affected even the wealthy; Prince Albert's untimely death from typhoid fever in 1861 seems not unconnected to the bad drains at Windsor.

With the passage of the decades the ill-health prevalent in the metropolis led Dr. James Clark to label the complex *cachexia Londoniensis*, and Dr. Cantlie pointed out that it was hard to find a third-generation Londoner; the strain was too thin and, apparently, degenerated in the urban environment. The poor clustered together in the southern and eastern parts of the city (Dennis, 1989; Hennock, 1976), and the well-to-do migrated west. The growing docks down river provided casual employment for thousands of porters; and so workers and families in the years before public transportation, like their northern factory cousins, huddled close to work in very poor circumstances. The writer, Jack London, (1903) termed them, the *People of the Abyss*. With the advent of trains and cheap tickets in the final decades suburban living was possible, but working-class folk generally needed to be near their work.

A family style of living followed the demands of work in other ways. Costermongers thrived in the streets that Mayhew described so colorfully in his 1851, "London Labour and the London Poor" (Quennell, 1969). Street peddlers sold patent medicines, dog collars, and fruit. Life was hard but brisk, and the health of the metropolitan population was one of stress with bouts of ill-health. The cholera epidemic of 1866 killed 4,000 people in three months of late 1866 due to the incompetence of the East London Water Company (Luckin, 1977); in a period of seventeen successive summer days no less than 100 East-Enders died each day. In the district of St. George's in the East the death rate peaked at 97 deaths per 1,000 of the population, and Camberwell was a close second at 89. In contrast, the mortality rates in Chelsea and Hanover Square were 4 and 2 per 1,000, respectively. In the patchwork that was nineteenth century London propinquity of middle class and poor was a frequent if unwelcomed fact of life. Wall (1974) presents several reports on housing in London and Dublin. *The Streets*. Conditions within ill-ventilated, poorly lit dwellings were not the only mechanism of exposure to infection. Today, we object to automobile exhausts and tobacco exhalations as sources of environmental pollution and personal discomfort. In some respects the Victorians were worse off. For them, the rough streets were polluted by horses. The problem created the job of crossing-sweeper who, for a copper or two, would clear aside the detritus of the streets. In all but the coldest weather, the smell and visual offense were compounded by quantities of disease-bearing flies ever ready to distract pedestrian and horse while also communicating infections to food and other surfaces on which they landed (Buchanan, 1985). The scale of this noisome problem may be appreciated by noting Schultz's (1989) estimate that the city horse was estimated to drop twenty two pounds (10 kg.) of manure on the streets per day; Milwaukee, he recorded, received one hundred and thirty tons per day. The New Yorker who traverses Central Park

South at Fifth Avenue gets an impression of the Victorian street and its hazards. This anachronism is less noisy and smoky than the diesel-engined bus or van, but the risk to health is probably as great. Victorian London, Manchester, Milwaukee or St. Louis, as a benchmark for urbanity—in the best sense, suggests our street problems are noisier, but less noisome or unhealthy. In the nineteenth century, many streets were unimproved, so that mud compounded problems of filth and waste water, while clouds of dust and flies characterized streets in dry weather.

A letter to The Times in July, 1849, signed by "J.", protested the condition of a busy Battersea Street, Plough Lane. The problem was an open ditch five hundred yards long which was a "cesspool of the most horrid kind." "J." ended his appeal to clean up this nuisance by recalling the role of another ditch widely held to have caused a fatal epidemic in Tooting. According to Gavin (1847), "the poison which causes death is not a gas, but a sort of atmosphere of organic particles, undergoing incessant transformations; perhaps, like malaria, not oderous, although evolved at the same time as putrid smells; suspended like dust, an aroma, vesicular water in the air; but invisible."

Metropolitan Model Housing

It should be noted that there were philanthropic efforts to house the poor. In London, there were developments exemplified by the Peabody Trust and the Guiness Trust, and there was the effort of Octavia Hill, supported by John Ruskin. Profit-making bodies with a philanthropic intent modulated by business acumen included the Society for Improving the Condition of the Labouring Classes, the Metropolitan Association for Improving the Condition of the Labouring Classes, and the Improved Industrial Dwellings Company. In most instances, housing above the level of the model boarding house was intended for families. They were expected to be orderly, and their children well controlled. Ever adept at living amidst their betters and exploitive landlords, the poor who were working learned to discriminate between their benefactors' degrees of supervision and interference. The poor who were feckless or out of work, that is the poor in greatest need, usually were not the object of philanthropic housing and frequently slept rough when necessary. Such people formed the residuum, and philanthropists thought them a bad risk, given that philanthropic housing could care for only a modicum of those in need.

On a different scale were the model communities built by industrialists. Titus Salt built Saltaire near Bradford, and nearby Sheffield was the site of Akroydon. A variation on housing was the theme of utopianism, which eventually saw the emergence of the garden city movement at Welwyn, Herts.

Philanthropic housing was a good, if limited, thing. It focused attention on the necessity for a social net under the deserving poor. In the fullness of time, it was succeeded throughout the country by housing sponsored by local municipalities. The need was probably greatest in Glasgow, with Dublin a close second.

Rural Housing

Our attention to housing in towns does not imply that life in Sweet Auburn was as serene as the poet implied. To many country folk, city housing and urban life amounted to a net improvement in their standard of living. They migrated from dwellings that were ancient, tumble down, and overcrowded, although in pretty settings. Some country cottages were little more than roofs supported by clay walls, and stone walls were not impervious to rain and moisture. Frequently, cottages lacked proper footings so that the stage was set for walls, doors, and windows to sag. From Fleischman's (1985) analysis of housing in Lancashire in the period 1811–1851, it is evident that the density of people per house was greater in rural than urban areas. Ten large cities in 1811 had a mean density per house of 5.35 people; in 1851 the mean was 5.20 people. In nine country districts the mean densities in the same years were higher at 5.85 and 5.72 people. Improvements, according to Fleischman, began in urban areas after 1821, and a decade later in rural areas.

In 1867, the Commission on the Employment of Children, Young Persons, and Women in Agriculture touched on the problem of housing. The picture which emerged was that of people living with improper sanitation, in smoke-filled rooms, and frequently several to a bed. Heath (1893) visited in 1872, shortly after the agricultural commission, a pair of dwellings in South Warwickshire. Each house was 8 feet wide and 15 feet deep and had two rooms. A woman and her five children slept in one room which was, presumably, 8 by 8 feet. Of course, there were exceptions as progressive landowners built model cottages from the plans of reformers.

Scotland and Ireland

In Scotland, agricultural workers frequently lived in bothies. A bothy was a structure of one room usually, but not exclusively, for unmarried males. It was small, crowded, and lacking in comfort.

Overcrowding in Glasgow was an enormous problem that persisted well into the twentieth century. The Gorbals was a substantial slum whose inhabitants lived at high risk of disease and other forms of morbidity. An 1895 study (Dawson, 1901) reported that one-quarter of Glasgow's population in 1881 lived in one room, and nearly one-half lived in two rooms. Smout (1986) described the typical one-room house as 14 by 11 feet, and added that, ten years later, one-tenth of such residences included a boarder. The death rate for these inhabitants was over twice that of more fortunate people.

Edinburgh's poor crowded in the streets of the Old Town around St. Giles cathedral were equally unfortunate. They lived in the Wynds in tall tenements, with up to ten floors, whose rooms were overcrowded. In 1851 a "Medical Gentleman" provided an account of the conditions in which adults and children lived. He entered a lodging in Blackfriar's Wynd consisting of "one room and two closets, the former about 10 feet by 8. One of the closets lodged five girls at least for that number was in bed . . . we had here eighteen individuals at least." Not all space was used for sleeping. The Medical Gentleman noted in the Cowgate that there were ten public houses in view while walking a mere 20 yards.

In Ireland, the registrar-general, Robert E. Matheson, presented a report on the state of housing in the six decades 1841–1901 (Matheson, 1903). He reported all houses in four classes, the worst of which consisted of one room, while the best class being better than an average farm house. This system, based on assigning numerical values to the number of rooms, windows, and durability, was first adopted in 1841.

During the sixty years, as the population fell the number of houses declined from 1.33 millions to .86 millions. The number of houses in the fourth, lowest, class declined from .49 millions to .13 millions in 1851 and to less than 10,000 in 1901. In contrast, first-class houses rose from 40,000 in 1841 to 75,000 in 1901; most of them were in cities.

In terms of residents, 42.26 percent, or nearly half, lived in fourth-class housing in 1841, a proportion that had fallen to 4.53 percent in 1901. The proportion in the best-class housing rose from 2.13

percent in 1841 to 7.46 percent in 1901. There were, however, sixty-eight dwellings of one room occupied by twelve or more persons. This alarming figure was, however, only half of the same problem, proportionately, in Scotland.

Ecology and Housing

An important aspect of the quality of housing was its relationship to the neighborhood and the process of growth in a district. Ironically, the biggest problem was probably progress. That is, widened streets and the advent of railways were possible only at the expense of existing structures. The poor, ever in competition for housing in expanding towns, competed for scarcer housing whose cost rose as a consequence. The purchasing power of the poor declined sharply. Railways affected housing even when not destroying them. They did so by creating deep cuttings which destroyed movement from one place to another. Railways also arrived on archways cutting off the circulation of air and access to sunlight for those fortunate enough not to have lost their dwellings; Glasgow provides an example evident even today.

Structure of Houses

Although it is useful to consider housing as so many units of particular sizes and with or without amenities, it is possible to look at housing as a micro environment with its own ecology. The physical structure of early nineteenth century housing for the masses is distinguished by poor construction; frequently, fly-by-night speculators threw up cheap and nasty housing for urban families. No less ill-used, however, were rural workers. In 1832, *The Penny Magazine* (of the Society for the Diffusion of Useful Knowledge) exhorted "the labouring man" to choose his dwelling away from a "low and marshy situation," to pursue "the free admission of light and air," and to avoid renting furnished premises since the money annually paid for furniture might well be the same as its initial cost to the landlord. In the 1840s commentators recalled that "wood and wattled houses, such as our forefathers built, are the driest and warmest of all" ("Condition of Labourers' Tenements in England," 1844). Stone was not impervious to water, and Berkshire cottages had floors of porous tiles; at Stratford, damp thatch propagated the miasma thought to create disease, and cottages everywhere lost heat through handsome, if excessively wide chimneys. An instance of urban housing and its problems in 1839 was given by Dr. J. Mitchell to the commission investigating the Spitalfields weavers. Describing the houses he said,

> Many of them are the worst that can be imagined, having no common sewers. The houses generally are of two stories, ground floor and one story above; the foundations of which were of laid upon the turf, or vegetable mould, and have no ventilation between the floors of the principal living rooms and the worst description of undrained soil immediately under such floors. The consequence is, that the exhalation arising from the garden-ground (for so it may be called) produces a dampness, from which the houses are exempt only during very dry weather. The roadway of the streets is of the most wretched kind, often composed of earthy and soft rubbish, and brick-dust saturated with moisture, and in many cases cut up by carts into a mass of mud, without any escape for the water but by soaking into the ground, from whence it makes its way under the houses, and joined by the oozings from the cesspools, frequently passes off in noxious vapour, and that through the sitting-rooms of the houses I have just described. The walls are of the thickness of required by the Building Act, but are in many cases constructed of bad material, half-burnt bricks, and mortar of very inferior description. The timbers are of the cheapest kind, and of course the least durable; and the scantlings the smallest that could be used. The roofs are covered with pantiles, and but few of them pointed, the pitch very bad, scarcely enough to keep them watertight.

A significant exception to the problem of housing is the city of Manchester whose slum district of Ancoats in the period defined by the censuses of 1851 and 1871 was studied by Rushton (1977). It appears that Manchester's housing stock kept pace with expansion of the population in the first half of the nineteenth century. However, Ancoats was still a slum and there was overcrowding; in this instance, it was related to the stage of family formation (e.g. the number of dependent children), which determined whether relatives and lodgers were taken in. In Preston, in 1851, a young female lodger would contribute nine to fifteen pence per week to the family, according to Anderson (1971). The overall pattern in Ancoats was for co-residence to decline; rent levels changed slowly thereby relieving family budgets in an era when wages tended to rise, except for the Hungry Forties and the cotton famine of the early 1860s. Lest it seem that Ancoats represents a tolerable minimum level of housing two points may be made; first, sanitation was bad and middens, piles of night waste trash and garbage, occupied public spaces. Second, worse than Ancoats was little Ireland into which immigrants poured raising levels of overcrowding in houses and their cellars.

It is noteworthy that in Manchester, and its vigorous rival to the east, Leeds, some housing for the working class tended to be built expressly for them. London, in contrast, frequently housed the poor in deteriorated middleclass housing from which the bourgeois single-family units had fled for more salubrious surroundings in (e.g.) Highgate and Holland Park.

Dr. John C. Hall wrote to *The Times* on September 17, 1853 describing Turner's Retreat in the parish of St. George the Martyr in London. Housing was particularly abominable there and deaths from cholera were high in the epidemic of 1849. Five years after Edwin Chadwick's (1842) great report on urban sanitation and health people continued to die in appalling surroundings. The cellars of Saffron Hill, St. Giles, and Jacob's Island, the rookeries in which people were crowded together like flocks of birds in a tree, were occupied by children and adults living amidst filth and darkness.

Micro Ecology

To live in such circumstances had a direct effect on the health of residents. *The Penny Magazine* (1844) reported the total demoralization of a tidy servant who, on marrying, occupied a miserable dwelling. Her benefactor found better housing and the woman recovered her former style of good housekeeping. Today, we know that dirt and overcrowding affect creatures great and small, and humans are no exception. In Liverpool at mid-century 118 Irish people in Crosbie Street lived in 150 square yards (Duncan, 1844). In the same period in Leeds one house in five or six occupied by the Irish had ten residents or more (Dillon, 1974). In *Ragged London* in 1861, Hollingshead gave statistics of housing density in the East End. In the 43 acres of St. George's in the East 13,300 people lived in 1,888 dwellings. Those numbers can be expressed as 7.05 persons per dwelling. More generally, the ratio of people to houses in Table 2.1 varies little across the century. I have calculated the decennial numbers for people and houses in England as ratios, and they vary around a mean of 5.34 persons per dwelling. Because the average dwelling was not large there was probably one person or more per room, with a quite large range of ratios for the extremes of quality in housing. However, when we consider Palgrave's data in Table 2.2 on Middlesex, that is, the country traditionally con-

TABLE 2.2 LIVING CIRCUMSTANCES, 1801–1911

Year	Number of[1] Inhabited Houses in Millions	People[1] per House	Persons per Dwelling						
			England[2]	Middlesex[2]	Westminster[2]	Manchester[3]	Leeds[4]	Low Moor[5]	Glasgow[6]
1801	1.57	5.66	5.67	7.25					
1811	1.79	5.67	5.68	7.29					
1821	2.08	5.76	5.76	7.48					
1831	2.48	5.60	5.62	7.52	9.84				
1841	2.94	5.41	5.44	7.59	9.79			6.79	
1851	3.27	5.48	5.50	7.88	10.04	5.80	4.81	5.34	5.08
1861	3.73	5.38	5.39	7.90	10.01	5.40	4.75	5.12	4.56
1871	4.25	5.34				5.20	4.69	4.03	4.31
1881	4.83	5.37				5.10			4.63
1891	5.45	5.32							4.01
1901	6.26	5.19							4.55
1911	7.14	5.05							4.61

M persons/rooms[1]
"County of London"
N Tenement Rooms

	1	2	3	4
	2.24	1.82	1.45	1.29
	2.04	1.74	1.38	1.24
	1.92	1.71	1.37	1.19

[1] Aggregated from tables in, *Census of England and Wales 1911* (1917).
[2] Palgrave (1869).
[3] Baker (1882).
[4] Hole (1866).
[5] Calculated from Ashmore (1964).
[6] Calculated from Butt (1971).

TABLE 2.3 TOWNS WITH HIGHEST AND LOWEST PROPORTIONS OF POPULATION PER ROOM ACCOMMODATION

One Person Or Less Per Room		Over One But Not Over Two Persons Per Room		Over Two Persons Per Room		In Tenements Of More Than Ten Rooms	
Town	Per 1,000	Town	Per 1,000	Town	Per 1,000	Town	Per 1,000
Highest							
Ilford	680	St. Helens	540	Gateshead	337	Blackpool	165
Handsworth	667	Wigan	528	South Shields	329	Bournemouth	162
Gillingham	662	Stoke-on-Trent	522	Sunderland	326	Eastbourne	155
Leicester	658	Warrington	512	Newcastle-on-Tyne	317	Ealing	144
Ipswich	652	Rhondda	507	Tynemouth	308	Bath	135
Hornsey	640	Edmonton	500	Plymouth	176	Hastings	119
		West Ham	500	St. Helens	169	Hornsey	112
Lowest							
Gateshead	254	Hornsey	215	Leicester	11	Aston Manor	3
South Shields	262	Bournemouth	253	Northampton	11	East Ham	3
Newcastle-upon-Tyne	270	Blackpool	260	Ipswich	13	Smethwick	5
Sunderland	270	Ealing	269	Bournemouth	15	Rhondda	8
St. Helens	282	Handsworth	279	Burton-upon-Trent	15	West Ham	8
Tynemouth	288	Oxford	280	Handsworth	15		
Wigan	332	Bath	281	Derby	18		
West Ham	339	Southport	281				

Source: *Census of England and Wales 1911. General Report with Appendices.* (1917). London. H.M.S.O.

stituting much of London north of the Thames, the ratio of people to houses is higher and actually increased across the nineteenth century. In 1861, Percy Greg pointed out that the London worker occupied one room for a rent yielding three bedrooms for an artisan in Lancashire or Yorkshire. In Westminster the density was still higher and also rose across the century. In the eighth column of Table 2.2 are data from Leeds calculated by James Hole (1866). Those ratios resemble the extra-London figures and show a slight decline over twenty years at mid-century. By the opening of the new, twentieth century there had been progress, but far from enough by the standards of today. In Table 2.3 are data on the frequency of overcrowding identified in the census of 1911. The highest frequency of more than two persons per room was Gateshead followed by three other towns in the northeast: South Shields, Sunderland, and Newcastle upon Tyne. Life for families in that area was well described by Lady Bell (1907) in *At the Works: A Study of a Manufacturing Town.*

Housing in Scotland was an acute problem in the nineteenth century. Smout (1986) described Glasgow housing in 1851 as composed of one or two room houses for half of the total stock of housing. Overcrowding was seven times more common in Scotland than in England.

In 1888, Glasgow's medical officer, James B. Russell, wrote an informative book, *Life in One Room.* Drawing on his personal experience and on data from the 1882 census Dr. Russell expanded observations previously offered by John Bright in his Rectorial Address to the university in 1884. For Glasgow as a whole there were 84 people per acre, a density exceeded only by Liverpool. However Glasgow was unique in its high proportion of one-room dwellings. Thirty percent of the residences consisted of one room, and a further 44 percent consisted of two rooms. In the Gorbals and other areas of Glasgow there were enclaves where density per room averaged 2.94 persons. Still more alarming was the presence of a lodger in 14 percent of the one-room dwellings and in 27 percent of the two-room houses.

In relation to the question of the degeneracy of health there was the alarming ambience within which children lived and died. Russell emphasized the Glasgow one-room houses of the 1880s, because

> Their exhausted air and poor and perverse feeding fill our streets with bandy-legged children. There you will find year after year a death-rate of 38 per 1000, while in the districts with larger houses it is only 16 or 17. Of all the children who die in Glasgow before they complete their fifth year, 32 per cent die in houses of one apartment; and not 2 per cent

in houses of five apartments and upwards. There they die, and their little bodies are laid on a table or on a dresser, so as to be somewhat out of the way of their brothers and sisters, who play and sleep and eat in their ghastly company. From beginning to rapid-ending the lives of these children are short parts in a continuous tragedy. A large proportion enter life by the side-door of illegitimacy. One in every five of all who are born there never see the end of their first year. Of those who so prematurely die, a third have never been seen in their sickness by any doctor. Every year in Glasgow the deaths of from 60 to 70 children under five years of age are classified by the Registrar-General as due to accident or negligence; and it is wholly in these small houses that such deaths occur. Half of that number are overlain by drunken mothers, others fall over windows and down stairs, are drowned in tubs and pails of water, scalded, or burned, or poisoned with whisky. I can only venture to lift a corner of the curtain which veils the life which is lived in these houses. It is impossible to show you more.

The mechanisms by which bad housing, alcoholism and child neglect operated may be illustrated in the Medical Gentleman's (1851) anecdote from Edinburgh's Old Town:

Shoeless and shivering in the raw damp of a chilly November night, might have been seen a few Saturdays ago, a woman, with one child in her arms and two little ones tugging at her gown—drunk, almost unable to stand—who, a few minutes before entering the dram-shop, had pawned her shawl for fourpence, in order to get a glass of the accursed liquor, the love of which had reduced her to the appalling condition in which we saw her. She was a bloated and besotted looking wretch. Her dress consisted of only a few rags, and her red and skeleton-like legs were bare to the thigh—her feet were thrust into a pair of old bauchles—her bosom was nearly bare—the children were crying for food, and while endeavoring to walk away from the door of the public house, she fell upon the greasy pavement, and was humanely hurried off to the Police-office, perhaps a better shelter for her poor children than the home she could taken them to.

In 1917, Dr. W. L. Mackenzie reported for the Carnegie United Kingdom Trust his analyses of the condition of women and children in Scotland. In particular, he presented photographs of dwellings in the isles that had the appearance of mounds of earth, lacking windows, and through whose doorways smoke flowed out for lack of a chimney.

TABLE 2.4   DECREMENTS IN HEIGHT (cm.) AT THREE AGES ASSOCI-
ATED WITH SCOTTISH DWELLINGS OF LESS THAN FOUR ROOMS

| | Rooms | | |
Age	Four to Three, Decrement	Four to Two, Decrement	Four to One, Decrement
5[1]	−1.79	−3.81	−6.09
9[2]	−1.77	−3.30	−6.09
11	−1.78	−3.82	−5.85
5–18[2]	−3.30	−3.81	−4.82

[1]Calculated from W. L. Mackenzie (1917), *Scottish Mothers and Children: Being Report on the Physical Welfare of Mothers and Children*. Dunfermline: Carnegie United Kingdom Trust.
[2]*Report of the Physical Condition of Children Attending the Public Schools of the School Board for Glasgow* (1907).

Barefoot children are present in his photographs. More analytically, Mackenzie presented data on the "child of the one-room dwelling," of which there were many in Scottish towns. One of Dr. Mackenzie's informative findings was that there was a demonstrable drop in the height and weight of children at ages five, nine, and eleven years as the number of rooms in dwellings declined from four to one. Mackenzie presented no information on the number of cases, and he excluded data from girls but added the comment that the pattern of heights and weights was the same. Table 2.4 may be read at each age from left to right showing the drop in height associated with a smaller dwelling. The criterion of four rooms in 1917 is far from luxurious by our standards, but it represents good housing in the large cities of Scotland in the period 1907–1917. The average reduction in height for three-room dwellings in Glasgow is 2.18 cm. (.85 inch), for two room dwellings it is 3.68 cm. (1.45 inches), and for the one room dwellings it is 5.71 cm. (2.25 inches), at all ages. It should be noted that the number of rooms is a covariate of the family's socioeconomic level. Even so, we can see that the number of rooms is a marker variable for height. Small children fell behind other children in height as they moved from age to age. The pattern for decrements in weight is quite similar, so that as the number of rooms declines the tendency for boys to be shorter and lighter increased. In 1963, Craig confirmed that housing and height were still connected. Within a given occupational group heights were influenced negatively by a high ratio of people to rooms (i.e., three or more persons to a room).

That height is but one component of health is evident when we translate data on home density into behavioral patterns. Watterson (1988) reported the effect of housing when income is held constant from an unplanned experiment. Drawing on data from the 1911 census she noted that in the period 1890–1910 soldiers enjoyed government housing, but sailors did not. Given their comparable economic state, Watterson noted that infant mortality in army families declined, but there was no decline in navy families. Similarly, Watterson reported that the income of miners exceeded that of agricultural workers, but the greater income was not accompanied by a greater decline in infant mortality; income alone did not determine the quality of life.

A persistent cry of the reformers called attention to the insalubrious effects of several households sharing external toilets with neighbors. Within overcrowded dwellings parents and growing children shared beds, and reformers called attention to the indifference to modesty that a lack of privacy created. They rarely were more explicit than that; Wohl (1978) pointed out that the few Victorian writers who investigated incest found it a refutation of the idealized view of the family as the repository of virtue; the contrary was simply not discernable. However, Peter Gaskell (1833) dropped some pretty broad hints about domestic vice in *The Manufacturing Population of England.*

The turn of the century reformer R. A. Bray described the impact of overcrowding on children based on his experience living in the Albany Dwellings in Camberwell along with C. F. G. Masterman (1901) and other men of social conscience:

> When a number of people inhabit a few rooms peace and order take wing, leaving behind a ceaseless babel of noise. With boys and girls varying in age, from the baby to the child about to leave school, and indulging in their respective amusements, nothing else is possible. From lack of calming influences there is a constant strain on the nerves which renders those living in this way intensely irritable, and the child develops a highly-strung, excitable nature. Children, possessing as they do a surplus of energy, are naturally easily excited; but town children are marked by this characteristic to a far greater extent than those who have their homes in the country.

Children sought recreation in the streets, especially as the door usually opened onto a flagstone pavement paralleled by the gutter. Teenagers, ever touchy in the brief, stressful years of maturing, were quick to turn to the streets for companionship and to avoid the turmoil of the household. Mayhew (Quennell, 1969) devoted a good deal of time to the process by which adolescent costermongers left the family roof to set up their own domiciles with or without churching; Fleischman (1985) quoted an inspector in the West of England to the effect that weavers married earlier than any other groups in the region. Town streets were the playgrounds for children, and the debris of urban life provided new material for play, imagination, and exploration. Shopping areas were more attractive, and home and church competed unsuccessfully for adolescents' attention. Forster's 1870 education act corralled most children of the towns; but the early school-leaving age and permissibility of work as "half-timers" (Mills, 1933) were powerful magnets drawing children into the public life of towns. From streets to pubs was an easy step, especially as children were used to being dispatched to the jug and bottle window of the local for a pitcher of beer. Drinking had been a major recreation since time immemorial, and public drunkenness was a common sight. The scope of abuse of alcohol was enormous and constituted a major complex of ill-health and neglect of children and the home by mothers and fathers.

Speculative Housing

Then as now the key to housing was control of the land on which it sits. In towns the ground rent was the base for leasing rather than sale; it was followed by renting entire dwellings to someone who then rented apartments, single rooms, and cellars. At each stage a profit was taken. For speculative builders land sold or leased was the basis for cheap construction, sometimes without footings on which to place walls or plumbing to provide sewage. In 1839, Dr. Mitchell described the houses of the poor as,

> erected by speculative builders of the most scampy class. The houses require constant repair to keep them any way fit for habitation. They may screen from the heat of summer as much as any of this class can be expected to do, but I do not consider that they sufficiently protect from the cold of winter. Altogether, they deserve the attention of the public authorities.
>
> The proprietors of the land being anxious to get an increased rental were glad to negotiate with builders, frequently men of no property, and they advanced to them a certain amount of bricks and timber, securing themselves as a remuneration by an exorbitant ground rent. Of course to such men the propriety of making sewers or drains, or in fact doing

anything beyond what was necessary to give an appearance of the property, never once occurred. ("Reports from the Assistant Hand-Loom Weavers' Commissioners," 1839)

Sewers and drains would not have been expensive; in Brown's (1990) analysis of the standard of living in Northwest England in the first half of the nineteenth century, the cost could have been recovered within the weekly rent at a cost to the residents of 2 d. or 2½ d. Building row houses that shared side walls was an economical step; frequently, the back wall was without door or windows to lower costs which, in turn, suggested that the back wall also be shared in a double row of houses sharing a common inner wall. Here was the "back-to-back" house, whose limited ventilation was the perfect site for tuberculosis and other airborne disases. The back-to-back house was uncommon in London, and Leeds gained the unwelcome distinction of having the most. The pattern became conventional; Ward (1962) presented a photograph of a terrace of half-back houses adjoining a property line. None of the back walls are pierced by windows and the end residence has blank back and side walls. Back-to-back housing was especially common in northern manufacturing towns and many were not pulled down until the mid-twentieth century. Cowlard (1979) provided the instance of John Lee, a nineteenth century Solicitor of Wakefield, who constructed shells of houses and left purchasers to finish the interiors on their own. Such housing would be imperfectly prepared for habitation and constituted a ready-made slum. In London's Thomas Flight, slum housing reached the zenith of speculation since he owned hundreds of shabby dwellings on which the profit was enormous. In the case of the infamous Boot and Shoe yard in Leeds the rent realized was £214 per annum (Baker, 1840); this handsome profit explains the aphorism that, "where there's muck there's money".

Throughout the industrialized world factory owners built housing for workers. To work for Krupp in Germany was to have a good job and house for life, if one were careful. Gaskell (1833) reported that factory "cottages," usually row houses described as terraces, were an additional source of profit for factory owners. On an outlay of £5,000 he reported an annual return of £800, which is 13.5 percent. Consols generally paid about 3 percent, so that housing was a sensible investment which could appear to be philanthropy. Rent was deducted automatically from the pay packet, and when combined with the company retail store, the "truck" system of payment in kind, workers became a source of retail profit as well as production.

At the end of the period addressed in this work, in 1913, Bowley and Burnett-Hurst (1915) conducted a study of the living conditions of the working class in four towns: Northampton, Reading, Warrington, and Stanley (near Durham). When pooled, they constituted a set of 2,150 working-class households (excluding 480 better-off households) composed of 9,720 persons, of whom 3,287 (34 percent) were children. One family in six, 13.5 percent, lived in Rowntree's "primary" poverty (to be distinguished from "secondary" poverty, due to improvidence). Relevant to this book is the finding that one in four children (27 percent) lived in "families which fail to reach the low standard (of living) taken as necessary for health." Thus, at the end of the period addressed here, the physical development of many working-class children remained compromised by the circumstances of life, even using the standards of that era. As an example, 729 (32 percent) of the working men studied earned less than 24s per week, a number roughly the same as that recalled by Mrs. Pember Reeves (1913) in *Round About A Pound A Week.*

Bowley and Burnett-Hurst also noted that secondary poverty, that due to the parent's self-indulgence, included betting and its corollary in Warrington, loan-sharking. Funds borrowed for drink, betting, and gambling generated interest due each payday of 25 percent per week; annually, that amounted to 1,300 percent interest.

Aesthetics and Morality

The concept of degeneracy addressed in this work is a question of health and physical development. However, the Victorians were conscious of another level of problem, one paradoxically concrete and abstract at the same time. On the one hand, vitiated air, overcrowding, and poor sanitation produced self-evident problems; on the other, the conduct of residents of bad housing, which is to say the poor, violated middle-class expectations for respecting property, being sober, and keeping the peace. The challenge was to disentangle cause and effect. The poor neglected their dwellings, were shiftless, and were given to rowdiness. Given the nature of their residences there was little to husband and less to take pride in. Until personal values improved nothing else would. But circumstances clearly shaped values, and so reform of housing and the broad assertion that public architecture affects individual conduct set afoot a process of reform.

Across the nineteenth century designers invoked Gothic design in competition with classic columns and pediments. Banks looked like temples and factories like anything else. Prisons looked like fortresses with crenellated walls and towers, although the historic function of those elements was to keep people out rather than in. A subtext argued that classicism was republican and democratic, while the Gothic was hierarchical and undemocratic (Schmieken, 1988). At the level of the individual home, the emerging theme was decoration; an improving economy permitted acquisition of religious and secular pictures with uplifting themes. Contemporary condescension towards this aspect of domestic decoration tends to slight the reforming theme that designers introduced into family life in pursuit of overall respectability. The latter encompassed repudiation of the violence, dirt, and disease, which appeared to be moral failure on the part of the poor. In that context, model housing aimed to reform individual moral degeneracy, as well as to provide healthy dwellings for the working man's family.

Planning

The Victorians were not unmindful of their problems and housing was a constant challenge to reform. One of the early movements culminating in the twentieth century's garden cities and corporation housing estates was the model housing movement. At the simplest level it consisted of philanthropically sponsored shelters where the homeless could sleep. Slightly more sophisticated were the model lodging houses for the separate sexes in which cooking and laundry facilities might be found. Model dwellings for single families were sketched abundantly in magazines. When it occurred, philanthropic housing was intended for the deserving poor and not for the undeserving, rowdy poor of bad moral character. Two figures who combined financial resources and energy to provide cheap housing were John Ruskin and Octavia Hill. In London, the complexes founded on the donation of Massachusetts philanthropist George Peabody are still occupied. On a larger scale were the model communities developed by industrialists for their workers: Saltaire near Bradford built by Titus Salt, Akroydon near Halifax built by Edward Akroyd, Bourneville near Birmingham developed by the Cadbury's, and Port Sunlight near Birkenhead developed by W. H. Lever. However, construction of housing on an appropriate scale for the poor and the working class was not really on the public agenda until after the 1914–1918 war. In that period Liverpool acquired 64,789 houses of which 58.3 percent were built by the municipality (Pooley and Irish, 1987).

TABLE 2.5   GROWTH OF POPULATION IN LEEDS, IN-TOWNSHIP, 1801–1901,[1] AND PARLIAMENTARY BOROUGH[2]

Year	In-Township	Parliamentary Borough
1801	31,000	
1811	36,000	
1821	49,000	
1831	72,000	
1841	88,000	152,000
1851	101,000	172,000
1861	118,000	206,000
1871	140,000	252,000
1881	160,000	
1891	179,000	
1901	196,000	

[1]M. W. Beresford (1967).
[2]D. Ward (1980).

Urbanization of Leeds

Leeds is a useful site for studying the process of urbanization. It is an old town having been known within the Saxon kingdom of Elmet and placed still earlier by Baines (1873) as the pre-Roman Loid. A center of the woolen trade it expanded and acquired engineering facilities in the nineteenth century. Originally a core town on ground rising north of the river Aire, Leeds was caught up in the mechanization of its historic wool trade. In the nineteenth century it had evolved into the center of a trading area as well as a manufacturing site. People migrated from surrounding towns, and in the early 1800s Leeds' mill owners paid a premium for workers for a time. The immigration of workers had no parallel in the size of the housing stock as various parts of the inner town expanded (see Table 2.5).

As the nineteenth century opened, the township of Leeds and its ten out-townships spread from the banks of the Aire that flows east from the Pennines to the Humber and the North Sea. Over the decades the out-townships north of the river attracted the middle classes in a pattern of growth that still continues. The core town lay on rising ground growing away from the river. The area to the east was comparatively level ground and became an area of residence for the poor. In the early nineteenth century erection of factories occasionally infiltrated residential areas in west Leeds. The well-to-do generally fled to the north and west into what is rolling ground rising eventually into Wharfedale and the moors. On the low ground south of the turgid river lay Holbeck and Hunslet, ancient townships, which became a district of factories and housing for the very poor. In his report to the Statistical Society of London, just established, Dr. Robert Baker (1840) noted the density of persons in Boot and Shoe Yard; originally a fold or enclave this small area expanded by consuming its own interior space, and it did so with no expansion of amenities. As a result, in 1839 there were thirty-four habitations with fifty-seven rooms and 340 residents. The ratio of people to houses was 10:1, and of people to rooms 6:1. The yard was razed in 1842.

About this time, development occurred in an area about 1 mile east of Briggate, to be crowned about a century later in the 1930s with Europe's second largest public housing complex, Quarry Hill flats. In that area the nineteenth century poor gathered to be joined by Irish immigrants. Housing stock was cheap and consisted mainly of the back-to-back construction for which Leeds became notorious. The houses in question can be seen in the photographs assembled by Caffyn (1986, p. 84).

In 1866, "Hole of Leeds", as he came to be known, wrote *The Homes of the Working Classes*. In that influential work he reported that

> the number of houses in Leeds increased from 1841 to 1861 rather faster than the population of the borough. While the increase in our population was some 36 per cent., that in the number of houses reached 39 per cent. In the Leeds township, while the increase of population from 1841 to 1861 was 32 per cent., the increase of houses was 33 per cent. Such facts simply might indicate that the population was not overcrowded, or at least that overcrowding was not increasing. It is really as fallacious, however, as it would be to take the total income of the inhabitants and divide it by the population, in order to ascertain the means of subsistence possessed by each individual. Notwithstanding the great increase of houses, overcrowding exists to a considerable extent. Cellars are now occupied as dwellings that, not long ago, were considered too bad for living in. The rents of cottage dwellings have advance latterly 15 to 20 per cent, and were even 2,000 or 3,000 additional cottages erected, there would be applications for them. Although nearly unfettered by building conditions— which in Bradford, and elsewhere, are made the pretext for the inadequate supply of these dwellings—the "demand" does not create the

"supply", and neither speculators, employers, nor philanthropists seem disposed to make the slightest move towards the supply of this great social necessity. Hence the lower class of tenants are glad to avail themselves of any shelter, however deficient in the proper conditions and applications of a home. (Hole, 1866)

The growth in population in Leeds, as in many towns, outstripped the supply of housing, especially with births exceeding deaths after 1770 (Yasumoto, 1973). In-migration from local villages and immigration of 5,000 Irish people by 1830 swelled the population. The magnet was work in textile mills that specialized in woolens and, to a lesser degree, in flax. As with all early nineteenth century workers before the development of electric tramways, living close to the mill was important and led to high demand. Hole (1866) reported that the number of houses in Leeds borough rose in the period 1841–1861 from 31,597 to 44,080, which is an increase of 39 percent. Even so, the ratio of people to houses in the twenty years merely changed from 4.81 to 4.69. Expansion frequently came narrowly in the form of back-to-back houses, sustaining the density of populations at a high level. Beresford (1971) documented that Leeds continued to build back-to-backs long after other towns abandoned them, the last being erected, according to Beresford, as recently as 1937. Two ironies, in this regard, are that to the west and southwest lay the nineteenth century model communities of Saltaire and Akroydon; while at the time that back-to-backs were still going up, the Quarry Hill flats were under construction to house 3,000 people.

From the point of view of health and human development the essential problem was the risk of air-borne diseases, tuberculosis, and water-borne diseases created by insufficiency of sanitary provisions. Several families shared outside toilets, which were supplemented by domestic utensils.

In all of this it is the density of population and correlated exposure to foul and diseased air that caused the degeneration of health to continue. Air-borne diseases were unavoidable because ventilation was poor in back-to-back houses and the sheer number of people in propinquity speeded the transmission of disease. In such circumstances parents with high personal standards of child care and hygiene waged an uphill fight against childhood disease and insect vectors such as typhus. Shaved heads with a little tuft in front were the hallmark of the inner-city boy whose parents fought the infestation of fleas and other vermin in overcrowded conditions.

Given that the original back-to-backs sometimes consisted of one room up and one room down, it can be seen that families faced infectious disease as a chronic problem within the family. Across the narrow street lay another row of back-to-backs so that privacy and quiet were luxuries not known in the locality. Drink became an escape for some men and women, and their children went neglected, untended, and ill-fed. In some respects the prevalence of back-to-back houses in Leeds had a unique origin. Beresford (1971) pointed out that the fold-type of development consisted of adding rooms against any existing wall creating a room with a solid rear wall. He suggested that this mode of adding three walls to an existing blank wall set the precedent for back-to-back houses with blank rear walls. In a culture that tended to be inward-looking, two-story back-to-backs constructed from scratch appealed to cost-conscious entrepreneurs who cherished their "brass." However, Caffyn (1986) pointed out that the back-to-back was configured in Bradford to create a rear window by running the rooms narrowly from front to back as two opposed, interlocking, L-shape dwellings. In Leeds the unenlightened version prevailed to the detriment of health and propagation of tuberculosis and other diseases as late as the 1940s.

It was not until 1910, however, that a full picture of the risk to life presented by back-to-back housing became available. In that year, Dr. L. W. Darra Mair completed a study of health in back-to-back houses in thirteen towns in the West Riding of Yorkshire. In an inquiry fortified by a design that took several factors into account, including modification of houses' layouts, Darra Mair demonstrated that mortality was raised even in the best of back-to-backs by about 20 percent. For through-houses, mortality from smallpox, scarlet fever, diptheria, and similar conditions was 1 per 1,000 (K) people; in back-to-backs it was at least 1.34 per K, and as high as 1.50 deaths per K. For all causes it was 13.89 per K in through houses, 16.40 in improved back-to-backs, and 17.25 per K for ordinary back-to-backs. When Darra Mair adjusted his data from 3,996 houses containing 6,784 residents for sex and age the corrected three death rates were through-houses = 16.15 per K population, ventilated back-to-backs = 18.60, and ordinary back-to-backs = 19.46. In the case of children under five years the mortality rate in through houses was 51.3 per K, but it rose to 66.6 in back-to-back houses. Deaths under age five due to diarrhea in through-houses were 7.23 per K and rose to 9.78 in back-to-back houses.

The development of public housing estates planned by local town councils between the wars illustrates that the city was the source of social evils, but also its own theoretical resource for their remediation. Housing estates as an element of public policy stand in contrast to Victorian efforts such as Cross's housing act. The policy of the interwar years required establishment of suburban dwellings to which inner city residents could emigrate. They left their old neighborhoods to be razed and, ideally, replaced with light industry. This component of public policy shows the evolution of thought and experience since the Victorian era. Then, the public heard denunciation intended to focus attention, as in the *Bitter Cry of Outcast London* (1883). Charity was evident in early model lodgings followed by (e.g.) the Peabody Trust's tenements. Utopianism had its place in Buckingham's model town of Victoria, and in the reality-testing of the Salvation Army's way-out of Darkest England by degrees of emigration. Today, urban policy is something of a battlefield, but it has come a long way since the first glimmering that urban problems were comprehendible within experience and probably solvable to a degree. Slowly, the concept of degeneracy yielded its social and intellectual vagueness to narrow specifications whose empirical elements promoted analysis and improvement.

Work

Work was the central fact of life in the nineteenth century. In the country small children were sent into the fields to scare off crows, pick up stones, and glean after the harvest. Adolescents were hired at country fairs to work for farmers. In the factory towns to which the surplus rural population moved, the hours of work no longer followed the sun. The factory whistle or bell marked the change of shift as one worker replaced another at tasks now standardized and monotonous. As a percentage of the work force in textile factories the incidence of employment for children peaked at 15.9 percent in 1835 and declined to 7.8 percent by 1890; conceivably, by the last date, those children still employed were half-timers, a group we shall address shortly. In the case of teenage males, the peak came a little later, 1838, and the low point of 7.4 percent of the work force, in 1878, was exceeded slightly in the next few years (Nardinelli, 1990).

The workplace could be dangerous and it could be unhealthy. Each occupation had its problems, and all shared long hours in a six-day work week. For people working in metal there was the inhalation of metal dust created by grinding. Mortality in the Sheffield cutlery trade had a high and early mortality rate. Survivors had congested lungs and chronic coughs. In 1867, Hall described the ill-health of boy file-cutters and "their complexion with its dirty, sallow, yellow-white hue . . . dropped wrist . . . blue line around the gums." Far worse was the health of steel puddlers whose average age at death was thirty one years (Pollard, 1959). In the fabric industries high temperatures were a common problem in drying rooms.

Across the nineteenth century there are frequent references to scrofula, a term with both the modern meaning of a tuberculous disease and a range of generic meanings. They connote everything from a heat-induced skin reaction to scurvy brought on by excessive reliance on bread and tea, to the detriment of vegetables, in the diet.

Of course, the sheer density of population in the workplace increased the exposure to communicable diseases. From fatigue, as well as disease spread by droplets, the working population suffered poor health chronically. Long hours of standing, with few breaks, produced curved spines and dropped arches.

Children

Early evidence that children had a place in the economy came from Daniel Defoe, the author of Robinson Crusoe, who reported his tour of the British Isles in two volumes in 1726. He noted that in the cottage industry of northern manufactory districts, "The women and children . . . are always busy carding, spinning, and etc. so that no hands being unemployed all can gain their bread even from the youngest to the ancient; hardly anything above four years old, but its hands are sufficient to itself," a phrase indicating that what we would term *preschoolers* had a little job to perform. Born on April 26, 1845, the anonymous mid-century collier known to us only as "A. Miner" (Simpson, 1988) began to work at a mill at age eight and then went into a coal mine at age nine. His older brother began work above ground at the mine at age four. As a "banksman," he guided the horse that drew up baskets of coal. He yielded this job to another brother at age six. The boss was the boys' father. This observation also demonstrates that "domestic economy," such as the weaver at his loom in the house, could be just as demanding of little children as the factory overseer. In his 1885 M.D. thesis on the health of Lancashire working people, Dr. William Stewart, of Bacup, noted that, "one old woman told me that, when she was a child, she was indulged by her parents, and had only to work from 8 a.m. to 8 p.m., and she was at the ripe age of five." Parental "indulgence" of children in the family economy persisted as a practice "across the nineteenth century." In 1896, Margaret Macmillan noted that "There are in Yorkshire and Lancashire today many men and women who remember well the terrible eye and thongs of the overseer who was their own father." Orphans and others dependent on charity had no advocate, and they were frequently abused by parish overseers and factory owners (Emmison, 1944). Robert Owen was probably the first large factory owner to see the work force as the site for a utopian vision of the industrial age. Owen introduced schooling into the mill he operated at New Lanark, near Glasgow.

In the 1830s there was evidence that children suffered when put to work. The First Report of the Factory Commissioners demonstrated that factory work was hard. J. Cowell (1833) showed that factory children were smaller than nonfactory children. Gaskell's (1833) book reported an unidentified survey of "2000 children taken indiscriminately from several large establishments," showing child workers to be,

> stunted, pale, flesh soft and flabby; many with limbs bent, in most the arch of the foot flattened; several pigeon chested, and with curvatures in the spinal column; 140 had tender eyes, in a great majority the bowels were said to be irregular, diarrhoea often existing, and 90 shewed decided marks of having survived severe rachitic affections.

Women

In addition to children, women working in factories, mines, and even in domestic service were at great risk for injury to health. The working day was long, and there were children to care for and a home to maintain once working women came home, then as now. It is no wonder that Friedrich Engels, in a passage identified by Marcus (1974), reported, "I cannot recall having seen a single healthy, tall and well built girl in the throstle room of the mill in Manchester in which I worked. The girls were all small, poorly developed or stunted" Frisch (1977) reported that "About a quarter of the women working in the mills suffered from either 'retarded or suppressed' menses" and went on to report that menopause came earlier than today. The picture, in brief, is one of overstrained women working long hours in difficult circumstances. However, the problem went beyond the factory women since, in Gaskell's (1833) study,

> The female, from certain specific causes, is the one upon whom these bendings and curvatures are likely to produce the most serious conse-

quences. The arch of the pelvis becomes contracted or made irregular in its outline;—the spinal column, when curvatures take place low down, encroaches on its dimensions, or forms such projections as effectually to block it up. To the natural difficulties and pains of parturition are thus super-added obstacles, not unfrequently fatal to the child, and in all cases exceedingly perilous to the mother, leading to the annual sacrifice of many lives, and an amount of human misery not conceivable by anyone, but those whose avocations have led them to witness degrees of torture, which humanity shudders to contemplate.

Ten years after Gaskell, Noble (1843) conducted a survey of conditions in Manchester factories. Noble made a point about ill-health, namely, that factories alone were not the evil; he concluded from his inquiries that a portion of the health problems of people, " . . . appertain to their domestic rather than to their industrial relations." The significance of this insight would be largely ignored for decades until a more fully developed public sensibility appreciated the potentials for health which repose in effective and conscientious parenting. Neglect of family health due to parents' abuse of alcohol is an example of the "domestic" sources to which Noble referred.

Slowly, a series of reforming acts protected women and child workers and reduced the length of the working day. The Ten-Hours Act of 1847 meant well, but canny employers introduced the split shift and circumvented the law. Throughout the century enforcement of labor laws was weak and sporadic.

Child study entered the picture with the system of physicians' certifying children, after a physical examination, as being of age to work in factories. Leonard Horner's 1837 collation of statistics from manufacturing districts (see Chapter Four) was an attempt to provide a normative basis in physical development for determining age. He noted, "I have found children certified to have the ordinary strength and appearance of thirteen years of age, who were manifestly, to the most common observation, not more than ten or eleven" ("Practical Applications of Physiological Facts," 1837).

Only slowly, beginning with denunciation of women and children working in coal mines in the 1840s, did the conviction evolve that developing bodies were not meant to work. Led by Lord Ashley, later styled Lord Shaftesbury, the evangelical conscience galvanized the attention of the middle class. Decade by decade, work yielded to the classroom as the place for growing bodies. As factory work declined so did correlated problems such as the incidence of flat feet.

Roberts (1876), for example, reported that the incidence of flat feet was five times greater in factory children than in country children.

At the intermediate level of part-time work by children, nominally a reduction of stress on child factory workers, problems remained. The vicar of Rochdale, in Lancashire, the Rev. Mr. Wilson, was a close observer of childrens' health in the early 1890s. From his inspection of growth data on Rochdale youngsters, Wilson noted what he called "the *half-time bend.* It was a decline in the rate of acceleration, or annual growth increments, in children spending (e.g.) mornings in factories and drooping over their desks in the afternoons (Mills, 1933). The half-timer's stress was compounded by schools' inordinate expectations of energy available to children already fatigued by factory work. Each of two masters probably expected more than one-half of the energy of growing boys and girls. The resulting stress on the growing bodies of half-timers was a decline in the acceleration associated with early adolescence and normal growth, hence the "half-time bend" in the growth curves.

Shortly after the new century opened, in 1903, Harry J. Wilson, formerly a factory inspector in Scotland, presented comparative data on the height and weight of boys and girls to the Interdepartmental Committee in 1904 (see Chapter Seven). Wilson's data came from children working half-time in the jute mills of Dundee, in the age range eleven to fifteen years. Wilson compared his measurements with norms reported by Treves in *Physical Education.* In each instance, the half-timers fell far below the comparative groups in height and weight. Boys between eleven and twelve years of age were shorter by 3.5 inches (8.89 cm.) and lighter by 7.2 pounds (3.27 kg.); at age fourteen to fifteen, other boys were shorter by 5.0 inches (12.7 cm.) and lighter by 1.5 pounds (.68 kg.). Girls between eleven and twelve years were shorter by 1.5 inches (3.81 cm.). At age fourteen to fifteen, other girls were shorter by 2 inches (5.08 cm.). Of course, the argument was that factory work contributed to diminished height and weight. Although that is probably true, we lack information about the prior habitus of these Dundee half-timers. It is likely that they worked due to economic necessity; probably, their diminished condition in the teen years was merely an extension of their previously unsatisfactory condition.

Five years later, in 1909, the Interdepartmental Committee on Partial Exemption from School Attendance took evidence from half-timers in Bolton and Blackburn in Lancashire and Halifax to the east in Yorkshire. When Bolton half-timers were compared with other Bolton children they also fell behind. In this case, the comparison children may have been the wrong group, because we would like to compare the half-timers with other children from poor circumstances. It seems likely that Edwardian Bolton's schoolchildren were quite homogeneous, however, and so we accept the proposition that Rochdale's Archdeacon Wilson was correct in his view that even part-time work was harmful to growing children. Dr. Nora Mills (1933) cited the description given forty years before of half-timers in Rochdale. They were slender, pallid children with one shoulder higher than the other due to carrying heavy objects and fatigued due to lack of rest. Half-timers were the last of the child factory workers; their regimen, according to Dr. Mills, could be followed by children as young as ten years of age. They might work from 6 a.m. to noon and then attend school. In alternate weeks they might attend school in the morning and work in the cotton mills for four hours in the afternoon. Photographs of working children including half-timers and little children learning to make lace are given in Horn's (1989) *The Victorian and Edwardian Schoolchild.* Photographs from the early 1900s are also given in *A Century of Childhood* by Humphries, Mark, and Perks (1988).

Slowly came the advent of positive steps, in contrast to the mere absence of negative influences such as work. In particular, introduction of exercise and games as a therapeutic, developmental act, as opposed to mere recreation, came slowly. Overall, work was inimical to the health of growing children, and the locus of work, the factory town, generated conditions that perpetuated the harmful effects of work. It did so in the form of disorganization of family life, never quite idyllic at any time, and the neglect of growing children. With the passage of the decades, the culture of the slum emerged with its elements of alcoholism, abuse, and neglect. Philanthropy and religion made inroads into the problem, but only slowly. Government, the organized bureaucracy we recognize, had little place until the end of our period and the reforms in the decade before 1914.

3

Circumstances of Life

The topics shedding light on the degeneracy question in this chapter are the Victorians' understanding of genetics, nutrition, and health. All address aspects of how young and adult Victorians developed in the face of a quality of life that varied by social class and region. The range of conditions of growth was wide, by present-day standards, and the gap separating rich and poor was enormous. The poor faced stressful, shorter lives and were always at the mercy of epidemics. The child of the middle classes was likely to be well fed, however, and several inches taller than his or her working-class counterpart. Exactly why one child was shorter was explicable in part to the Victorians, but the complexities that led nature to produce redheads, twins, and families of recurring prodigy, like the Galtons, Wedgwoods, and Darwins—all intermarried—were beyond their grasp. They speculated that acquired traits such as low stature and susceptibility to disease would be transmitted to following generations.

Genetics and Evolution

As the nineteenth century opened thoughtful people had begun to appreciate that the world had not been created in one week, around 4004 B.C., as the eighteenth century divine, Bishop Ussher, had calculated. From the cliffs of Lyme Regis and similar sites, fossilized living things demonstrated that organisms had a history and presented both identical and dissimilar evolved forms. Species were discernible in the natural world and the similarities suggested changes from a common

59

antecedent. At the practical level, people had known that selective breeding of horses, dogs, and sheep led to recognizable, stable changes. As with all unknowns, formulating the problem was a major task. It consisted of attempting to understand the scope of changes in living things and to discern the mechanism by which similarities and changes occurred from one generation to another. If changes observable in the health of working-class people also occurred in their children the evident deterioration or degeneracy might be part of an irreversible process. Absent from nineteenth century commentaries appears to be acknowledgement that ordinary people were superior to their cave-dwelling ancestors rather than inferior. That observation implies that humankind had progressed from a primitive state far worse, originally, than the factory towns. The deepest worry was that once a generation was stigmatized its ravages must appear in successive generations. In Gaskell's (1833) formulation, "bodily deformity . . . will not be transmitted. But an universal weakness and want of tone in all organs (the child) has, an heir-loom . . . weakened constitution, attended with all its liabilities to physical inferiority." Mazumdar (1980) reported that the Swiss scientist Forel traced a variety of disorders to blastophthoria, a descriptive rather than explanatory term, conveying that several deficiencies were transmissible through the "germ plasm." History was not reassuring; in the early centuries of colonization the population of Iceland shrank in stature, and the colony in Greenland disappeared in the face of changes in climate. Today's Icelanders are tall by comparative standards, according to Tanner (Harrison, Weiner, Tanner, and Barnicot, 1964).

Charles Lyell recalled in 1872, that he had set forth in 1832 the question of, "whether it is conceivable that each fossil flora and fauna brought to light by the Geologist may have been connected, by way of descent or generation, with that which immediately preceded it." In his 1839 *Elements of Geology*, Lyell took note of Charles Darwin's observation of the specialized, adaptive claws of the Galapagos marine iguana. He also reported in disingenuous style Agassiz's observation about the phylogenetic distance between fossil creatures. In that speculation, which Charles Darwin found exciting, is the thought that quite different organisms in separate strata were nevertheless connected. Differences in that formulation would express continuity over time, a process of evolving differentiation. Here, we encounter the first Victorian milestone in the process of understanding the scope and the mechanisms of change in the biological order. The first reverberation was theological since it appeared inescapable that the Creator had

formed mountains and seas in forms not restricted to those around the Victorians. The world appeared not to have been created in seven days, and findings in the Neander valley in Germany suggested that humankind was comparatively old, certainly older than Genesis, overconstrued, might dictate. On Thomas Huxley's voyage on the *Rattlesnake*, and Charles Darwin's voyage on the *Beagle*, followed by Alfred Wallace's field research in southeast Asia, it became apparent that species evolve in ways that express adaptability, with survival being the prize for those most efficiently adapted. These views were muddled by the original presumption that modifications easily arrived at would be easily transmitted genetically.

To understand the views held by commentators on the apparent degeneration of physique, it is helpful to note the absence of a knowledge base in biology. As examples we cite the condition of embryology and plant morphology and genetics. Embryology suggested that evolution of the fetus caught echoes of ontogeny recapitulating phylogeny; accordingly, primitive states had not been left behind. Down picked up this element noting in his 1866 paper (Jordan, 1966) that some mentally retarded individuals were "analogues" to non-European races; in the case of a particular boy, Down thought it, "difficult to realize that he is the child of Europeans." Plant morphology acknowledged phylogeny, but biologists were unable to settle the question of whether change was abrupt or continuous, a critical mechanism in evolution. It may be noted that the search for intermediate forms in fossil materials remains far from complete. The overall state of affairs was that evolution and genetics needed a mathematical-statistical model; that innovation in the twentieth century made it possible to distinguish evident changes in human materials of a transmittable nature from temporary or mutable traits created by circumstances.

In the absence of rigorous design to avoid faulty deductions it appeared reasonable that once physical deterioration set in, it must manifest itself in subsequent generations. Further, in the form of social Darwinism, the best adapted people should prevail, a notion supported, unfortunately, by the apparent greater fecundity of the worse-off layers of society. In that respect, Nature should be allowed to take her course, and charity amounted to interference in The Plan; temporarily, Man and God were reconciled, but at the demographic price of a proliferating, unhealthy plebs. Shortly after the *Origin of Species* had appeared W. R. Gregg (1868) noted,

> We are growing daily more foolishly and criminally lenient to every natural propensity, less and less inclined to resent, or control, or punish

its indulgence. We absolutely refuse to let the poor, the incapable, or the diseased die; we enable or allow them, if we do not actually encourage them, to propagate their incapacity, poverty, and constitutional disorders.

Even so, there was hope in Darwinism; Wallace (1892) and Bulman (1902) argued that evolution could be counted on to breed the drinking problem out of the population. In fact, the drinking problem had already shrunk considerably by the turn of the century, based not on Darwin but on the marketing of cheap, soft drinks and tea, plus rising taxes on alcohol (amounting to 60 percent of the income anticipated in the budget for 1893 [Williams, 1894]).

More fundamental was the sequence of thought leading through Francis Galton and his protegé Karl Pearson to the eugenics movement of the twentieth century. Middle-class people saw the poor as a seething, breeding mass whose evident moral and physical degeneration evident in alcoholism, crime, and family disorganization was perpetuated by heredity. In 1877, R. L. Dugdale reported the "degenerated" Jukes family, and in 1912 Henry Goddard reported the eponymous Kallikak family. Eugenics deteriorated into pseudo-science and racism and was expressed in immigration quotas for various groups by American law in the 1920s. Kingsland (1987) pointed out that eugenics was eventually taken over by nonscientists, but they were no worse than the scientists. For example, Karl Pearson fulminated against Russian Jewish immigrants entering Britain to escape the endemic antisemitism evident even a century later in eastern Europe. The study of mental retardation was confounded until quite recently by laws and social policies expressing the excess of the eugenics movement (Jordan, 1976).

The level of thought on heredity as late as 1880 is illustrated by Dr. J. Mortimer Granville's (1880) paper in *Lancet*, "A Note on Intention in the Determination of Sex, and the Mental and Physical Inheritance of Children." There the younger Granville wrote that the sex of children,

is determined by the relative ardency of the two parents. A preponderance of impulse on the part of the male parent produces female offspring, while excess of the part of the female parent produces male progeny. Facts commonly observed in relation to the human species show that the same law governs the determination of sex in man. Among those may be mentioned the following: (a) The first children of quickly married parents are generally females. This is particularly noteworthy in the case of men marrying with a strong feeling of personal affection, or an especial desire for heirs. (b) Children born as the result of unions in which the female parent is not a consenting party, or is averse from the union, are almost invariably females. (c) Female children commonly resemble their male parents in early life, and at the successive periods of change occurring in the course of development and decadence. On the other hand, the offspring of unions, or periods in which the female parent is more ardent are nearly always males.

Put at its broadest, Granville summarized genetics as a process in which,

1. There is a force operating to produce an animal of the class Homo, in obedience to the law of the development of species. 2. There is another force gravitating upon this, the outcome of geographical, climatic, and racial energies and influences, which tends to give the animal so produced a national type. 3. There is a force, of which we have been speaking—namely, the energy of family exclusiveness. 4. There is the individual entity, which embodies the sum of the ancestral energies so far as these have been transmitted.

Given such views legitimated in *Lancet* it is not surprising that the stage was set for the subsequent emergence of eugenics and the sense that physical decline would be transmitted as "ancestral energies," in Granville's phrase. To Charles Darwin, as to his predecessor Lamarck, inheritance lay in pangenesis. Each organ had a very small replica or gemmule, something like a homunculus, which could be altered by exercise or disuse and then transmitted to the next generation in modified form. According to Wallace (1892; 1893), Galton tested Darwin's theory of gemmules by transfusing large amounts of blood from black to white rabbits, and vice versa, noting that "in every case the offspring resembled their parents and showed no trace of intermixture." He then developed a new theory that the germinal material passes directly from parents' organs to offspring, a theory also put forward by Professor Weissman in Germany. In his last years, John Beddoe still reasoned that small brains in lower-class people were due to heredity, "larger-brained people having risen in the social scale" (Beddoe, 1904).

Only slowly did the idea of inheritance of acquired deficits yield to biological data, and Mendel's ideas finally prevailed in the core idiom recognizable today in a highly evolved form. An example of the challenge to understand children's disease originating in their parents' disease may be found in Lomax's (1979) study of infantile syphilis. She observed that the term *heredity* was construed in the nineteenth century to embrace events from gestation to delivery and included what we now discriminate as congenital. The term *heredity* was quite unrelated to our post-Mendel, molecular idiom. Degeneracy, to the nineteenth century mind, was a condition of biological deterioration sometimes evident early in the life cycle. The concept needed no precise grasp of cause in an era that could not emphasize prophylaxis. The Victorians sought valiantly for clinical relief of suffering by children and adults. To sociomedical reformers and innovators the focus was therapy on a scale ranging from the individual to collective humanity. Scarce beyond individual, sporadic efforts to understand human pathology was today's notion of organized inquiry at the basic as well as the applied level. *Degeneracy* was a term valued less for its analytic meaning than for its generic nature. It summated an array of human problems and so allowed innovators to move onto treatment of group and individual problems. As an example, the autobiography of Dr. A. B. Granville records ingenious relief of symptoms.

Regrettably, progress in understanding evolution and genetics, and bringing them together in a single formulation, came after the eugenics movement had run its course. Eugenics led to some nasty social engineering, such as sterilization of the mentally retarded and, ultimately, genocide in the 1940s. Nor had Galton's (1886) concept, "regression toward mediocrity," had time to sink in. By that statistically derived concept the more extreme instances of traits are followed by less extreme manifestations which resemble the average rather than the outlandish. Exploitation of the Mendelian model and deciphering the DNA code came much later. As a result, our period of interest ending with the Great War of 1914–1918 did not see the degeneracy question settled on the basis of a completed picture of genetics and probability theory within evolution. Darwin's glimpse of discriminable forms of species on the Galapagos islands had been fundamentally correct. A degree of separation led to circumscribed mutations whose adaptive value was locally significant. Lacking a knowledge of genetics until dissemination of Mendel's forgotten paper of 1866 in 1900, by Hugo deVries, the Victorians could only observe and speculate. By 1900, biologists knew of chromosomes, having known some of the functions of the cell's nucleus since Brown's work in 1833. The Victorians and Edwardians could have done more, however, because the British Association study of heights and weights in 1883 has not been repeated, although Knight generated useful data in 1984. Also, see Rona and Chinn (1987). Survey of British children through the works of Tanner and his colleagues and pursuit of the 1946, 1958, and 1970 birth cohorts have provided useful information on growing children. The New Zealand study of Silva and associates (Silva, 1991) has been, perhaps, the model prospective research program on children of British stock.

In general, the Victorians were ill equipped to deal with the hypothesis of degeneration as a heritable stress across the generations. The medicosocial reformers were empirical in that they gathered facts in the Benthamite tradition. But descriptive empiricism is a hit and miss affair. What was lacking was a general theory, a set of propositions from which predictions may be made and tested, to guide selection of facts. Within that context there was a hiatus in the form of a mathematical model, or a data language, to treat information about people. Such formulations, however, are not free from the cultural biases of any age, and it seems likely that models of generations and development would have started with some Victorian truths about the immutability of social classes—perhaps better described as a caste system at the time. As with the mental testing movement (Jordan, 1987), delay was perhaps propitious. An informative exposition of how science and the times influenced each other, with attention to eugenics and social Darwinism, was given by Bowler (1991).

Slowly, statistics emerged as an applied form of mathematics. Probability theory, the basis for statistical tests and genetics, developed, and with it the possibility of making intergroup comparisons. By 1890, the pages of the statistical society's journal began to lose the emphasis on public health, and mathematical articles began to appear. In 1911, R. A. Fisher could draw on the correlation coefficient to discuss Mendelian genetics in a paper (Bennett, 1983). The biometric research of Karl Pearson (1903) was also influential, but he became enmeshed in some of the excesses of the eugenics movement. The result is that only as the Great War approached were people equipped to discuss the degeneracy question at a reasonable scientific level. In 1930, R. A. Fisher wrote *The Genetical Theory of Natural Selection*. It had taken ninety years to get from Lyell's flirtations with evolution to reach Fisher's infusion of evolution with a relatively sophisticated, mathematical, representation of genetics.

Nutrition

Whatever the predisposition to longevity and to body type contained in the genetic endowment of Victorians and Edwardians, the realization of potentials for physical health depended on nutrition. At the beginning of the period of interest, brown bread was replaced by white bread and the tradition of pure grain cereals began to erode. Around 1800, the first of the infamous Corn Laws protecting domestic producers of grain was introduced, and the price of grains remained unnecessarily high until repeal in 1846. Meat had always been scarce in the diets of the poor, and potatoes flavored with a little bacon were a large portion of working people's diets.

In the case of growing children, the diets of the poor frequently were not sound; Floud and Wachter (1982) concluded their study of boys' heights in the period 1770–1870 with the observation that malnutrition was the most salient environmental explanation for markedly low heights. We know from contemporary accounts (Jordan, 1987) that ignorant mothers frequently fed infants wholly inappropriate food ranging from souplike concoctions of starches and milk to meat from the table. Toward the end of the century some commentators observed that maternal incompetence was probably the major cause of children's problems.

In the early Hungry Forties William Neild (1842) of Manchester reported family food budgets for 1836 and 1841 in the *Journal of the Royal Statistical Society*. Bread accounted for a large portion of budgets, and food was about half the total budget. In Scotland, potatoes, oatmeal, and milk were important, especially in rural diets. In 1868, it was evident to Robert Hutchison that oatmeal was highly nutritive and its use was widespread. In contrast to England, beer was little used in rural Scotland. Hutchison concluded that the Scottish agricultural labourer bought more nutritious food at a lower cost than his English counterpart.

The French sociologist, Frederic Le Play, developed a picture of annual expenditures on food from four working class families in the 1850's (Le Play, 1878). Three of the heads of households were in Sheffield and its environs, and the other lived in London. In each case, there were several consistencies; cereals and meat took about one quarter of annual expenditures apiece, milk products about eight percent, and fruit and vegetables about five percent. Drink absorbed 13–16 percent of three budgets, but only one percent of the fourth. For the next decade, the 1860s, Oddy and Yudkin (1969) analyzed the chemical content of diets and compared them to those of a century later. They found that the Victorian diets had 50 percent less fat, sugar, and calcium, but about 20 percent more iron.

Hardy (1988) has called attention to the apparent paradox of mortality due to tuberculosis apparently beginning to fall in the period before food became cheap and wisely selected. In his 1871 address, "On a Progressive Physical Degeneracy of Race in the Town . . . " to the Social Science Association, Dr. Henry Rumsey named food and drink as the first of three causes; the other two were labor and residence. Absence of milk, abuse of alcohol, and adulteration of food were evident to Dr. Rumsey. Sixteen years later, in 1887, Lord Brabazon observed that bad bread and alcohol lead to "decay of bodily strength in towns." Summarizing his clinical view of elderly people in Lancashire, in 1885, Dr. W. Stewart concluded, "when one compares the hale old men and women with their fresh colour and good teeth, with the present generation, white, puny, and with bad teeth, one is inclined to think that the mode of living in the past, when they worked hard in their cottages, brewed their own ale, and were content to live on porridge and milk was much more beneficial."

It is conventional to speak of an improvement in the level of nutrition of the British population in the nineteenth century. The inference rests on a declining death rate, rising wages, and repeal of the Corn Laws. In the case of the last of these three, it can be argued that government interference in the operations of a free grain market was counterproductive until it ended in the 1840s. The origins lay in the rising price of domestic grains during the French wars and the wish of agricultural interests to maintain their protected status in the postwar years. Between 1804 and 1846 a series of reformers, among whom the name of William Huskisson is eminent, strived to repeal the protectionist legislation. Over the period of interest, insensitive but well-meant tariffs closed British ports to foreign grains. The population suffered under high bread prices for about thirty years and so were denied "the staff of life" needlessly. North American grain was available, and Ireland exported food stuffs even during the potato famine of the 1840s. The problem was one of pricing caused by supply, to which was added the burden of the failed British harvests from time to time; for example, the summers of 1841, 1842, and 1856. In their old age people remembered the stress of malnutrition under the Corn Laws. Charles Robinson, of Surrey, born in 1821 remembered seeing children pick up potato peelings and a bit of bread from the street to eat. To drink there was tea, but it often turned out to be hot water poured over loaf crusts toasted until black. Under the Corn Laws a loaf of bread cost about 10 percent of a farm laborer's weekly wage. Rural people depended on potatoes plus a little bacon and were driven to eat turnips stolen from the field when money ran out. The British agricultural population of laborers and families came quite close to the total dependence of the

Irish on the potato. As in Ireland, the potato crop failed, beginning in 1836 in Scotland (Withers, 1988) but the effects were less destructive than in Ireland, a decade later, for most families. To Dr. Arthur Newsholme, in 1905, the drop in the price of wheat had made all the difference. He argued from the relationship since 1838 between wheat's price and the rate of mortality for tuberculosis. When (e.g.) wheat's price rose by 21 percent in 1851–1855 phthisis deaths rose by 26 percent; when they fell by 13 percent in 1881–1885 the deaths declined by 19 percent. In only two of nine periods, 1871–1875 and 1876–1880, were the directions of prices and mortality not highly correlated.

Complicating the problem of nutrition was the adulteration of food. Additives were substituted for the real thing so that the profit would be greater. Milk was watered, beer was artificially flavored, and flour was extended by a variety of substitute powders. Smith (1864), an expert on nutrition, favored and recommended adulteration of coffee with 20 percent chicory. Few loaves of bread were composed of wheat alone. The consequence of adulteration for growing young people was a loss of nutrition. Mis-nutrition, providing the wrong food, also had a part. As late as 1898 Helen Bosanquet could report an inquest in Shoreditch on a six-month-old child. When not breast feeding the little girl, the mother had fed her fried fish, pease pudding, and biscuits. Clearly, ignorant mothers posed a danger quite as formidable as the summer fevers and diarrheas that killed children. But a young woman, barely literate and tied to the workplace would hardly be a model for Mrs. Isabella Beeton to cite. Nor, indeed, did the Mrs. Beetons of the period address working women directly. On the other hand, the problem of ill-prepared young mothers was well recognized, and home visitors attempted to educate women to proper ways to nourish their children. A frequent first step was to persuade mothers to stop feeding gin and opiates to babies. Clearly, whatever the contribution of the factory system to the degenerate health of children, the domestic system prevailing was no less stressful. See Fildes [1992] for a discussion of breast-feeding in London, 1905–1917.

In consideration of the place of nutrition in domestic economies the contribution of a mayor of Victorian Manchester, William Neild, and his colleague Mr. Graham (1842) is particularly useful. Conveying the challenges to ordinary people's resources is the comparison Graham calculated with 1836, five years earlier. In the interval, flour rose 27 percent and tea fell 17 percent. In the case of flour there was considerable variation as the price fluctuated up to 55 percent above its 1836 cost. The families, described as "of sober and industrious habits," must have been hard pressed to adjust to inflation and fluctuations in price based on supply and demand. By 1841 six families out of seven in the Dukinfield district of Manchester had gone into debt to the local grocer, although none of them had been so hard pressed in 1836. Ahead of them and their descendants was the cotton famine of the early 1860s precipitated by the civil war in the United States. In Table 3.1 is a list of expenditures in 1836 and 1841 for an "Overlooker; Family 6 individuals." (See Mackenzie, 1962.)

In 1836, the total income of the family was 34 s. (£1.14.0.), and it was the same five years later. Expenditures, however, rose from 24s. and 3d. (£1.4.3.) to nearly 28s. (£1.7.10.) over the five years, a rise of about 15 percent. In Table 3.1 we see a list of consumable items plus rent; absent are such purchases as clothing and shoes—the overlooker probably did not wear clogs—medical services, transport, and other items.

In Table 3.1 we see that flour consumed 13.2 percent, rising to 16.9 percent of the budget. Meat nearly doubled over the five years. Eggs, milk, soup, salt, coffee, candles, and coals remained stable, and tea and cheese dropped slightly as a percentage. Rent went down, but that may be misleading because Neild adjusted rents to accommodate widespread nonpayment in 1841. It seems likely that the family of six included four children whose food consumption undoubtedly rose over the five years, placing more demands on the family budget for food. The striking item, of course, is the high cost of bread, which was replaced progressively by potatoes until the potato failure of the mid-1840s.

In 1861, a budget was sent to the editor of *The Penny Newsman* by a London worker who signed his letter, "Working Man" (Hollingshead, 1861). The budget, which is given in Table 3.2, amounts to 28s. and 1 d. Of that amount 17s. and 4d. are assigned to food and the amount rises to 18s. and 6d. when beer for the evening meal is included. At that level, food is approximately two-thirds of the domestic budget. By present-day standards food was very expensive; in contrast, housing was cheap, but the budget is for a family of six living in two rooms. The "sick club" item was a highly prudent expenditure but it was not cheap at 9d. a week. Sickness of one of the (presumably) four children was inevitable, but sickness of the wage earner was the real risk. A family could drop swiftly from the working class into the "residuum," the stratum of the homeless and abandoned, due to economic reverses. This chronic stress has been discussed in the context of craftsmen working in York, 1801–1851, by Armstrong (1974).

TABLE 3.1 AVERAGE INCOME AND HOUSE EXPENDITURES FOR ONE WEEK: MANCHESTER OVERLOOKER'S FAMILY, 1836 AND 1841

Articles	Weekly Expenditure of the Family						Weekly Expenditure per Individual						Percent of Expenditure on the Total Income	
	1836			1841			1836			1841			1836	1841
	£	s.	d.	£	s.	d.	£	s.	d.	£	s.	d.		
Rent	0	6	3	0	5	0	0	0.	0½	0	0	10	18.3	14.6
Flour or Bread	0	4	6	0	5	10	0	0	9	0	0.	11½	13.2	16.9
Meat	0	2	11	0	4	8	0	0	6	0	0.	9¼	8.5	13.8
Bacon	0	0	3	0	0	4	0	0.	0½	0	0.	0¼	.7	1
Ham														
Oatmeal														
Butter	0	1	6	0	2	0	0	0	3	0	0	4	4.4	6
Eggs	0	1	0	0	1	0	0	0	2	0	0	2	3	3
Milk	0	0	10	0	0	10	0	0.	1½	0	0.	1½	2.5	2.5
Potatoes	0	1	1	0	1	8	0	0.	2¼	0	0.	3¼	3.2	5
Cheese	0	0	9	0	0	9	0	0.	1½	0	0.	1½	2.2	2.1
Tea	0	1	2	0	1	0	0	0.	2¼	0	0	2	3.4	3
Coffee	0	0	6	0	0	6	0	0	1	0	0	1	1.5	1.5
Sugar	0	1	4	0	2	0	0	0.	2½	0	0	4	3.9	6
Treacle														
Tobacco														
Soap	0	0	6	0	0	6	0	0	1	0	0	1	1.5	1.5
Candles	0	0	6	0	0	6	0	0	1	0	0	1	1.5	1.5
Salt	0	0	0½	0	0	0½							.2	.2
Coals	0	1	2	0	1	2	0	0.	2½	0	0.	2¼	3.5	3.5
Total	1	4	3½	1	7	10	0	4	7	0	4.	0½	71.5	82.1

Source: W. Neild (1841).

TABLE 3.2   WEEKLY EXPENDITURE FOR SIX PERSONS DEVELOPED BY
A "WORKING MAN"

	£	s.	d.
Rent for two rooms	0	4	0
Bread and flour	0	5	4
Meat and suet	0	5	0
Butter and cheese	0	2	8
Tea, sugar, and milk	0	2	4
Vegetables	0	2	0
Coal and wood	0	1	4
Candles, soap, etc.	0	0	9
Children's schooling	0	1	3
Sick club	0	0	9
Beer for the man at work	0	1	0
Beer at supper for man and wife	0	1	2
Tobacco	0	0	3
"Newsman"	0	0	1
Halfpenny for each child as a treat	0	0	2
Total	1	8	1

Source: J. Hollingshead (1861).

The budget proposed by a "working man" is a prudent draft probably expressing his own condition. Also in Hollingshead's *Ragged London in 1861* is a letter from a factory manager who used the pen name
"Scrutinizer." He argued, in his letter to "The Penny Newsman," that
working people were prudent and careful with their incomes and that
children were fed and cared for. He conceded that the habit of adjourn-
ing to the beer house was common, but pointed it out as a place of
warmth providing a little temporary pleasure when housing was overcrowded and cold.

In 1864, Dr. Edward Smith could provide his, "Practical Dietary
for Families, Schools and the Labouring Classes." Smith calculated the
nutritive value of food as grams of nitrogen and carbon. In particular,
he provided a table of carbon and nitrogen yielded by 1 pennyworth of
thirty-one food items. Smith provided model diets for the poor and prepared handbills to disseminate these diets among them. Smith observed that, "the best guide to a poor family will be . . . to obtain
plenty of skimmed milk, bread and potatoes; to add thereto as much
meat, bacon or herrings, and fat, as they may be able to afford." He
thought exemplary prudence was demonstrated by a farm labourer in

Okehampton, Devon, with a wife and three children and a weekly income of 10 s. (c. 1875). Their weekly dietary was "Flour, 35 lb.; peas 4 lb.; rice, 2 lb.; treacle, 1 lb.; very cheap butter, 1 lb.; bacon 3 lb.; cheap pieces of meat 4 lb.; skimmed milk 10½ pints; eggs 3 (from their own fowls); tea 1 oz.; total cost weekly 10s 7d." The 7d. that put them over budget allows nothing for clothing, medicine, and so forth and seems to exemplify Wilkins Micawber's observation about solvency and happiness.

Most discussions of diet address the situation of urban dwellers. Fussell (1929) provided an account of agricultural laborers' diets over two centuries. In Table 3.3, which is an abstract, we see data from 1774 to 1912 at six dates. The term *standard unit*, equals one working laborer, a statistical figure who ate comparatively little meat across the period. The highest level was reached in 1902 at 1.9 lb. Bread was a staple at all four dates averaging a consistent 10 lbs. per worker, as were potatoes at 25–27 lb. per family. Sugar increased within the diet, as did milk. In the period of interest, 1805–1914, potatoes had taken up a portion of the diet previously occupied by bread, at a lower cost. Addressing the diet of Leeds' children, 1840–1871, Shaw (1975) concluded that they generally received, "a dull diet, overweighted with bread . . . watery porridge and treacle, and lacking meat, green vegetables, fish and fruit." By way of comparison, Buss (1990) reported weekly consumption of bread at about 2 lbs. (1.9 kg.) and noted that British consumption of fruit and vegetables is among the lowest among developed countries. Returning to consumption of bread there is the report of food selected by British navvies constructing a French railway at Rouen in the 1850s. The Belgian statistician, Edouard Ducpétiaux (1855) reported that the navvies took thirty percent by weight of their solid foods as "pain blanc." In the case of the Simkins family of Manchester, at mid-century, thirty six pounds of bread cost four shillings and sixpence; bread absorbed twenty six percent of the seventeen shillings and twopence halfpenny John Simkins brought home to his wife and five children in Home Street, Ancoats (Rushton, 1977).

In 1871, Richard Heath reported on one of a series of studies in the journal *Golden Hours*, on English peasants (Heath, 1893). From Wooler, Northumbria, Heath gave the annual budget of a rural hind (servant) as £37. Of that £20 went for food, and the budget given by Heath lists the expenditures for potatoes, oats, barley, peas, and wheat. It is noteworthy that 53 percent of the whole was spent on food, and there is no item given for meat. Within the grains and potatoes, 30 percent was spent on oats, a superior nutrient, as today's generation is

TABLE 3.3 FARM LABOURER'S WEEKLY DIETARIES, 1774–1912

Item (in lbs.)	1774	1863 Family	1863 Standard Unit	1902 Family	1902 Standard Unit	1912 Family	1912 Standard Unit
Bacon		4.55	1.2	7.15	1.9	6.53	1.7
Total meat	1.2	4.55	1.2	38.83	10.2	39.61	10.4
Bread	10.5	55.75	14.7	1.25	0.3	1.56	0.4
Oatmeal and rice		27	7.1	25.75	6.8	25.75	6.8
Potatoes		1.5	0.4	1.2	0.3	1.08	0.3
Cheese	0.75				0.5		0.5
Butter, lard, margarine, and drippings	0.22	1.56	0.4	2.07	1.1	2.07	1.2
Tea, coffee, or cocoa		0.14		.61		.66	
Sugar (in pts.)		2	0.5	4.31		4.57	
Milk: New		1.75	0.5	4.5 or	1.2 or	4.5 or	1.2 or
Skimmed				8.75	2.3	8.75	2.3

Source: Adapted from Fussell (1929).

rediscovering. To nineteenth century observers, the excellent habitus of Northumbrians was due in part to retention of oats in their diet.

In the last several decades of the nineteenth century came an innovation in food still evident today. The rise of fish and chips as an element in working-class diets, especially in Lancashire and the West Riding of Yorkshire, was spectacular. Walton's (1989) study of Preston showed 22 shops in 1885, 100 in the last few years of the century, and 133 in 1913. The number of profitable enterprises in relation to the size of the population was phenomenal. Relatively cheap to buy and already cooked, fish and chips was a dish of great appeal, occasionally supplemented with peas and beans and generally sprinkled with salt and malt vinegar. Fish provided protein and the chipped potatoes were carbohydrate. Offsetting them was the excessive amount of fat contributing to what recent decades have seen as the cholesterol problem. However, in the context of our period, fish and chips was a hot meal accessible to the poor at comparatively little cost. In Wenlock's (1990) view, based on a survey of 3,200 schoolchildren, ages ten and fourteen, consumption of chips remained excessive, was pronounced in the North, and was related to low consumption of milk.

Disease

Communicable diseases such as cholera, which reached Britain from its historic source in northern India on several occasions, such as 1849, spread rapidly. Tuberculosis, then known as phthisis, was so common in families that it was cited as evidence that degeneracy was abundant, progressive, and hereditary. The front page of *The Times* for Wednesday, June 12, 1872, lists the death, "On the 3rd June, at Hastings, of consumption, Ethel Mary, eldest child of the late John James Tallant of Ivy Lane, Paternoster Row, and Lewisham, dearly loved and deeply mourned."

In an era when informality was the prevailing mode for the provision of goods and services ordinary people purchased relief from sickness at the doorstep. Thomson and Smith (1877) gave a description, with photographs, of "crocusing," the trade of street doctors. From a suitcase they sold cough lozenges (which have not improved greatly in over a century, it must be conceded) and remedies for serious afflictions such as eye diseases. Thomson and Smith noted that for the poor who were chronically ill the palliatives of the crocus man who went from door to door were highly convenient; they added that, by 1877, the crocusing trade had gone into a decline. It should be noted, however, that this change in an itinerant trade was not occasioned by a decline in the prevalence of ill health. The thesis of Thomas McKeown (1979) that some serious diseases were declining despite the absence of innovations in therapy has been challenged in recent years (Szreter, 1988; Mercer, 1990). In either case, those who became sick were not radically benefited by hospitalization. Surgery posed the threat of infection and shock—iatrogenic illnesses—plus exposure to all manner of communicable diseases in an era when noisome, offensive odors were still considered indications that (miasmic) disease-bearing organisms were generating. Treatment by street doctors was a kind of institutionalized placebo effect in an age when Morison's Vegetable Universal Pill and Daffey's Elixir were acclaimed as sovereign remedies. Altick (1991) provided an account of the widespread invocation of such medications in popular literature. Conceivably, the elixirs, which were opiates or alcohol, might have provided temporary respite for people with psychological burdens then as now (Openheim, 1991).

However, once sick, child and adult were likely to stay sick because there were no antibiotics, and aspirin had not been invented. Physicians relied on sedatives and opiates to bring rest to the sick. Most draughts contained alcohol in generous amounts and that was among the least noxious agents. Infants and children were frequently tranquilized, and occasionally killed, by use of Godfrey's Cordial and similar opium-based medications (Jordan, 1987a). In 1991, the *New York Times* (Shapiro, 1991) reported that the nineteenth century British nostrum *gripe water* was still available in New York, to the chagrin of the Federal Drug Administration, which noted the presence of alcohol (as well as sodium bicarbonate) as a threat to babies. Another reason for chronic illness, or at least extended convalescence, was that selected organisms, especially scarlet fever, were more virulent in former times. Improvement in health across the century depended less on therapeutic innovations than on a general rise in the standard of living. Another influence was the increasing availability of safe drinking water. This innovation began with Edwin Chadwick's health of towns report and his emphasis on providing cheap, piped water and sanitation to ordinary folks' houses.

Tuberculosis

Across the nineteenth century and well into the twentieth, tuberculosis cast its baleful shadow. In 1838, according to McKeown (1979) the annual mortality rate stood at 4,000 per 1 million people (see Figure 3.1). Even at that high level people were a little better off than

FIGURE 3.1 RESPIRATORY TUBERCULOSIS: MEAN ANNUAL DEATH RATES (STANDARDIZED TO 1901 POPULATION); ENGLAND AND WALES

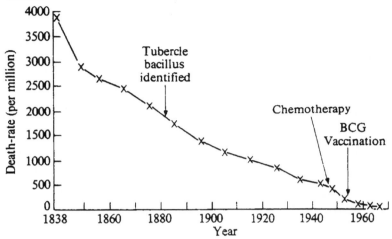

Source: T McKeown (1979).

at the end of the seventeenth century; Smith (1988) quoted Gideon Harvey who observed in 1672 that it was hard "to arrive at one's grave in this English climate without a smack of consumption." By 1848–1850 the mortality rate had dropped to 2,901 cases per 1 million population and was more than halved, at 1868 cases, by 1901. For purposes of comparison McKeown (1979) caps the series in 1971 with a death rate of 13 fatalities per 1 million. In 1862, Dr. Edward Smith reported to the British Association for the Advancement of Science meeting at Cambridge the results of examining the characteristics of 600 male and 400 females with tuberculosis examined at the Brompton hospital. One in every four was under twenty years of age, and half had lost one parent. Their average age was twenty-eight years when they presented themselves for treatment; presumably, that would have been a comparatively late stage of the disease, since the condition is without apparent symptoms until coughing, loss of weight, and elevated temperature provide clinical signs. Fifteen years after Smith, Dr, Ransome's (1887) report to the British Association accurately described the environment in which tuberculosis flourished, while thinking that the TB organism was "derived from the atmosphere."

In the nineteenth century, a culture complex accreted around the TB bacillus associating it with social refinement and a convalescent's delicacy. In fact, as drinking water infected by sewage produced cholera, so overcrowding and a lack of ventilation accounted for pulmonary tuberculosis. Today, tuberculosis is amenable to a rational chemotherapy (e.g., streptomycin); but in Victorian days its prevalence and fatality were a constant worry. Given the combination of crowded streets and houses, ineffective and frequently preposterous therapies, and a malnourished population, tuberculosis spread quickly through the population of towns. A study by the Manchester Statistical Society in the stressful 1840s, according to Rushton (1977), found that tuberculosis was the cause of death in many occupations; phthisis killed excise officers - 66%, soldiers - 55% and teachers - 46%. Common to all three occupations was association with people and the diseases transmitted by air-borne droplets. Rural residents were not spared communicable diseases, but they were less vulnerable to many diseases, of which tuberculosis is an example. To the eminent John Simon at the Privy Council office, in 1858, the connection between tuberculosis and the degeneracy question was clear. In his report of June 1858 to the Board of Health, Simon cited a study by Dr. Greenhow of St. Thomas's Hospital. Dr. Greenhow's words are, "Whatever tends to increase tubercular disease among the adult members of a population must be regarded as assuredly tending to produce a progressive degeneration of race" In this assertion we glimpse the stress on public health that tuberculosis presented to thoughtful analysts of disease within the population at mid-century.

Few diseases have been feared as much as the damage produced in the lungs and in other organs also, when the bacillus identified by Koch in 1882 invaded the body. Only late in the progression of the condition did the patient begin to cough up blood, and at that stage, virtually nothing could be done. The prevalence of phthisis was construed as evidence of degeneration in the population. Familial incidence led to grave suspicion that it was hereditary. In Table 3.4 the distribution of deaths due to tuberculosis is presented by Cronjé (1984). There, we see that in 1851–1860 tuberculosis was a prime cause of death, which is the ultimate state of degeneracy. About one death in seven was due to tuberculosis, and among adolescents and young adults age fifteen to thirty-four about half the deaths came from this single disease. In passing, we note the problem of accuracy of diagnosis

TABLE 3.4   TUBERCULOSIS DEATHS AS A PERCENT OF TOTAL DEATHS FOR MALES AND FEMALES AT ALL AGES AND AT YOUNG ADULT AGES (15–34), ENGLAND AND WALES, 1851–1910

	1851–1860	1861–1870	1871–1880	1881–1890	1891–1900	1901–1910
Males, all ages	15.2	14.2	13.6	13.0	11.7	11.6
Females, all ages	16.3	14.9	13.5	12.4	10.3	9.9
Males, 15–34	44.2	43.3	40.6	40.2	37.5	38.2
Females, 15–34	49.3	48.5	44.9	42.5	37.3	37.9

Source: G. Cronjé (1984).

in both the pulmonary and nonpulmonary forms, but the statistics seem reasonably appropriate.

By 1901–1910 the rate for all ages and sexes was down about one-third, with a less promising trend among the fifteen- to thirty-four year olds, and women's mortality declining faster than men's. Across the period, the peak death rate, as analyzed by Cronjé, rose more extensively in males for whom it reached 45.54 years in 1901–1910; for females the 1851–1860 peak age of mortality was twenty-five to thirty-four years and rose only to thirty-five to forty-four years in 1901–1910. Rural death rates were slightly lower than urban rates. It is not clear why tuberculosis rates declined across the nineteenth century, and the twentieth century started with high mortality rates for this disease. Emphasis on fresh air and good nutrition and exercise probably did no harm. However, the condition is a communicable disease whose organism is now fought successfully by chemotherapy, although drug-resistant strains appeared in the early 1990s. In that paradigm, heredity dropped away and the superfluous connotation of degeneracy in the species has faded as the legacy of "the white plague".

Scrofula

A less fatal form was the condition known as scrofula. It was produced when the bacillus invaded the lymph system. It too had a culture complex surrounding it and had been known as "the King's Evil," a term referring to the mythical cure rather than the cause; it was once thought that the touch of a king, like Charles I, was enough to cure the condition. Lest that seem too fanciful, it appears no more unsuccessful than the sanatorium treatment of the early twentieth century for the pulmonary form of tuberculosis.

Scrofula was a widespread disease, recognizable in the disfigurement of face and neck. Smith (1988) observed that the lymphatic form of tuberculosis had also begun its retreat by the 1840s. However, Benjamin Phillips (1846) in the Hungry Forties found that 24 percent of a large sample of working class children under sixteen years displayed symptoms of the disease. Above that age, the incidence was 8 percent, and Phillips reported that, at any time, up to 3 percent of the population were being treated for this disfiguring, lymphatic form of tuberculosis. As high as the rates were, they appear to be lower than rates in continental countries. In the case of children and adolescents, an incidence of one in four youngsters seems very high. Bridges and Holmes, in 1873, reported an incidence of 2.68 percent in some districts, and a still lower incidence among people not employed in factory districts. In fairness to Phillips, his reported rate of 1.3 percent among adults is not unlike the incidence reported by Bridges and Holmes.

Cholera

A major threat to life was the occurrence of cholera. Apart from transmission by the people who handle food, a major mode of infection arises when the disease is transmitted in contaminated water and so, even today, a supply of pure drinking water is our best protection. Such a guarantee came slowly in the nineteenth century (Evans, 1987; Meckel, 1990). Cholera originated in India reached Britain in 1831, via Russia and Poland (Evans, 1988). London experienced major outbreaks in 1844 centering on Southwark in 1854 and in the East End neighborhoods in 1866. In Glasgow during the outbreak of 1854–1856, the reformer and architect, Alexander ("Greek") Thomson lived in the subsequently infamous Gorbals district. Mr. and Mrs. Thomson lost four of their children during the epidemic (Schmieken, 1988). Cholera is due to the action of the vibrio organism, which acts rapidly and reduces the victim by fever and dehydration; people sickened and died within hours in extreme cases. The value of hydration therapy had been noted in 1832 by Dr. T. A. Latta, but appears not to have been widely adopted. Infants and children died swiftly, and those who survived had long periods of weakened health and susceptibility to other diseases. It should be noted that the death of adults also afflicted children; it did so by depriving them of one or both parents and so set the stage for neglect and malnutrition. Cholera was the disease traced by Dr. John Snow in 1849 to the Broad Street pump near Golden Square in one of the great investigations of sanitation (The Broad Street Pump, 1866).

Evidence of the truism that collective memory is good for about fifteen years lies in the 1866 outbreak of cholera. Despite Snow's work in 1848 the public, and even physicians, were not sure of the connection of disease and the quality of the water supply. In the 1866 outbreak in London the culprit was the negligence of the East London Water Company, according to Luckin (1977). Mortality per thousand residents reached 116 in Stepney, 89 in Poplar and 97 at St. George-in-the-East. Eventually, satisfactory separation of sewage and drinking water created an effective but breachable defense.

Scarlet Fever

This air-borne disease frequently confused with diphtheria was a substantial cause of death in the nineteenth century. Its decline cannot be traced to an innovation in medical therapy, and McKeown, Record, and Turner (1975) point out that no chemotherapy was available until 1935. Indirectly, the rise in the nineteenth century standard of living probably contributed to greater power of recuperation. The remaining element is the nature of the organism, and there is reason to believe that it mutated into a milder form, rather than believe people acquired an immunity or resistance not supportable by evidence. Still, the outcome was benign since mortality from scarlet fever declined. It remains to point out that children who acquired the disease were very sick, even if they did not die, and needed a lengthy period of recovery from the streptococcal-based sore throat and related symptoms. The great Victorian biologist, Thomas Huxley, lost a child to scarlet fever. In Mercer's (1990) view, the rise in mortality after the 1830s might have been due to a more lethal strain of streptococcus brought by famine refugees from Ireland.

Typhoid

In the nineteenth century the term *enteric fever* was used for typhoid until the condition was more finely discriminated. A preventable disease, this condition led to dehydration and death. For infants and small children "summer fever" was a risk and led to much loss of life. The mode of transmission is infected water, usually urine

(El Shabrawy et al, 1988), which in conveyed by sewage and contaminates drinking water. It is instructive to note that the 340 residents of Boot and Shoe Yard in Leeds had no water supply within a quarter of a mile to flush sewage away from three "out-offices," as Baker (1839) termed them. It is an ill wind that blows no good, and residents' exposure to air-borne vectors of disease was not compounded by a linkage to well or piped drinking water. For the population in general, however, contaminated drinking water was a perennial risk.

Measles

Considered a routine childhood illness today, although not without the risk of complications, measles had lost its former place among cause of mortality in children. In McKeown and Record's (1962) exposition, measles fell in sixth place as a fatal infection, but before diphtheria and smallpox. In the last five decades measles mortality rose slightly in the final twenty years, peaking in the years 1891–1900. As there are iatrogenic diseases, that is, conditions associated with being in hospitals, so measles was probably school centered, in the years after Forster's 1870 education act. It is worth recalling that an argument against schooling for all was the increase probability of communicating disease through the high density of population in classrooms of children with poor habits of hygiene. Even today, head lice infestations are not unknown in middle-class school populations, and the risk is due to the inherent overcrowding that schools create.

Smallpox

From the research of Landers and Monzas (1988), it is evident that smallpox underwent a significant decline as a recognized, recorded cause of death just prior to our period of interest, 1805–1914. From being a severe childhood affliction for which all children were at risk, smallpox declined in virulence, effectively. In three periods beginning with 1750–1754 smallpox mortality declined from 10.0 percent to 5.8 percent, a drop of nearly one-half. By the mid-nineteenth century, diphtheria emerged for the first time as a major cause of death, and schools were considered a major source of infection (Hirst, 1991).

Typhus

Relevant to the preceding consideration of crowding is typhus. This disease is distinguished by high fever and depression of body and mind. The organism rickettsia is the cause, and it is transmitted from body to body by lice. Clearly, the greater is population density the higher the risk of infection. Fundamentally, control of lice in the nineteenth century was a matter of individual hygiene. When hygiene was at a low state in a crowded place, and schools are still a fair example, typhus would spread from person to person. As the standard of comfort (living) rose across the nineteenth century and houses had an adequate supply of water for residents the disease yielded to rising standards of sanitation and individual cleanliness. However, personal cleanliness was no protection if others were contaminated and spread their parasites.

૨ે.

In all these overviews of specific diseases lowering the health of the population there lies the generalization that the Victorians' health was not very good by our standards. Babies sickened and died, children were weakened and stressed by acute illnesses, which were sometimes preventable when public health considerations governed town life. People experienced a series of illnesses, and weakness after one bout predisposed them to the next. Health degenerated as propinquity speeded infection. It is likely that the prevalence of ear infections and colds in winter would be very high. Dr. Crichton-Browne reported an assessment of children's hearing acuity in 1902. The admittedly gross whisper test for hearing was failed by 521,000 schoolchildren attending poor-law schools.

By 1902, the health of the population, although far from perfect, had improved greatly over the preceding decades of the nineteenth century. Only summer—but with the risk of fevers—would bring relief from bronchitis, colds, and other air- or droplet-based diseases. Victorians were probably sickly people, with higher and lower rates of incidence varying by personal age, place of residence, and standard of living. The poorest in the worst parts of factory towns had markedly shorter life expectations than their fellows in better circumstances.

Mortality

Despite appalling living conditions in Victorian Britain the population of ordinary folk grew (see Table 3.5). The birth rate fell steadily, beginning with the middle classes, but despite that fact the number of people alive at any age, and living longer, increased. Figure 3.2 shows the change in the population; there, we see falling birth rates and death rates and rising population over the period 1841–1915. What is especially noteworthy is that the changes in the nineteenth century

TABLE 3.5   BIRTH AND DEATH RATES IN ENGLAND AND WALES
PER K, 1801–1915

Year	Births	Deaths	Year	Births	Deaths
1801		24.7[1]			
1811		14.3[1]			
1821		14.1[1]			
1831		30.2[1]			
1841–1845	35.2	21.4			
1846–1850	34.8	23.3			
1851–1855	35.5	22.7			
1856–1860	35.5	21.8	1855–1859	33.8	20.4
1861–1865	35.8	22.6	1860–1864	35.1	22.2
1866–1870	35.7	22.4	1865–1869	35.1	21.8
1871–1875	35.7	22.0	1870–1874	34.9	22.5
1876–1880	35.4	20.8	1875–1879	35.1	21.1
1881–1885	33.5	19.4	1880–1885	33.5	19.8
1886–1890	31.4	18.9	1885–1889	31.9	18.7
1891–1895	30.5	18.7	1890–1894	30.6	19.1
1899–1900	29.3	17.7	1895–1899	30.1	18.1
1901–1905	28.2	16.1	1900–1904	29.4	17.5
1906–1910	26.3	14.7	1905–1909	28.1	16.3
1911–1915	23.6	14.3	1910–1914	25.9	15.3

Source: L. Cook and J. Stevenson (1983).
[1]Source of these figures, for Manchester, Hammond, (1928).

were not traceable to medical breakthroughs; very few innovations occurred beyond vaccination and the appendectomy. We trace the changes in mortality to the general rise in the standard of living. McKeown attributed the 40 percent of the drop in mortality, 1848–1871, to the reduction of airborne diseases.

An invisible portion of the degeneracy of health in the form of death was the widespread occurrence of stillbirths and infant mortality. Even today fetal wastage, the loss of life before birth, usually in the first trimester, is not fully grasped. Werner, Bierman, and French (1971) calculated that 1,300 conceptions were needed to yield 1,100 live births in Hawaii. In the nineteenth century the rate of fetal loss was undoubtedly, but unmeasurably, higher. Stillbirths are those instances where death of the fetus is recognized at delivery; the fatal antecedents may have developed in utero, but may also have been the consequence of trauma in delivery. The rate of stillbirths was high in the nineteenth century. For the period 1818–1828 Dr. William Farr (1865) reported

85

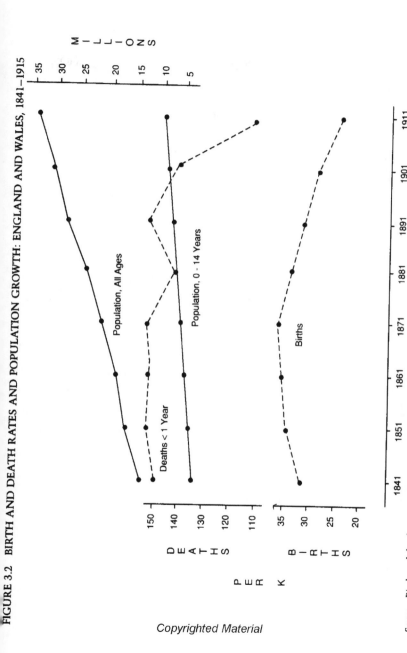

FIGURE 3.2 BIRTH AND DEATH RATES AND POPULATION GROWTH: ENGLAND AND WALES, 1841–1915

Source: Birth and death rates: Office of Population Censuses and Surveys (1985) Tables 1 and 2. Population growth: Mitchell (1962), p. 12.

that 128 women had 305 miscarriages. Undoubtedly, there was a range from many to few, so that we refrain from calculating an undoubtedly misleading average per woman. Dr. Cowan of Glasgow (1840) reported an incidence of one stillbirth in every 14.59 deliveries in 1831. Thirteen years later, the Health of Towns commission was told of 251 fetal deaths in 100 families.

In the case of infant deaths, many children died from infections causing diarrhea (Buchanan, 1985). Each summer saw deaths from "summer fever," deaths we can prevent today, even in Third World countries, by intravenous supply of liquids and electrolytes at very little cost. Among the diseases of childhood measles and scarlet fever wrought destruction.

Explored with difficulty is the phenomenon of infanticide (Behlmer, 1979; Forbes, 1986; 1988); but it seems clear that the slaughter of the innocent was wreaked swiftly and silently by malice, neglect, and by soporifics across the decades of the nineteenth century. In the depths of parents' alcoholism, infants died due to having been "laid over," during the night (Wilson, 1905). Such deaths, deliberate or accidental, were returned as accidents by coroners with regularity; today, we label such deaths *sudden infant death syndrome,* or SIDS. Forbes (1988) reported that a coroner's inquisition revealed suffocation, but the coroner recorded the apparent homicide as, "death by visitation of God."

In 1874, Charles Ansell, actuary of the National Life Assurance Society produced a study of infant mortality and of some aspect of family life among "the upper and professional classes." Based on 49,000 cases the study reported that infant deaths were least among clergymen's families and highest in physicians' families up to age fifteen; from fifteen to thirty-five years of age the order of magnitude was reversed, however. Ansell attributed the low infant mortality rate of clergymen's children to living in the country; we might say that Barchester was healthier than Coketown for the newborn. One of Ansell's findings was the high rate of mortality on the day of birth— "as much as 10 per cent of the total mortality of the first year of life in the case of males, and 8½ per cent in that of females, occurring on that day." Mortality in general was very high among children whose birth order was seventh or later in the first eight years of life.

In Table 3.6 are figures on child mortality rates between birth and age nine for the years 1840 to 1915, by sex, for England, Wales, and Scotland. There we see, per thousand children, that the death rate in the four countries of Great Britain varied by place, age, sex, and year. For England and Wales the rates of mortality by locality are given in

TABLE 3.6 CHILD MORTALITY RATES PER THOUSAND, ZERO TO NINE YEARS, 1840–1915

Year	Less Than 1 Year — Both Sexes			0–4 Years — Boys			0–4 Years — Girls			5–9 Years — Boys			5–9 Years — Girls		
	EW	Ireland	Scotland	EW	Ireland	Scotland	EW	Ireland	Scotland	EW	Ireland	Scotland	EW	Ireland	Scotland
1840	154			75.4			64.5			10.8			10.6		
1845	142			66.5			56.5			8.2			7.8		
1850	162			66.8			57.4			8.1			8.1		
1855	125		118	71.5			61.3			8.2			8.1		
1860	127		127	67.3		37.4[1]	57.2		37.4[1]	6.8		9.1[1]	6.9		8.8[1]
1865	160	98	125	75.0			65.1			8.1			7.8		
1870	160	95	123	75.0	38.0	35.2[1]	64.2	34.2	35.3[2]	8.9	5.4	9.8[1]	8.3	5.4	9.3[1]
1875	158	95	132	71.9			61.2			6.9			6.4		
1880	153	112	112	69.2	40.0	29.5[1]	59.2	36.1	28.8[1]	6.4	5.3	7.8[1]	6.0	5.8	7.3[1]
1885	138	95	95	60.6			51.0			5.1			5.1		
1890	151	95	131	62.9	38.3	27.5[1]	53.3	34.5	27.1[1]	5.0	4.1	5.7[1]	5.0	4.7	6.0[1]
1895	161	104	133	66.0			55.2			4.1			4.2		
1900	154	109	128	61.6	39.4	22.8[1]	51.8	35.0	21.5[1]	4.2	3.9	4.3[1]	4.2	4.8	4.8[1]
1905	128	95	116	50.3			42.1			3.4			3.5		
1910	105	95	108	39.7	34.7	17.8	33.1	30.2	16.8	3.0	3.2	3.7	3.1	3.7	3.8
1915	110	92	126	42.0		22.2	34.4		20.6	3.9		4.1	3.8		3.9

Source: Mitchell and Deane (1971).
[1]1870–1872 et sequelae.
[2]1–4 years.

Figure 3.3, developed by Woods and Hinde (1987), for 1861. Across the seventy-five years spanned by Table 3.6 mortality rates fell for both sexes by about one-quarter in England and Wales after peaking quite late in the period—1895. For Ireland, fewer figures are available, and the rate followed the time pattern with the peak rate occurring five years later in 1900. For Scotland, the picture is less clear due to rapid fluctuations in which the last twenty-years resemble the middle years, 1860–1875, of the nineteenth century. Among children zero to four years old, boys have a slightly higher mortality rate, which fell by almost one-half across the period after peaking in the third quarter of the nineteenth century. The rate in England and Wales was well above the rates of mortality for little children in Ireland and Scotland. In Ireland the drop in rates, at a lower level initially, was not great. Among children aged five to nine years the rate was much lower, the period of greatest peril to life having passed. Across the period 1840–1915 the rate for boys and girls in England and Wales fell steadily from approximately 11:1,000 to 4:1,000. Each of the summary statistics in Table 3.6 represents children, and a knowledge of death among the young was an everyday reality for families.

When we turn to the causes of death in the nineteenth century the data assembled by Logan (1950) and presented in Table 3.7 are useful. The period 1842–1872, that is, the middle third of the century, includes the Hungry Forties and the subsequent period of relative economic well-being. In Table 3.7 we see that infectious diseases were the prime cause of death, and respiratory diseases were about half as prevalent. Among children in the first year of life developmental and wasting diseases accounted for about one-fourth of the total, followed by nervous, infectious, and respiratory diseases. For the ages one to four infectious disease was clearly the chief cause, followed by respiratory disorders. In the major span of childhood, ages five to fourteen years, infectious diseases was clearly the prime cause of death, with "violence," added for the first time, a distant second cause. Much the same pattern is apparent among adolescents and young adults fifteen to twenty-four years of age. In the vigorous years, twenty-five to forty-four, infectious disease remains prime, but less prevalent; and violence drops to third place behind respiratory diseases. In the age group forty-five to sixty-four infectious diseases are prime, at a lower rate; and circulatory diseases appear for the first time.

For a consideration of mortality in an early year there is the report of Dr. George Gregory in 1840. Addressing the Royal Institution Gregory described death in London. Half of all boys were dead by age

FIGURE 3.3 LIFE EXPECTATION AT BIRTH, ENGLAND AND WALES, 1861 (SHOWN BY REGISTRATION DISTRICTS WITH BOTH SEXES COMBINED)

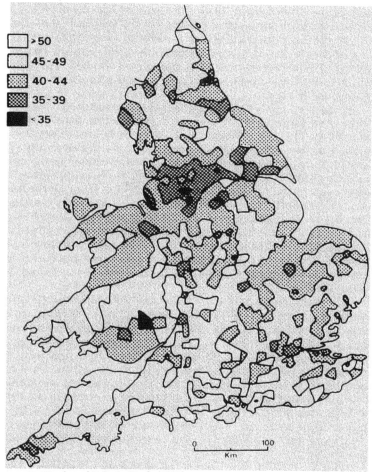

Source: R. Woods and P. R. A. Hinde (1987).

seven, and girls in the same proportion by age seventeen. That winter, Dr. Gregory spoke in March, had seen a terrible epidemic of scarlet fever. In the first three weeks of December 1839 82 people died; in the first three weeks of January 1840, there were 345 deaths of which 326 were persons under fifteen years of age. For the year as a whole, however, deaths due to tuberculosis were twice as frequent as any other cause. Six years later, in 1846, Wigglesworth (1846) provided data from 1,987 families on mortality by age and gender of children. The highest probability of death was for boys at age one year whose chances of dying were one in eight.

In the view of McKeown and Record (1963) the major cause of a decline in deaths was the drop in the mortality rate associated with tuberculosis. This is a welcome but curious phenomenon because no specific cure was introduced; commentators have tended to rely on a general feeling that better nutrition explains the decline in the death rate, a view subject to revision (Mercer, 1990). However, the period included a rise in the adulteration of food, including watering the milk, so that the mortality decline for tuberculosis is not wholly explained. When declines associated with scarlet fever and typhoid-typhus are added the result, according to McKeown and Record, covers 90 percent of the mortality decline in the years 1850–1900. For the twentieth century, the first period of which is within our span of interest, the decline in deaths due to airborne diseases was primary (McKeown, Record, and Tavner, 1975).

In a two-part paper, Woods, Watterson, and Woodward (1988) offered three criticisms of McKeown's approach; they are failure to appreciate age- and place-specific data, use of two long periods of several decades, roughly 1840–1900, and 1901–1971, and overattention to tuberculosis with attendant slightings of childhood. More positively, the investigations offered several ideas to explain the decline in infant mortality of the end of the period of interest. They are the consistency by social class and place of the decline in infant mortality in the 1890s and 1900s; the marked decline in urban areas; postnatal mortality; a temporal focus of decline—the mortality increase of the 1890s was due to hot summers; and breast feeding, which protected infants from some illnesses.

Winter's (1982b) commentary on McKeown emphasized three points, beginning with the view that medical intervention viewed broadly was a positive influence. Winter suggested that advice on personal conduct and environmental management were helpful. That view seems appropriate in view of the state of personal hygiene early in the period. In 1834 *The Penny Magazine* reported the "astonishing

TABLE 3.7   THE LEADING GROUPS OF CAUSES OF DEATH IN 1848–1872, RATES PER THOUSAND DEATHS FROM ALL CAUSES

Age	Disease	Male		Female	
All ages	Infectious diseases	321	(146)	338	(155)
	Respiratory diseases	148		134	
	Nervous diseases	129		117	
	Digestive diseases	83		85	
Under 1	Developmental and				
	wasting diseases	266		269	
	Nervous diseases	210		196	
	Infectious diseases	178	(64)	193	(62)
	Respiratory diseases	150		141	
1–4	Infectious diseases	554	(118)	557	(105)
	Respiratory diseases	172		171	
	Nervous diseases	85		81	
	Digestive diseases	63		64	
5–14	Infectious diseases	618	(164)	600	(192)
	Violence (excluding suicide)	103		68	
	Nervous diseases	72		62	
	Respiratory diseases	59		41	
15–24	Infectious diseases	619	(433)	678	(501)
	Violence (excluding suicide)	118		53	
	Respiratory diseases	55		48	
	Nervous diseases	53		48	
25–44	Infectious diseases	487	(370)	509	(400)
	Respiratory diseases	102		78	
	Violence (excluding suicide)	92		75	
	Nervous diseases	82		73	
45–64	Infectious diseases	232	(157)	212	(137)
	Respiratory diseases	197		170	
	Nervous diseases	126		154	
	Circulatory diseases	124		129	

Source: Adapted from Logan (1950).
Figures in parentheses are for tuberculosis (all forms).

fact that few countries in the world are so badly supplied with proper bathing places as England, and that (taking the people in the mass) there are few among whom the use of the bath is less general than among the English" ("Cleanliness," 1834). Winter also emphasized the value of anesthesia, antisepsis, improved nutrition, and health administration.

Mercer (1990) included among possible explanations for the decline in mortality attention to ventilation, smaller families, isolation of the sick, and decreased susceptibility secondary to reduction in the incidence of cholera, smallpox, and similar diseases.

It should be pointed out that an assessment of death in the nineteenth century is more difficult than in the present era. Diseases now differentially diagnosed were, in the period under study, less clearly grasped. Typhoid and typhus are not the same disease, and the terminal cause of death is not necessarily the original condition, for example, influenza leading to pneumonia. Diseases change, and scarlet fever apparently mutated into a less virulent infection. Convulsion was a frequent category for recording children's deaths, and it is not clear what we would call it today. We would not classify teething as a cause of death but Dr. Husband (1864) found convulsions and teething orthodox causes in the records of the registrar-general. Death due to wasting was probably due to opiates in some infant deaths.

A second observation is that there appears to have been a cultural lag between the decline in child mortality and an appreciation of the facts of the situation. Despite well-developed skill at generating facts on popular health, understanding of facts was inevitably deluged. A result was the paradox of rising clamor over degeneracy at a time when mortality was in decline, especially due to tuberculosis and scarlet fever.

Our major observation on death, the ultimate state of stress in the nineteenth century population, is that it declined across the years of interest. Death of infants and children became less likely, and the probability of death before age five for up to 50 percent of the population was replaced by more familiar, lower rates. However, death rates remained high by current standards as the prewar years of the early twentieth century faded one by one.

Teeth

A major change in diet in the nineteenth century was the expansion of sugar in the diet. Unlike tea, which superseded alcohol in the everyday diet, to good ends, sugar brought with it decayed teeth, caries. In the first decade of the nineteenth century per person consumption of sugar was 19.12 lb.; by 1860 it had almost doubled at 30.30 lb. and had tripled by 1879 to 68.09 lb. (Taylor, 1975). Thus, to the traditional problems of wisdom teeth and progressive gum disease in the years of maturity was added the juvenile problem of decayed and lost teeth in childhood, for which only ineffective remedies existed (Reichart, 1984). In 1873, Bridges and Holmes reported to the Local Government Board, in their important study of work in factories, that one of the health problems of workers young and old was bad teeth; in this instance, factory work and factory owners were not the direct cause of the health problems. Twelve years later, in 1885, Dr. William Stewart had also noted the contrast between the teeth of the elderly and the inferior teeth of younger people (in a passage given earlier in this chapter).

Across the century the dental problem grew worse; ironically, this health problem was sometimes at least as extensive among middle-class as among lower-class children. Sugar consumption in the form of sweets and desserts was more accessible to children with pocket money, and so caries was a greater problem among families with discretionary funds. By 1904, the range of incidence of tooth decay in schools of various social backgrounds was wide. According to Smyth's (1904) citation of data gathered by Dr. Hall in Leeds, the incidence of bad teeth was no less than 11 percent, and reached 60 percent in one school. In Edinburgh, as the new century opened, the problem was more extensive among middle-class children than among the poor (*Report of the Interdepartmental Committee on Physical Deterioration*, 1904). In a special memorandum stimulated by the Interdepartmental Committee (*Memorandum in Regard to Condition of the Teeth*, 1906) the "debauch of sweet stuffs" was so widespread that the author referred to it as sacchoromania. In the decade 1891–1902, the army found that the condition of young men's teeth had deteriorated greatly. The rejection rate for recruits rose from 10.88 percent to 49 percent, and the *British Medical Journal* attributed the increase to the prevalence of bad teeth ("National Health and Military Service," 1903). At the extreme, bad dentition meant more than toothaches; it meant reduction in the capacity to take in nutrition except through soft foods. Bad teeth meant a distracted recruit during a period of intensive physical training. Subsequently, it meant a drop in the proportion of men fit for duty, as the Boer War in South Africa demonstrated.

The problem of bad teeth continued to progress in the twentieth century. In 1911, 85 Rochdale children, all of whom had slight constitutions (M = "19.97 ounces per inch of height"; MacMaster, 1911) had an 85 percent incidence of decayed teeth; that is, only thirteen had sound teeth.

Wall (1989) reported the following prevalence of bad teeth, defined as four or more decayed teeth, for 1913 and 1914:

	Boys	Girls
London	10 percent	9 percent
Cardiff	24 percent	32 percent
Cheshire	32 percent	34 percent

One year later, in 1914, the percentages were

	Boys	Girls
London	9 percent	8 percent
Cardiff	32 percent	34 percent
Cheshire	25 percent	25 percent
Nottingham	40 percent	38 percent

In his history of the Scottish people, Smout (1986) put the incidence of bad teeth in 1914 at 67 percent, rising ten years later to 87 percent in 1924. In the case of teeth, deterioration of health certainly became increasingly widespread with the passage of time.

Poverty

In many respects most demonstrable causes of poor health and diminished stature in the nineteenth century were correlates of poverty. From that single source flow virtually all the forms of social malaise that appear as symptoms. The poor ate less sensibly and paid higher prices for what they got. They dressed badly and used clothing as a source of temporary wealth via the pawn shop. Unchanged clothing was a seasonal convention, and poor mothers sewed up their children's clothing into a single, fused garment to contain heat well into the twentieth century. The poor were most susceptible to infestations of vermin, and head and body lice transmitted typhus. In that regard, thoughtful people saw a trade-off in the expansion of schooling in the early 1870s for poor folk's children; against the growth of literacy was balanced the propagation of disease through crowding. Even today, the childhood diseases, measles, diphtheria, and so on are spread primarily through the concentration of population in classrooms; although education is vital in an era of effective health care, the density of children in schools is a cause of ill-health and potential interference with growth. The writer recently encountered a school in which teachers and children had many cases of tuberculosis. Even today, this disease has not disappeared entirely; there has been a resurgence among people with the HIV virus involving drug-resistant strains (Altman, 1992).

However, not every illness is communicable. In the case of the health of girls there was the risk that their poor nutrition would affect their skeletal development in ways whose harmful consequences would not be evident until maturity. A pelvis deformed by rickets presented the substantial risk for problems many years later when the formerly ill-fed girl gave birth. The connection was, in fact, mechanical but it appeared to be transmitted by a diseased "germ plasm," to use the idiom of the time. In Dr. Greenhow's medical report to the Privy Council for 1860 he quoted the comment of Dr. Bouthroyd of Hanley, in the Potteries, that, "each successive generation of potters is more dwarfed and less robust than the preceding one." He was joined in that view by Dr. McBean who "had observed a marked degeneration especially shown in diminution of stature and breadth." In 1865, Dr. J. H. Langdon-Down observed that puny children were the offspring of pale, small women and asserted, "How, moreover, can it be expected but that the mother . . . should propagate an enfeebled race?"

In the nineteenth century getting to school presumed clothing and footware. Such clothing was not always available, and the absence of footware was a problem into the twentieth century. For several decades, Leeds ran a charity providing footware by soliciting contributions to buy, "Boots for t'Bairns." Children without satisfactory footware were susceptible to colds, and it seems likely that bad winters, like that of 1837, produced colds and bronchitis on an epidemic scale. Poverty made recovery a slow process, with depressed resistance to other diseases as people breathed the same air in crowded dwellings. Woods (1978) found a high correlation ($r = .77$) between the prevalence of measles and the percentage of back-houses in Birmingham in the 1880s. The poor were even more badly served in the matter of sanitation. Lack of sewers and toilets insufficient to the numbers of people were routine into the twentieth century. Soil saturated with human waste led to infected water and typhoid. Outbreaks of gastrointestinal disorders led to death by dehydration for infants. However, even those above the poverty level were not immune to the problems. It seems likely that flies prevailed in clouds in horse-filled streets and could transmit disease through milk and food. Only with prevalence of the internal combustion engine over the horse did this problem end. Relief from toilet problems was mostly a matter of providing the clean water and toilets advocated by Edwin Chadwick in 1842.

Climate

An influence on health to be touched on lightly but necessarily is climate. Unlike his descendants the Victorian was more likely to be wet and cold. Dwellings were heated less efficiently because most heat went up the chimney as coal smoke. Walls and windows let heat escape, and the poor were always ill protected from the elements. The impression one gets from meteorological records of the first two-thirds of the nineteenth century is that winters were long and hard, increasing the prevalence of colds, influenza, and pneumonia. Mortality data from London analyzed by Buchan and Mitchell (1875) spanned the period 1845–1874. Although the three decades produced no major therapies, there were refinements in the taxonomy of diseases, and Buchan and Mitchell took them into account. Overall, death rates peaked at about 1,400 per week in mid-January and mid-December, with two slightly lower peak rates in late March and late July. November to April was the peak period followed by a briefer period from mid-July to mid-September. In the case of phthisis (tuberculosis) the year-round rate was constant, although slightly elevated in March, April, and May, but with no weekly rate more than 13 percent above average. Rather different was Asiatic cholera, which came as epidemics but killed many people in the years 1848–1849, 1853–1854, and 1866 (Luckin, 1977).

Six years after the work of Buchan and Mitchell, William Guy (1881) addressed the Statistical Society on the connection between seasonal temperatures and mortality rates. Guy divided the year into three periods of four months: hottest, coldest, and temperate. The coldest four months, December to March, yielded the greatest proportion of death, 37 percent. March was slightly more fatal to children under two years, and children in that age group provided about one-third of all winter deaths (34.13 percent); those between two and five years contributed about the same number as the adult decades of age, from this briefer range of three years. However, the number of deaths ages three to five was about one-fifth of the number under age two. September was most fatal of the summer months to those under two years.

Further consideration of the role of climate came in the study by Woods, Watterson, and Woodward (1988) of the role of temperature and rainy days in the year's third quarter on infant mortality in the years 1870–1911. Both variables were highly significant ($P < .001$) in a regression model that was itself highly significant ($R^2 = .60$).

In the case of children in London, death due to premature birth, a condition we analyze by birth weight and length of gestation today, the year-round rate was constant, with slight elevations in January–February and in July–August. For all infants less than one year of age death rates peaked in the periods November–April and July–August; in this last period the mortality rate for little children doubled very quickly due to diarrhea. The rate of death due to diarrhea was sixteen times greater among the under-fives than in the rest of the age range combined. Among the under-fives the rate was highest among those in the first twelve months of life. The November–April period was one of cold, wet weather.

The best set of weather observations appears to be derived from observations at Oxford beginning in the year of Waterloo, 1815. Data on temperatures at Oxford between 1815 and 1934 were extended to 1942 by Lewis and presented by her in that year (see Figure 3.4). Lewis's data, which employed a twenty-year moving average, were distributed around an average winter temperature of 39.3° F. From 1815 to about 1848 the trend was to colder temperatures in the period December–February. The trend for 1848–1885 was for rising mean temperatures, followed by a trend to lower temperatures in the period 1885–1898. In the final period, 1898–1916, temperatures rose again. The second cold period, 1885–1898, reached a much lower average around 1898. Drummond (1943) identified the winters of 1878–1897 as the coldest recorded at Kew in the period 1783–1942. Drummond's Kew data resemble Lewis's Oxford data, and both were based on twenty-year moving averages. The subsequent period of increasing mean winter temperatures, 1898–1916, was much warmer than the first warming period, 1848–1885. Across the century, mean winter temperatures did not reach the overall average of 39.3° F until around 1868, but stayed well above the mean line until 1888. From the point of view of child health, cold and less cold winters came in series lasting about thirty years. The sequence of series may be summarized as cold (< 1868), less cold (1868–1885), and cold (1885–1911). The early period to 1868 was potentially harmful to child health at a time when economic circumstances were not good, until the positive developments beginning around 1850 emerged. In the final period, the standard of living had

FIGURE 3.4   MEAN WINTER TEMPERATURES AT OXFORD, 1815–1920

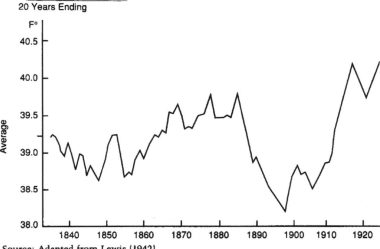

Source: Adapted from Lewis (1942).

risen, but purchasing power of wages was in decline. Horn's (1989) study of Victorian and Edwardian schoolchildren shows graphically the extent of sickness in school populations through photographs.

It may be noted, in passing, that another aspect of climate that might affect children is the number of hours of daylight. Unfortunately, this variable is site specific, so that the location of children must be specified, thereby reducing the relevance of many extant data sets from the nineteenth century. Two twentieth century studies that addressed the effect of daylight hours in long summer and short winter days are the work of Bransby and Gelling (1946) and Marshall (1975). Bransby and Gelling studied children on the Isle of Man and found a positive correlation between hours of sunshine and height increments. Marshall studied children on the Scottish island of Orkney, which is in the latitude of Stockholm and Hudson's Bay, but with milder temperatures. Marshall found little effect on childrens' growth rate due to variations in sunlight.

In the case of Victorian children, any connection between sunlight and height increment would, of course, have been confounded by the smokiness of the factory towns. Even into the middle of the twentieth century, burning solid coal in British towns created light-decreasing pollution in the air. Such opacity was complicated by weather, leading to the once-familiar, never-to-be-forgotten, pea-soup fogs; in them, buses and people were reduced to virtual groping, even in daylight. Thus the question of meteorological factors in the growth of Victorian youth is restricted to temperature, because the data requisite to analysis of the role of daylight is not manageable. On the other hand, as early as 1929, Nylin demonstrated that growth in height could be stimulated by exposure to artificial light of narrow, selected wavelength. It seems reasonable that our species' circadian rhythms might be responsive, in the developmental phase, to the length of the day, as a genotypic trait.

Eveleth and Tanner (1976) have shown that there are seasonal variations in growth. Height increases fastest in spring and summer, and weight in autumn and winter. The connection between climatic trends across the nineteenth century and illness and mortality is harder to gauge. The Christmas season of 1860 was the coldest in fifty years with "twenty-two degrees of frost" noted by Queen Victoria in her correspondence (Bolitho, 1964)—a frigidity likely to increase susceptibility to illness in young and old, foreshadowing Prince Albert's death in the next Christmas season. Buchan and Mitchell's (1875) data for the preceding three decades suggest that a very cold winter may account for the phenomenally high London death rate from influenza in 1847; in that year, the mean temperatures recorded at Kew were 33.4° F, 35.9° F, and 36.5° F (Drummond, 1943); influenza mortality for the year was 1,126 deaths compared to 115 in the preceding year. Of course, influenza, a "miasmatic" disease to the Victorians, is spread by droplets and a bad winter provided an occasion not a cause. In addition, influenza is less likely to kill than to debilitate. We may reasonably infer that the high number of influenza deaths connotes extensive sickness among the general population due to influenza in 1847. Deaths dropped by one-half in 1848, but were still far above 1849's 127 deaths. Apparently, the phenomenon of influenza deaths occurred in an epidemic that took two winters to run its course. During that period, the poor and the young would have had their health undermined by the strain of the influenza virus for which they had no prior constitutional immunity. Presumably, a new strain invaded the population in 1848 for which the 1837 outbreak, described by the footman, William Tayler (Wise, 1962), provided no immunity in adults. Children under twelve years would, of course, have had no immunity to the 1837 strain, in any case.

When illness occurs we know that there are direct consequences for the velocity of growth in height. Tully's (1924) study of Glasgow childrens' heights in 1921–1922 is persuasive in the conclusion drawn from study of 3,995 boys and girls ages five to thirteen; Glasgow was long a site of poverty, and Tully discovered that serious illness in the previous year was followed by lowered heights. Accordingly, the line of evidence and logic demonstrates that attention to winter temperature constitutes inclusion of a major predisposing variable in the ecology of health and auxology.

Climate also affected people's health and development by influencing the food supply. Good, dry summers led to bumper wheat crops, but wet summers meant late harvests and poor yields and made hay making a slow process. When a cool wet summer led to a small harvest the poor felt the effects in the following winter. In the years before 1846 when the Corn Laws were repealed, the growth of cheap North American grains could provide no relief. There were riots in years of low grain supply, and the people's heavy reliance on expensive bread in the diet lowered nutrition and resistance to disease. For years preceding the period of interest here, 1805–1914, Lee (1981) was able to develop a relationship between wheat prices and mortality rates some months later. Of course, repeal of the Corn Laws and adoption of free trade led to more affordable bread, and so to better nutrition and health, even when British harvests failed. Climate affected the growth of other foodstuffs and the price of grains was probably a great influence on the health of adults and the growth of children and adolescents.

Population Growth

An aspect of the health of society is the size of the population. In the years for which the best census data are available, 1841–1911, the population of England, Scotland, and Wales in the age range birth to nineteen years grew from 4.27 millions to 8.19 millions—a doubling across the decades. Proportionately, Scotland grew at a slower rate than England and Wales, increasing by about one-half. Table 3.8 lists the population by gender for the three kingdoms at eight census dates.

The size of the juvenile population is important for consideration of health because of the susceptibility of the young to infections. In the first five years of life, mortality rates were high, reaching the 50 percent level, cumulatively, for those years. By juvenile age, the population levels dropped in any year as death culled the ranks at increas-

TABLE 3.8   GROWTH OF POPULATION, IN THOUSANDS, AGES ZERO
TO NINETEEN YEARS

Year	Gender	England and Wales	Scotland	Total
1841	Male	3663	612	4275
	Female	3667	612	4279
1851	Male	4064	670	4734
	Female	4046	660	4706
1861	Male	3646	711	4357
	Female	4538	699	5237
1871	Male	5193	793	5986
	Female	4111	595	4706
1881	Male	5997	882	6879
	Female	6019	862	6881
1891	Male	6554	937	7491
	Female	6019	914	6933
1901	Male	6823	985	7858
	Female	6919	965	7884
1911	Male	7168	1006	8174
	Female	7202	993	8195

Source: From census data.

ing ages. For those not eliminated by death, illness interfered with
health, and resistance to disease was undermined by poor nutrition. It
seems probable that many more young people were sick than we recognize in our own generation. Chronic ill health in an age before antibiotics was common. The population was shorter, and lighter, than
today's young people, a condition traceable in part to the cumulative
effects of a higher population density constituting a greater repository
for disease and delays in growth. Growth in population increased density and is clearly demonstrated in the early maps of disease presented
by Gilbert (1958).

Population, Climate, Mortality, and Height

Next, we bring together three variables in the ecology of growth
that constitute a formulation of factors potentially influencing height.
In each instance, the variables were beyond individual's control.
Population is the annual figure interpolated from census data and represents density with proportional risk of infection. Climate is the
mean temperature of the three winter months December, January, and

February recorded at Kew (Drummond, 1942). In 1991, Campbell, Rodrigues, Macfarlane, and Murphy reported that cold weather was raising infant mortality almost a century after the Victorian era; sudden infant deaths rose sharply in February 1986, and the four investigators traced the excess deaths to "the unusually cold weather during that month." The relationship between infants and diarrhea is discussed in Buchanan (1985). Mortality is the annual rate of live-born children dying before the first birthday per thousand. Table 3.9 presents a description of the data set by gender and social level. The dependent variable is height in cm. indexed to the "urban artisans" series of the British Association's Galton Committee report in 1884. Data were checked for the absence of autocorrelation and lagged effects.

The technique for relating the hypothetical influence of the three predictor variables—population, temperature, and child mortality—to heights across the 105 years is multiple linear regression. The technique is also employed in Chapter Six, in which economic variables are added to the three ecological variables employed as covariates (ceteris paribus).

In Table 3.10 are six analyses composed of three social groups for two genders; Table 3.9 provides a description of the variables. The results in Table 3.10 analyze the contribution of any particular variable, in the presence of the other two predictor variables, to Galton height indexes. Results from analyses using non-working-class subjects are presented for completeness, primarily, due to the limited numbers of cases, especially for females.

The topic of this work is child development, and it draws on an era before our own to generate a perspective across decades and invoke quantitative data describing stress in society generated by rapid social and economic changes. Choice of statistical conventions when analyzing numbers depends largely on the analyst's métier. To some, slope, intercept, and evaluation of regression weights is the way to decipher the regression of a criterion on predictor variables. To others, reductions in R^2 (criterion variable) is paramount and attention to regression weights is imprudent, except when orthogonality of predictor variables is fully demonstrated (McNeil, 1991). I subscribe to this latter convention and select multiple linear regression (Bottenberg and Ward, 1963; MacNeil, Kelly, and MacNeil, 1975) to analyze data, a technique proven useful in other analyses (Jordan, 1980; 1991d).

Multiple Linear Regression

In multiple linear regression, an equation, or model, composed of a number of rationally selected variables is developed to predict a

TABLE 3.9 DESCRIPTION OF THE VARIABLES

Group	Variable	Males			Females		
		N	M	σ	N	M	σ
All	Population	96	36.37 (mill.)	6.08	52	38.22	5.68
	Mean winter °F		40.08	2.07		40.46	1.76
	Mortality rate		139.60	16.57		137.15	14.02
	Galton index		.97	.03		.98	.02
Working class	Population	64	35.41	6.10	42	37.95	6.04
	Mean winter °F		39.96	2.17		40.43	1.84
	Mortality rate		142.70	15.80		137.42	15.09
	Galton index		.96	.02		.97	.02
Non-working class	Population	32	38.30	5.64	10	39.38	3.85
	Mean winter °F		40.32	1.87		40.59	1.46
	Mortality rate		133.40	16.56		136.00	8.62
	Galton index		1.00	.02		1.00	.02

Note: Winter temperatures are not lagged.

TABLE 3.10 MULTIPLE LINEAR REGRESSION ANALYSIS OF GALTON-INDEXED HEIGHTS 1805–1914

Group	Model	Deleted Variable	Males				Females			
			N	R^2	F	P	N	R^2	F	P
All	I. Full		96	.05		.18*	52	.06		.37*
	II. Restricted	Population		.01	3.46	.06		.001	3.11	.08
	III. Restricted	Mean winter temp.		.05	.02	.88		.06	.002	.96
	IV. Restricted	Mortality rate		.04	1.11	.04		.02	1.78	.18
Working class	I. Full		64	.23		.001*	42	.06		.47*
	II. Restricted	Population		.01	17.58	.00009		.002	2.45	.12
	III. Restricted	Mean winter temp.		.23	.01	.91		.06	<.01	.93
	IV. Restricted	Mortality rate		.11	9.25	.003		.04	.88	.35
Non-working class	I. Full		32	.37		.003*	10	.73		.03*
	II. Restricted	Population		(−).13	10.84	.002		.72	.39	.55
	III. Restricted	Mean winter temp.		.36	.58	.45		.65	1.96	.21
	IV. Restricted	Mortality rate		(−).27	4.55	.04		.28	10.15	.01

*Significance of the difference from zero.
(−) = negative regression weight.

criterion, such as height at a particular age. The equation accounts for some proportion of the variance of the criterion measure; this equation containing all the variables one wishes to use to explain the criterion is called the *full* model. A second model is then constructed that is reduced, or *restricted*, by omitting a variable of theoretical interest. For example, given a full model of sex, race, and height at four previous ages, one might develop several restricted models, each of which deleted one or several of the variables. Each restricted model also accounts for variance of the criterion. Comparing the proportion of variance of a restricted model (R^2 restricted) allows us to test statistically the effect of omitting the variable of interest.

The basic model may be illustrated as $Y = a_0 u + a_1 x_1 + a_2 x_2 \ldots + a_n x_n = e$, where Y = a criterion of continuous or discrete data, u = a unit vector when multiplied by the weight a_0 yields the regression constant, $a_1, a_2, \ldots, a_n$ = partial regression weights arrived at by multiple linear regression techniques and calculated to minimize the error sums of squares of prediction (e^2), $x_1 x_2 \ldots x_n$ = variables in continuous or discrete form, and e = error in predicting a criterion. Two sources of information on multiple linear regression are Bottenberg and Ward (1963) and MacNeil, Kelley, and MacNeil (1975). The format in which results are reported is one of two patterns. Here, the style emphasizes criterion variance accounted for and the related F-test, with attention to the statistical significance from a model of zero information. An alternative, used for example in economic circles but probably less informative to the nonspecialist, emphasizes slope and intercept, presenting constants and evaluating regression coefficients with t-tests. The latter may be exemplified by the study of British heights 1750–1980 by Floud, Wachter, and Gregory (1990). Both modes of presentation draw on a common technique, regression of a criterion, like heights, on a set of predictor variables. The choice of mode of presentation seems to be a matter of preference across disciplines with parallel but not identical objectives in inquiry.

Table 3.10 shows the results of applying the three-predictor model to Galton-indexed heights drawing on ninety-six male and fifty-two female data sets of heights between 1805 and 1914. The entire corpus of studies is summarized in Figure 3.5. In Table 3.10, the regression model of three ecological predictors is presented six times; each gender is analyzed by three social-class markers. This formulation, which is repeated in Chapter Six, uses unequivocal identification of young people as working class as the central description. Non-working-class subjects are generally middle and occasionally upper class, although there are instances in which there are working-class subjects. An example is the heterogeneous population who paid Francis Galton to measure them at the Health Exhibition in 1885. Subjects are best understood as constituting a dichotomous (1/0) concept in which working-class membership equals one. The majority of subjects are working class, as they were the object of Victorian inquiries, primarily. The term N refers to data sets of mean heights and height indexes, not to individuals.

Males

For all males, the R^2 of the full regression model of three predictors is an insignificant .05 ($p = .18$), and none of the three predictor variables significantly reduced the R^2. For working-class males, the R^2 is greater, at .23, and reaches statistical significance ($p = .001$). The predictor, population size, was highly significant ($F = 18.03$, p = .00008). The third of the predictors, the mortality rate, dropped the R^2 in the third restricted model from .25 to .11 ($F = 9.25$, $p = .003$); it has a negative beta weight. For non-working-class subjects, the R^2 of the full model is .37, which is quite significant ($p = .003$). Two predictors, annual population and annual mortality rate of infants and small children, are significant. Deletion of population size dropped the R^2 from .42 to .13 ($F = 10.84$, $p = .002$), and deletion of annual mortality rate dropped the R^2 from .42 to .27 ($F = 4.55$, $p = .04$).

Females

Drawing on the fifty-two female data sets schematized by year of collection in Figure 3.5, the R^2 for all females is .06, which is not significantly different from zero. When the corpus is disaggregated by social level the three predictors demonstrate no relationship to the criterion of Galton-indexed heights. For working-class females the R^2 drops a little when the population size is deleted; however, the decline in R^2 is not statistically significant. In the case of the small group of non-working-class females ($N = 10$), mortality rate is an influence ($F = 10.15$, $p = .02$). That finding is gravely compromised by the small variable-to-cases ratio and would normally be set aside on the grounds that the regression line is overfitted. On the other hand, mortality rate is also significant among males of the same social level. That double outcome—not a cross validation of weights or a replication—is noteworthy, however.

107

FIGURE 3.5   VICTORIAN MALE AND FEMALE DATA SETS

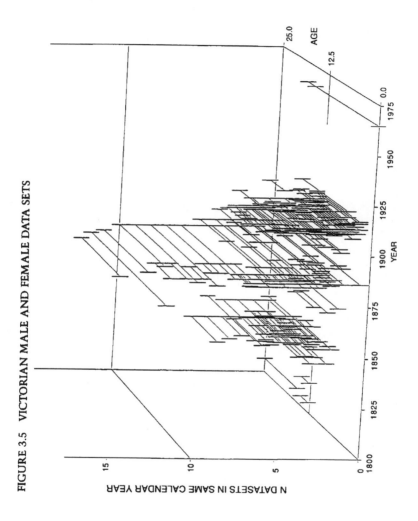

Commentary

This empirical analysis of variables in the ecology of nineteenth century height suggests several things. The first is that the impact of population size, winter, and mortality rate differs by gender and social class. Female heights indexed to Galton's 1884 data from urban artisans seem less susceptible than those of males to circumstances; only mortality rates appear relevant and that finding is suspect due to the low number of observations.

Victorian Index of Children and Youth

So far, we have considered a variety of discrete elements constituting the ecology of children's growth. In an attempt to provide an overall estimate there is the Victorian Index of Children and Youth (VICY Index), which covers the quality of life in the 100 years 1815–1914. The index was assembled by identifying twelve variables in three domains (see Table 3.11); index numbers and their development are described elsewhere (Jordan, 1991b; 1992). For the purpose of this chapter, it is necessary to know the domains that are listed in Figure 3.6 and Table 3.11. It will be evident that the greatest weight is given to health factors, with lesser allocations of factors from the social and economic domains. (See Jordan, 1992a,b,c.)

All variables are indexed to 1914; there are index numbers for the overall VICY index; and for each of the three domains there is a subindex. Because the period covers 100 years, the ordinate or Y-axis can be used to determine when particular variable levels were reached. Strictly speaking, the term *percentile* should be invoked to describe elements of a frequency distribution, not an index number. In the interest of interpreting the VICY index for the nonspecialist, I have chosen, also, to describe social change in the years 1815–1914 by using the terminology of percentages to describe annual approximations toward the 1914 value of 100, in Table 3.12, Part A. Readers may wish to keep this nontechnical idiom in mind since it is employed in the interest of broad communication.

Figure 3.6 presents four indexes, each of which must reach 100 percent in 1914. In the top left quadrant is the twelve-variable, overall VICY index. The graph begins at 35.58 in 1815 and makes a pronounced spurt in the 1840s. Thereafter, the index advances in zig-zag fashion to a level above an index value of 90, around 1900, and then climbs steadily toward 100 in 1914. In the case of the health subindex,

TABLE 3.11   DOMAINS AND VARIABLES

Domain	Variable
Health	Birth rate
	mortality < one year
	Winter temperature °C
	Summer temperature °C
	Galton height indexes
Economics	£ GNP per capita
	£ wage index
	Cost of living index
	Commodity price index
Social	Elementary school enrollment
	Female rates of literacy
	Size of households

the line starts at 76.06 in 1815 with plateaus induced by limitations of data in the early and late years. The line fluctuates sharply reaching its apogee in the early twentieth century. The social subindex is much calmer and rises sharply after a fairly modest rate of increase until about 1850, after beginning at 3.11 in 1815. Finally, the economic subindex begins at 27.56 and increases steadily, with fairly minor deviations, until 1914. In Table 3.12 Part A are dates that illustrate the relative degree of progress across the century in the three subdomains and in the total of all three, the VICY index, toward the 1914 index values of 100. The shape of the health index should be interpreted by noting that deviations from the overall shape of the other three indexes are increased by the reduced range of values on the ordinate or *Y*-axis. It is helpful to recall that the index is keyed to 1914 values, and the ninety-ninth percent level was generally reached a little before that date. The twenty-fifth percent levels generally came early, with the exception of health, which started out with an index number of 76.06. Part B of Table 3.12 is more conventional. There, quartiles of the annual data points for 100 years are presented. The first quartile or twenty-five data point-years end in 1839. In that second year of young Queen Victoria's reign, the overall VICY index was nearly halfway toward its 1914 level at 43.01, but there was a long way to go. In the case of the three subindexes, the range in 1839 was wide. The health index number was 76.06, the economic index number was 48.51, and far in the rear was the social index number of 4.44. The year 1864 marks the

TABLE 3.12 PERCENTAGE AND QUARTILE VALUES OF THE VICY INDEX AND THREE SUBINDEXES, BY DATE

Part A

			Dates for Subindexes		
	Percentage	VICY	Social	Health	Economic
	25	>1815	>1815		>1815
	50	1851–1852	1871–1872		1848
	75	1884–1885	1891–1892	1814–1815	1887
	99	1911–1912	1908	1895–1896	1911–1912

Part B

Quartile Dates		Index Numbers			
First	1839	43.01	4.44	76.06	48.51
Second	1864	54.77	15.72	89.36	59.23
Third	1889	78.47	68.94	85.64	80.82

second quartile or midpoint. The overall VICY index stands at 54.77, which is about what we might expect, and continues to resemble the economic index number of 59.83. About the same level of increase can be observed for the social and health index numbers, which increased by twelve to thirteen points to 15.72 and 89.36. Finally, as the final decade of the nineteenth century approached, in 1889, the VICY index stood at 78.47, much like the economic index number of 80.82. The social index number had risen sharply in the years 1864–1889 to 68.94. In contrast, the health index number fell back of 85.64. In that regard, it is helpful to recall that in some places the infant mortality rate reached its highest level in the closing years of the nineteenth century.

The major comment these data lead to is that social change in factors affecting the quality of children's lives was not uniform or consistently progressive. According to the three subindexes the period began with quite differing levels of quality of life for children (a picture due in part to limitations in some of the data), a state of affairs still evident in 1839. By 1864, the three domains increased at about the same rate, but the social index was low. By 1889, progress was evident, but health quality retreated rather than advanced. For the years 1889–1914, a modest amount of progress was achieved in the economic sphere, in the social sphere to a greater extent, and health had to recover ground in the face of retrograde developments. It appears that

FIGURE 3.6   VICY INDEX AND THREE SUBINDEXES OF CHILDREN'S
QUALITY OF LIFE, 1815–1914

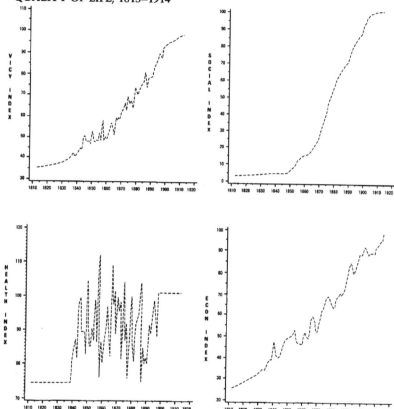

stress in the lives of children, judged by 1914 standards, was inconsistent in the earliest years and relieved at quite differential rates of social change across the years beginning with Waterloo, in 1815.

When considering the index numbers, it should be kept in mind that the input data were selected not to represent a domain as a whole, for all people, but to concentrate on children. Accordingly, the domain subindexes may not be generalized beyond children's quality of life and may not coincide with more narrowly conceived indexes for the respective domains. The overall VICY index is the salient variable.

However, balance requires that the limitations of this quantitative approach be acknowledged. Nineteenth century data often fall short of current standards, so that the VICY index should be viewed as an estimate, but one phrased numerically as an approach to description; in that respect, it is no worse than impressions expressed traditionally in prose, and perhaps better since it invites quantitative evaluation of the era and refinement of instruments for measurement. This work is a study of childhood and stress, and the quantitative approach to children has been the primary tool of child study for over a century. Extension of the quantitative mode to childhood over time is appropriate and overdue.

It is useful to represent the overall state of affairs in three domains with twelve contributing variables because that complex of information summarizes the changes in Georgian–Edwardian Britain from the point of view of children's welfare. The degree of stress in children's lives varied a little by domain, suggesting differing rates of social change within the republic of childhood. In all four instances progress was, in the long run, steady. Of course, the 1914 marked the end of an era.

The period beyond that watershed year is no less interesting for study of stress in children's lives. Winter (1979; 1982) documented the changes associated with the Great War, the reduction of infant mortality, and the processes of the 1930s. Clements (1953) focused on height and weight changes from 1883 to 1950. Boyne and Leitch (1954) cited data from Wolverhampton showing that boys' and girls' heights increased by 4.5 inches (11.43 cm.) and 6.5 inches (16.51 cm.) in the five decades 1901–1949. Smith, Chinn, and Rona (1980) reported height gains from England and Scotland. Rosenbaum's (1988) survey of 100 years of heights and weights is an excellent source. Finally, Harris (1989) reviewed medical inspections and children's nutrition in the years 1900–1950. He reported that five-year-old boys grew 3.35 inches (8.51 cm.) between 1911 and 1965, and girls grew by 3.04 inches (7.72

cm.) in the same period. Harris also reported geographic differences in growth in the twentieth century. Heights at given ages began to increase before 1914 in Croydon and in Bradford, but not until after the 1939–1945 war in Wakefield, Bradford's neighboring town.

In this chapter we have discussed the social and intellectual framework within which the phenomena of observed attainment of height took place. Nineteenth century Britain was diverse; small market towns grew into concentrations of industry, and the population shifted from a preponderance of comparatively low density in picturesque if unsanitary villages to living cheek by jowl in the "Cottonopolis" of Manchester and in other industrial centers. Whatever the place, there was the growth of population, which became a catchment for communicable diseases. Over all was nature, and climate influenced health, mortality, and growth through cold, wet winters and fluctuating harvests; the latter was less of a problem after 1846 when the Corn Laws were repealed.

To this discursive approach we have added an empirical consideration, the VICY index, and we have applied three elements in the ecology of growth, the size of the population, the mean temperature in the winter and the infant mortality rate to Galton-indexed heights. The result has been a differentiation of the impact of these three variables by gender and social class (see Table 3.10). In Chapter Six we will extend this perspective by introducing economic factors connoting the impact of the nineteenth century economy on the lives of the population as a form of stress.

Height and Body Mass of Children

Concepts

*I*n study of the processes of human development, known to specialists as *auxology*, there is a range of formulations of growth. There is the obvious matter of height, followed by weight, and there are indices of the proportions of one of these to the other. There are also specific components of the body exemplified by the proportion of body fat for which subcutaneous fat acts as a proxy; it is usually measured on the upper arm (triceps) or on the rib cage (subscapular), although there are more sophisticated ways of deriving body fat, such as weighing the entire body in water. There are also measurements based on specific anatomical sites. Examples are the Frankfurt plane for morphology of the skull, biiliac (hip) width, and sitting height.

Steckel (1983) demonstrated with contemporary data from around the world that, "height is a measure of economic welfare that is sensitive to the consumption of basic necessities, particularly food and medical care." That detached statement may be brought to life by citing the description of sixteen-year-old Alfred Webb of Birmingham. Sent to prison at age sixteen he was described as "so small that he does not look more than twelve or thirteen" (Allday, 1853). By our standards he would be as tall as a boy younger by still a few more years—say, eight or nine. A quarter century later, Thomson and Smith (1877) presented a photograph of a group standing around a vendor of fish in the slum of St. Giles. A barefoot boy of seventeen, "Little Mic-Mac Gosling," lived by making himself useful to stall keepers; his height is

115

given as 3 feet and 10 inches. Similarly, in the records of the convict transport, *John Renwick*, which reached Van Diemen's Land (Tasmania) in 1843, nineteen-year-old George Abbey of Middlesex, a laborer, is described as 4 feet 3½ inches tall (Jordan, 1991e). A hazard of such anecdotes is that they may be true statistical "outlayers" in the distribution of heights or might be cases of (e.g.) achondroplastic dwarfism. However, their existence is incontrovertible, and illuminating, even if not representative of the distribution of heights in the middle decades of the nineteenth century.

A dynamic aspect of growth is its velocity, usually expressed as the difference measured at fixed intervals of time for height and weight. Also, there is the rhythm of that process evident in rapid growth in infancy followed by a slower period, then the quickened pace of adolescence, and the attainment of maximum height on early adulthood. (Later, there is a process of contraction associated with aging.) Menarche and menopause in females and puberty in males are examples of developmental milestones determined by biosocial rhythms. Bone age determined by inspection of X rays also illustrates the individuality of growth patterns; dental age, more accessible to simple inspection, is another example.

The preceding items are twentieth century concepts of growth, and their application to nineteenth century questions is, in some respects, an anachronism. Indeed, even birth weight below 2500 gm (5.5. lb.) was standardized as a developmental concept within memory. In early nineteenth century Paris an infant delivered to the Foundling Hospital weighing 6 lbs. had a chance to survive; "if a newborn infant weighs less than 6 lbs., there is little hope of rearing it" ("Practical Application of Physiological Facts," 1837). About all we can hope for in historical files is to find height and weight data. But that expectation presumes a systematic interest in the assessment of the body, a topic for which Tanner (1986) called attention to the work of Christian Friedrich Jampert who died quite young in 1758. Although the question seems interesting, it is difficult to identify measurement earlier than the series of annual measurements on his son taken by Philibert Gueneau de Montbéliard between April 11, 1759, and November 11, 1776. There followed a period of indifference until Quetelet's work began being published in the 1830s.

In addition to the major study of Marine Society boys' heights in the period, 1770–1870, by Floud, Wachter, and Gregory (1990), there are other programs of studies in the late twentieth century of eighteenth and nineteenth century heights. Komlos (1985; 1986; 1989) analyzed

Austro-Hungarian records, and Nicholas and Steckel (1991) analyzed British heights through Australian data on transported convicts. They reported an advantage in height for rural-born males that was most apparent between fourteen and seventeen years of age, with the growth spurt delayed at fourteen to fifteen years. The third program is the study of heights, c. 1800–1815, of men recruited into the army of the East India Company (Mokyr and O Grada, 1993).

My consideration of adult male convict heights (Jordan, 1991e) excluding non-working-class occupations, analyzed heights from the transports *John Brewer* (1842) and *John Renwick* (1843). For ninety-five men between the ages of eighteen and forty-three years the mean height was 164.16 cm. (64.62 inches). Expressed as a percentage of the British Association's 1883 Galton report, using the "town artisans" series for a reference, the average height becomes a Galton index of only .97. These mid-nineteenth century convicts were small by virtue of their sociooccupational backgrounds, and they were smaller than average within the broad occupational group represented by the Galton town artisans of 1875–1883. That criterion is, perhaps, less satisfactory than the corpus of 14,946 adult male convicts, analyzed by Nicholas and Shergold (1988). Some of them were born in the decade 1810–1819, and they would have been about twenty-five years old when *Renwick* and *Brewer* transported their human cargoes. Nicholas and Shergold place the mean height of 3,080 such men at 167 cm. Even by that criterion, the convict men of 1842 and 1843 were below average by 2.94 cm. (1.05 in.). Their mean height constitutes an index of .98 by the Nicholas and Shergold criterion.

In 1872, a new phase of anthropometry began. Dr. Nicholls of Boston told the medical society that he had been measured semiannually (presumably by a parent) from the age of six months to twenty-five years. If Dr. Nicholls were only twenty-five at the time he commented on Bowditch's important paper (Bowditch, 1872), the study of his development by anthropometry would have commenced in the late 1840s; were he older in 1872, this first post-Montbeliard study would be dated earlier, in proportion.

Weight is more problematic because it is subject to a series of temporary influences so that, like blood chemistry, we need to know the precise circumstances surrounding the measurements. Height is not without its ambiguities, and babies defy the concept of reliability of measurement as they contract and expand.

A challenging problem is to find data sets to address the problem in the early decades of the nineteenth century. I have developed two additional data sets from the indents (records) of ships transporting convicts to Australia. The first is a set of women transported on the ship *Harmony* in 1829; by contemporary accounts the ship was probably highly misnamed (Jordan, 1990b). The second set is for boys ages thirteen to nineteen on the convict transports *Frances Charlotte* (1832) and *Lord Goderich* (1841) (Jordan, 1985) dispatched to Hobart, Tasmania. The significance of these data on 306 boys and 100 women is that they were poor folk. Indeed, some of them probably fell into what the Victorians called the *residuum*, a social stratum at the very lowest level where sheer survival on any given day was the objective. However, most of the convict women were domestic servants, and the boys old enough to provide an occupation described themselves as "labourers." Such people are the unglimpsed but large portion of populations against whose supporting roles the eminence of major players, statesmen and generals for example, is highlighted. These are the ordinary people whose lives tend to be invisible and unreachable. In the case of the women and boys they afford a glimpse into individual lives in stress in early Victorian Britain. Obliquely, we can gain a little insight into the nurturing patterns of the residuum and working class through the admittedly nonrepresentative practices of women convicts who had been transported to Australia. Elsewhere (Jordan, 1990b) I have reported such a group of women in passage; however, Gandevia (1978) addressed child care by convict women more directly. He noted that some infants accompanying their convict mothers died from neglect, and that mothers of older children were inattentive when participating in educational programs for their children. In Australia, maternal venereal diseases killed a number of infants and blinded others among the children of women convicts.

Reservations about these items of information are that they arose under the stressful circumstances of life on a convict ship and in the developing settlements of early Australia. On the other hand, the mothers were Britons and living under the Union Jack. In that sense, they represented to a fair degree their sisters in the United Kingdom and the patterns of child care, and neglect, frequently practiced among the poor and criminal.

To describe some assemblies of numbers as "data sets" is to underreport the procedural difficulties they present. A data-centered approach to study of development in the nineteenth century, especially in the early decades, calls to mind John Graunt's description of his own efforts in 1662 to analyze the Bills of Mortality as, "buzzling and groping." Steckel (1979) transcribed and systematized records of slaves moved by ship from one American port to another. Ships manifests in the age of sail are not obvious, self-deciphering documents. Similarly, convicts transported to Australia (Jordan, 1985; 1990b; 1991e) were described in indents with emphasis on features by which the authorities would identify runaways. A large archive brought to usefulness by Floud and Wachter (1982) consists of Marine Society records of boys trained to be seamen in the period 1770–1870. Fogel et al. (1983) presented a data set of heights on men serving in the Revolutionary War. Two archives developed for twentieth century use were the set of heights and weights of men entering the Ecole Polytechnique between 1801 and 1954 (Sutter, Izac, and Toan, 1958) and men entering West Point by Komlos (1987).

An interesting foreruner is the data set on 17,000 children from factory districts analyzed by Factory Inspector Leonard Horner in 1837 ("Practical Application of Physiological Facts," 1837). Of particular interest are entries listing paternal occupation in ten groups approximating social strata. Comparable are studies of heights of Danish conscripts 1852–1856 (Boldsen and Kronberg, 1984) and Australian convicts (Jordan, 1985; 1990b). In each instance analysis was preceded by intensive work to extract items from records and organize them into a data set. Rarely do pre-twentieth century archives yield easily to contemporary standards for data or to rearrangement for data processing.

An archive which may be mentioned in passing, because it conveys the riches which exist to be developed on living organisms, is the set of records amassed by the Hudson Bay Company. Elton and Nicholson's (1942) study of lynx pelts trapped in Canada drew on annual reports ad hoc first filed in 1635. This study, little known outside animal ecologists, indicates the richness which accumulation of careful records over time can provide.

Another procedural aspect is that we present data sets gathered in the period of interest or constructed from fragments. The consequence is that not every group of subjects is present to the same degree. An example is the absence of heights from non-working-class girls prior to about 1870. Our presentations are keyed primarily to working-class children as they bore the brunt of the social processes described in Chapter Two. In selected instances we can contrast working-class data with non-working-class data, but not in every case, nor to the same extent. As with the VICY Index, we are developing an estimate rather than an X-ray of an era.

Equally bothersome are the archives that resist analysis. Many fail to provide the number of cases at any given age; this omission limits analyses of data and interferes with evaluation and commentary. Sharpey and Boyd (1861) combined lengths of children studied post-mortem into a single set of observations for the age range seven to fourteen years. Boyd (1861) developed tables of heights from 2,086 examinations of poor people in the Marylebone Infirmary between 1839 and 1847. Aitken (1862) thought them excellent and referred to them as "the average height of the mature human being, as now accurately determined in this country by the observations of Dr. Robert Boyd." Unfortunately, *Philosophical Transactions* presents two pages of text, but not the tables. Boulton (1880a) appears to refer to a ten-year prospective data set of repeated measures, but I have found no data from it in any of his publications. Stephenson (1888) combined the norms of Bowditch in Massachusetts with those of the Galton committee as the "standard for the English-speaking races." Hall (Smyth, 1904) and Greenwood (1913) gathered data on boys and girls, and then proceeded to lump the sexes together in an unusable aggregate.

Quite different, and praiseworthy for its scope and the authors' analyses, is the set of male heights based on British military and philanthropic archives assembled and studied exhaustively by Floud, Wachter, and Gregory (1990). Based mainly on data in the Public Records Office, the Royal Military College, Sandhurst, and the Marine Society, this file was statistically adjusted to allow for (e.g.) the truncation of height distributions due to exclusion of recruits below minimum requirements. The study by Floud, Wachter, and Gregory drew interesting inferences for male heights, in the years 1750–1980, in terms of a variety of social factors. Major conclusions were that the concept of a secular trend did not apply to the height data of the period; that inequities between groups shrunk; that urbanization and disease explain much of the irregularity of increases in height across the period; and that, after 1870, improved nutrition contributed to increasing heights. Two late twentieth century studies of British heights which can serve as reference points are the work of Rona and Chinn (1987) on children, and Rosenbaum and Skinner (1985) on adults beginning at age sixteen.

Heights 1805–1914

For this chapter and for Chapter Six I will draw on archives consisting of data sets on height and weight (and, occasionally in the later years, strength and sensory acuity) on children, adolescents, and young adults. For the purpose of this book, whose central topic is *stress* in the lives of the young across decades of social change, we need an array of circumstances. Especially salient is gender, because females' auxology to maturity differs from that of males. Immediately we encounter problems because the Victorians placed a lesser emphasis on females of all ages and employed rigid gender roles in the home and workplace. As a result, data on females across the wide period of just over a century considered here is scanty. That limitation will be evident later in this chapter when the study of body mass is unavoidably limited to males. A second factor is social class. Interest leading to collection of empirical data arose from social problems so that middle-class individuals were of interest only infrequently. Not the least challenge is the comparative lack of interest in biosocial questions early in the period. The ethos of the early phase was unconcerned with analytic techniques, although propagandists began to appreciate the persuasiveness of numbers in the process of reform of, for example, factory conditions. When we combine the dimensions of period, gender, and social class in a three-dimensional box of twenty-seven theoretical cells, the gaps become evident. Height data are available across the period for working-class males (with a concentration between ages five and seventeen years). For other cells, there are substantial gaps. The lacunae represent reality in the data set employed in this work, rather than errors of sampling. Even so, the data file composed of small and large data sets includes females and middle-class subjects of both genders. The original documents often fail to list the number of cases, and some sets of measurements were excluded because they combined genders and otherwise lumped together incompatible groups.

The corpus of height studies is schematized for males and females in Figure 4.1, which presents a three-dimensional image in which the age ranges and frequency of data sets in any given year is displayed. Ideally, we would have data sets for each year that cover the entire developmental span. However, gathering the data sets was not an exercise in sampling but a search for every accessible data set. Study of height was an enthusiasm of Victorian gentlemen, not an organized scientific program; and so we describe reality when we list studies in some years and none in others. Also, we would like all kinds of people described, but we find more male than female studies and more working-class samples than higher social groups. The composition of groups by social level is also vexatious because it too reflects Victorian informality. There are tidy data sets, however; Komlos (1989; 1990) has drawn on German and Austro-Hungarian archives to describe social-class influences on height in the eighteenth and nineteenth centuries. Figure 4.2 illustrates the point by showing the two most different

FIGURE 4.1 VICTORIAN MALES

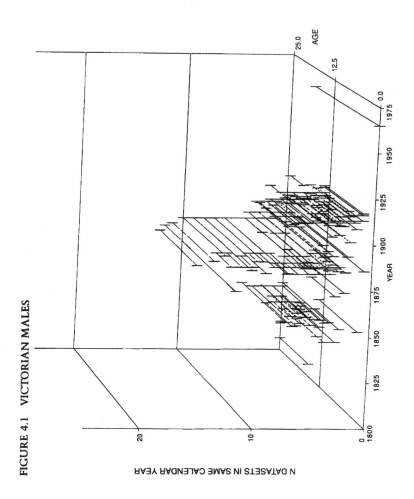

FIGURE 4.2 WORKING-CLASS MALE AND NON-WORKING-CLASS FEMALE DATA SETS

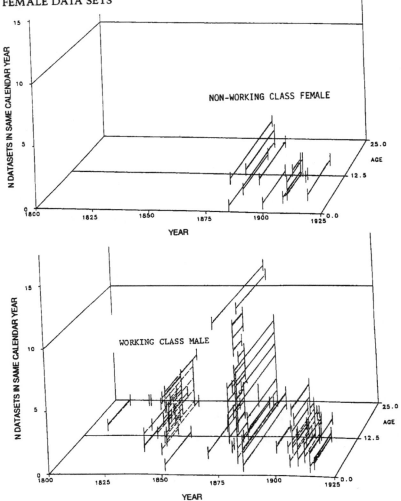

subgroups in the corpus. Working-class male data covers the entire century and its midpoint is approximately at mid-century. In contrast non-working-class female data are comparatively infrequent and were gathered in the last one-third of the period of interest. Military data are generally excluded from the data file.

In Figures 4.1 and 4.2 we describe data sets of heights of males and females in the period 1805–1914. The scale of years along the abscissa of Figure 4.1 covers 175 years. It begins in 1800, and the period ends in 1975 to include data from Tanner, Whitehouse and Takaishi (1966). The heights in the figures that follow were selected for several reasons from a total of forty-eight theoretical age entries for each of which some data exist in the corpus of studies. The ages seven to fourteen years, seventeen years and young adult are ages at which data frequently exist in the form of mean heights. The ages reflected have an additional rationale. Age seven (et sequelae) occurs after the high mortality rate in the nineteenth century in what we now call the *preschool period*. The spurt of adolescence is represented by ages fourteen to seventeen.

In the earliest period, data sets of heights occur at intervals of approximately a decade and become much more frequent in 1870. The mean heights have been translated from feet and inches into centimeters and, subsquently, indexed as percentages of the urban artisans' heights of Galton's 1883 report to the British Association meeting in Southport and to the data of Tanner, Whitehouse, and Takaishi (1966). The size of the groups from which the means are calculated is far from evident in the early decades. Indeed, even in the last forty years of the period there are problem statistics exemplified in use of the word *average*, which sometimes turned out to be the mode or value of highest frequency in the original data.

Appraising Social Level

A major descriptor of data sets in the corpus is socio-occupational information. For this variable, the tidier label is *working class*, which covers appropriate children and those still lower in the "residuum." *Non-working class* refers to people who were largely middle class, although there were occasional instances of working-class subjects. An example is the set of people tested by Galton at the International Health Exhibition in South Kensington (Galton, 1885; Ruger and Stoessiger, 1927; Elderton, Moul and Page, 1928; Johnson et al., 1985).

Employing the category of working class–non-working class to stratify young persons is practical due to limited descriptions in nineteenth century reports and, in this instance, is probably adequate as most of the data come from reports on males and are unambiguous. However, it is appropriate to point out that use of two, three, or five (Neale, 1972; 1981) classes that are discrete variables, or constitute a 1–3, or 1–5 continuous variable, is a satisfactory approach when the objective is to discuss ideology rather than to conduct empirical research. In the case of the latter option, one would hope for a continuous variable with a broad scoring range.

An example I have found useful in prospective longitudinal study of children and their families (Jordan, 1980; 1991g) McGuire and White's (1955) system based on occupation, education, and source of income (among several other variables); these three factors yield a continuous variable ranging from sixteen to eight-four points, a range of sixty-eight points which provides a sensitive barometer of social status. Comparable techniques are (United States) Duncan (1961), Greene (1970) and Stevens and Cho (1985); (Canada) Blishen (1967) and Pineo, Porter, and McRoberts (1979); (Great Britain), Osborn and Morris (1979) and Osborn (1987); (France) Brichler (1958); and (New Zealand) Elley and Irving (1972).

The Victorians, ever sensitive to social niceties, themselves essayed the classification of people: John Stuart Mill in 1839, according to R. S. Neale (1981) placed two levels of people in the "privileged" class, and then consigned to the "disqualified" class seven groups of people among whom were five sets of individuals we today might view as middle class. At the bottom of Mill's model were two working-class groups distinguished by slightly different ideologies and by their respective sites in London or the North. The Anthropometric Committee of the British Association (Final Report, 1884) placed people into five groups: they were, by male occupation, professional (outdoor and indoor), and commercial class, constituting together "nonlabouring classes." Three "labouring classes" were labourers, artisans, and industrial classes.

Lindert and Williamson (1982) reported on earlier system of fifty-one categories devised by Massie in 1760; he defined one stratum as "families which drink tea, coffee or chocolate morning and afternoon."

In the late twentieth century, Neale (1972; 1981) set forth a five class system for the nineteenth century. There is an upper class and a middle class, but there is also a "middling class" of "aspiring professional men," such as lawyers and physicians. Neale split the working class into an *A* and a *B* group; the former was an industrial proletariat, and the children I have aggregated here fall into Neale's working class *A*, for the most part. The connotation of that linkage is that such children may be described as members of a group with a particular sensibility. Children would observe an ideology increasingly nondeferential and collectivist, as the decades passed, in the industrial context. Implicit is Dahrendorf's (1959) theme of a process of conflict derived from the tension between authority and subordination in group relations. In another place Dahrendorf (1982) discusses the modern British working class in terms relevant and informative for understanding their ancestors studied here in their childhood and adolescence. Returning to Neale's formulations, however, there is his *B* group of working class people who were deferential, and dependent, working in agriculture, domestic service, and low-paying factory jobs.

Slightly different, but of interest due to its attention to classifying occupations is Armstrong's (1972) classification of nineteenth century jobs. The system emphasizes the skills underlying job titles, which is useful in view of the surfeit of titles encountered in (e.g.) the textile industry. Armstrong introduced the following five skills levels: (1) professional, (2) middling, (3) skilled, (4) semiskilled, (5) unskilled. More recently, Nicholas and Shergold (1988) applied ten categories to 19,711 individuals transported as convicts to Australia. The categories were (1) unskilled urban, (2) unskilled rural, (3) skilled building, (4) skilled urban, (5) skilled rural, (6) dealers, (7) public service, (8) professional, (9) domestic service, (10) occupations not classified elsewhere.

The children discussed in this work span about a century of social and economic flux. The precise connotations in ideology and world outlook for them vary with the era within the nineteenth century that defines their childhood and their maturing sense of identity with a reference group. Religion and geography combined with the local economy to shape the particular ethos distinguishing their lives and relationships in any given decade. This theme may be pursued more fully in the recollections of young people themselves provided by Burnett (1982), Thompson (1988), Roberts (1971), and Mayhew (Quennell, 1969), and, to a degree in Jordan (1987b, Chapter Four).

Data

The data (criterion variable) consist of 107 sets of mean heights from males and 57 sets of mean heights from females, converted into centimeters; the total of 164 data sets, containing data points from

1805 to 1914. (The list of data sets in the corpus constitutes Appendix 1.) The later nineteenth century data are quite modern and fully recognizable to today's reader. That is, data are reported as means, and there are modes and ranges. There were lapses, however, as in Sharpey and Boyd's (1861) grouping of heights of children between ages seven and fourteen as a single group; in Roberts's (1876) emphasis on the mode as the best measure of central tendency; Kerr's (1897) concentration of Bradford school children's heights without specification of neighborhood or social class; and in Greenwood's (1913) pooling of male and female data. The earliest data are quite informal; in Parliamentary Papers of the 1830s and 1840s data are sometimes reported by summing individuals heights for groups of children. For example, in the case of Symons's (1842) report, a value of 44 feet 6 inches for ten boy colliers was the basis of comparison with the total height of a second group of boys. A different style of reporting is evident in the work of Brent (1845), who described Marylebone paupers, amateur rowers, and Cornish wrestlers as, tall, middling, or short. One year before, in a paper presented to the British Association, Brent (1844) put the average height of Englishmen at 67.5 inches, based on "the measurement of some thousands of individuals . . . chiefly by the personal labour and expense of the author." Another example of the vagueness we encounter in nineteenth century studies is a muddle over the ages of children. Youngsters between eleven and twelve are sometimes best represented as 11.5 years, but they might, according to the vagaries of the text, be better reported as eleven or, sometimes, as twelve years old. In many instances, the number of individuals measured and the circumstances of measuring (with or without shoes) are not reported; weight and clothing are equally susceptible to misconstruing.

From the point of view of the person seeking to scan the nineteenth century broadly there is the classic problem of lacunae. Floud and Wachter (1982) reconstructed data on boys in the Marine Society, and I have reconstructed data on convicts transported to Australia in the 1830s and 1840s (Jordan, 1985; 1990b; 1990e). In the first half of the nineteenth century, data exist only sporadically, and the first sixty years are, perhaps, best represented at intervals of a decade. In contrast, the years from 1870, beginning with Roberts's (1876) studies, up to 1914, contain data sets that are both national and large in Europe and in North America.

There is the question of which people to study. In the 1830s children in factories were a topic of interest as Disraeli's idea of Two Nations, later raised in *Sybil* (1845), occupied the attention of Young England, a set of thoughtful men. In the first several decades, there were virtually no studies of middle-class children, and adults were rarely studied unless they were soldiers (Army Contractor, 1817; Aitken, 1962; Wachter and Trussell, 1982a) or felons (MacGrigor, 1857; Danson, 1862; Jordan, 1985; 1990b). Across the century data sets on females are uncommon although I have reconstructed some and collated others. In that respect, it is important to note the upsurge of anthropometry (Beddoe, 1870), which led to the British Association report of 1883 (Final Report of the Anthropological Committee, 1884). There was, subsequently, a spate of studies in the next three decades.

The studies provide heights clustered at three dates, c. 1840, c. 1880, and c. 1905, broadly speaking. One-third of the data sets are on females, and the most frequent category is working-class males. By age, the corpus represents well the years seven to seventeen, centering on age twelve years, although there are studies that survey the full developmental span to adulthood; an example is the anthropology report to the British Association associated with Francis Galton in 1884. On a smaller scale, Kerr's (1897) prize-winning essay based on Bradford school children measured youngsters from age three to fourteen. Given the formulation of the target population, Kerr's age range was commendably comprehensive, especially at the younger ages.

Selected Studies

Across the period of interest, there are many studies in the corpus. A few are distinctive by virtue of studying both genders. In 1837, Leonard Horner, the redoubtable factory inspector, contacted seventy-two physicians certifying children to work in factories. In total, Horner and his colleagues assembled weight and height data from 8,469 males and 7,933 females from ages eight to sixteen years ($N = 16,402$). The data were presented originally in *The Penny Magazine* (Horner, 1837) of the Society for the Diffusion of Useful Knowledge.

There appears to be no comprehensive study of urban and rural children until Charles Roberts's report of 1876. At that time, Roberts presented heights from a variety of towns and other sites convenient for sampling. The mean Galton index for boys in the series is .91, ranging from .93 at age 9.5 years to .89 at age 13.5 years. The data are the sum of Roberts's samples of working-class children. Roberts's appreciation of the value of describing his subjects in terms of their place of

130

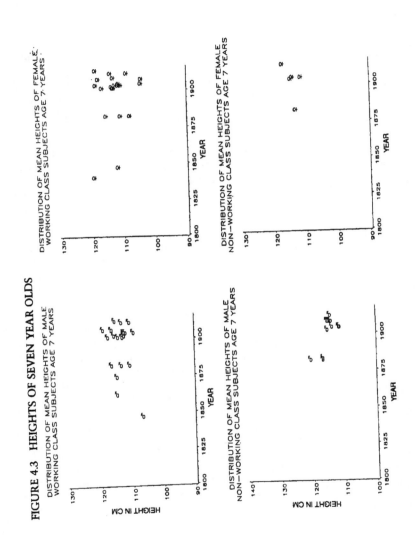

FIGURE 4.3 HEIGHTS OF SEVEN YEAR OLDS

residence is important because it relates growth to the habitat or social context of life. However, some of Roberts's data are presented without specification of the gender of the children reported, on occasion.

In 1883 came the British Association study of anthropometry, using 42,190 subjects from age two years to adulthood. Dr. Charles Roberts and Sir Rawson Rawson drew up the report usually known by the name of the committee's chairman, Francis Galton (Galton et al., 1884). Beginning in 1875 the British Association's Anthropometry Committee had set out to examine height, weight, chest circumference, and other features for a total of twelve measurements. When combined with data previously gathered by Dr. Roberts the committee "had observations made on a total number of about 53,000 individuals of both sexes and all ages, from which to construct their tables and to base their conclusions." When we evaluate the broad range of Galton's data against the Tanner, Whitehouse, and Takaishi (1966) heights we find that the mean Tanner index for males is .96, and the range is from .94 from age 13.5 years to 15.5 years to an anomalous 1.03 at age six years. For the laboring classes of considerable relevance to the purpose of this chapter, the Tanner indexes are lower and have a mean of .93 for Manchester subjects.

At the end of the period is Dr. Ethel Elderton's (1914) study of 63,776 Glasgow children under thirteen years of age. It should be noted that Glasgow had unique problems in the years of interest. As late as 1951, according to Smout (1986), Scots were seven times more likely to live in stressful, overcrowded conditions. In 1888 J. B. Russell described *Life in One Room*; of 100 dwellings five had five rooms, fifteen had three rooms, forty-four had two rooms, and thirty had only one room. "No less than 14 per cent. of the one-roomed houses and 27 per cent. of the two-roomed houses contained lodgers." In Elderton's data on males from 32,811 subjects the mean Galton index is .92 and the range is from .89 at age fourteen to .94 at age five.

The preceding four figures describe both genders. There are some informative studies of a single gender in the period of interest. I have excavated and reported (Jordan, 1982; 1985; 1987b) the physical condition of factory children and boy convicts transported to Australia in 1832 and 1841. Yeats (1864) reported the physical development of 400 boys in the London suburb of Peckham attending the Birkbeck school in 1863. This comparatively early study is interesting because Yeats (an LL.D.) related weight to height, calculated increments across ten months, and presented an informative graphic summary of his data set.

Another interesting report is Steet's (1874–1876) study of boys who wished to deliver telegrams. The occupational-vocational choice of the lads aged thirteen to nineteen is the basis for the study, which has a ring of modernity. In 1904, Bennett reported to the Interdepartmental Committee on Physical Deterioration the heights of boys in Southwark. A little further up the social spectrum was Clark's study of boys in York reported by Galton in 1884. (Public school boys at Cheltenham and Charterhouse were studied by Davis in 1889 and by Williams in 1914.)

Females

I have analyzed heights of convict women shipped to Australia in 1829 on the ship *Harmony* (Jordan, 1990b). Their average height across a range of ages from the teens to the forties was 61.74 in. (156.82 cm.). In 1842 Samuel Scriven studies girls employed in Halifax worsted mills. At the end of the period under consideration, in 1914, Williams, Bell, and Pearson measured girls at the Royal Soldiers Daughters Home in Hampstead. There were few studies of middle class girls in the period of interest, although there are females in the early studies of factory child workers (e.g., Horner, 1837; Symons, 1842).

Heights of Victorians

In considering the corpus of studies assembled over several years it should be noted that the heights are approached as Galton-indexed percentages. The Galton indexes are mean heights expressed as percentages of the means given in the Galton Anthropometric Committee report of 1884 to the British Association. The "urban artisan's" means are employed to calculate Galton indexes because that social stratum seems to represent a middle ground, although heights of females exist only to age sixteen. It has seemed vital to employ a Victorian norm to standardize heights as comparable when drawn from times separated by several decades. (The corpus includes a "Tanner index" based on the P_{50} norms of Tanner, Whitehouse, and Takaishi [1966]).

Also, as a matter of consistency, I have treated twentieth century data series on children (Jordan, 1980) in their original ranges, not seeking to interpolate or extend data beyond its pristine range by means of sophisticated methods to remedy sampling problems. Statistical extrapolations and interpolations are estimates, a concept whose respectability I acknowledge (Rosenbaum, 1988) but view cautiously, since it compromises the merits of original measures. In this instance, numbers are satisfactory for all males, all females, working-class males, working-class females, and non-working-class males. Thus, the critical population groups were recovered and only non-working-class female groups consistently provide less than adequate numbers. They are reported for completeness even when scanty.

As a preliminary examination, Figures 4.3, 4.4, and 4.5 present heights at three ages. There are both genders and three social groupings at ages seven, eleven, and fifteen years. The 1966 p_{50} value for one age and gender established by Tanner, Whitehouse, and Takaishi is indicated by means of the letter T (Tanner) for boys and for girls at each age in Figure 4.4.

In this section we draw on the entire corpus of mean heights from studies, some of which include several data sets. The purpose is to use data to examine the question of stability, rising or falling of mean heights at six odd-numbered ages from seven to seventeen years across the period of interest, 1805–1914 as evidence on the subject of degeneracy. The data in Figures 4.6–4.11 are grouped by gender and by social level. In that regard, it is important to recall that the labels *working class* and *non-working class* are not quite reciprocal. That is, the category of working class is an unambiguous description, but the non-working-class label is not. Some of those subjects probably are middle class and working class, such as boys at the Friends School at York studied by Clark in 1857; others are clearly middle and upper class, such as the Malborough boys measured by Galton (1876), and the Cambridge students measured by Venn (1889). A third example is the set of people who were measured by Galton at the Health Exhibition at South Kensington in 1884. (An amusing aspect of that project is that Galton persuaded his subjects to pay him, a rare but inspiring event in the annals of researchmanship.) Thus, the non-working-class designation is mostly middle class, with the probability that other folk were included. For the purpose of examining stature across the century the heights of the working class in the developmental years is relevant. The other, generic category is informative and has comparative value.

Figures 4.6 to 4.11 each present both genders in two social classes, across the decades of interest, for each of six ages: seven, nine, eleven, thirteen, fifteen, and seventeen years. The number of means varies by gender, age, and social class. Table 4.1 shows the means of the various groups.

134

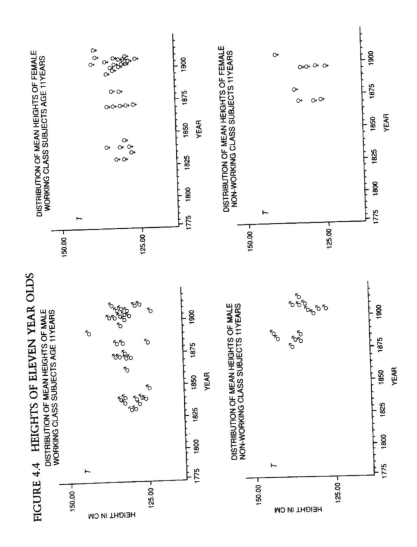

FIGURE 4.4   HEIGHTS OF ELEVEN YEAR OLDS

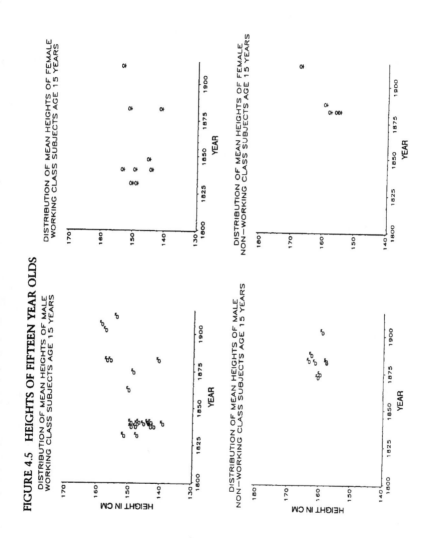

FIGURE 4.5 HEIGHTS OF FIFTEEN YEAR OLDS

Heights and the Degeneracy Question

The value of a time series of mean heights is the light that it can shed on the empirical state of stature across the decades of the nineteenth and early twentieth centuries. The youngest children whose mean heights are recorded in the corpus in numbers sufficient to plot are seven year olds. In Figure 4.6 there are a few non-working-class girls and considerably more boys of the same generally middle-class background. All the girls, and almost all the boys, were measured

FIGURE 4.6   HEIGHTS OF WORKING-CLASS BOYS AND GIRLS AND NON-WORKING-CLASS BOYS AND GIRLS AT AGE SEVEN YEARS

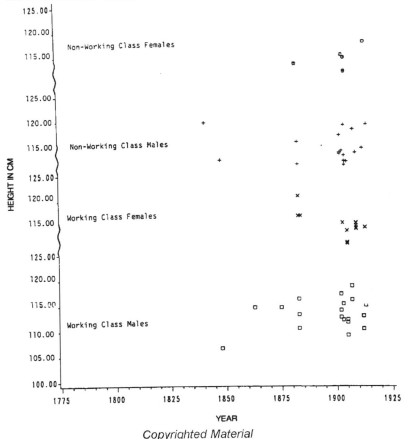

after 1885. In the case of working-class girls, the same observation applies, while the boys' series begins considerably earlier. The scatter of mean heights in cm. tends to be below 115 cm. for working-class subjects, with more non-working-class boys and girls above that level, comparatively speaking. In the 1884 Galton Committee urban artisans' series, seven-year-old boys and girls averaged 113.28 cm. and 110.64 cm., respectively. The 1966 standards of Tanner, Whitehouse, and Takaishi are 120.50 cm. for boys and 119.30 cm. for girls, respectively.

At age nine years, much the same scatter by date is evident in Figure 4.7, although the population of working-class youngsters measured and recorded before 1850 is larger than that of the seven year olds. Boys of non-working-class background tend to have heights in the 120–125 cm. range; the handful of girls' means is scattered, and they are, perhaps, a little shorter. The working-class girls' heights scatter between 120 cm. and 125 cm., and there is a break in the distribution by date. There are enough observations to suggest a trend to increased heights across the nineteenth century. The boys' means show much the same picture, centered around 135 cm.; the Galton averages at this age are 124.15 cm. for boys, and 120.29 cm. for girls, respectively; the Tanner, Whitehouse, and Takaishi (1966) averages are boys 131.60 cm. and girls 133.50 cm. A trend across the decades to slightly higher mean heights can be discerned.

At age eleven years the scatter of non-working-class girls' heights, in Figure 4.8, is quite broad, centered on 135 cm., and none appears before about 1880. Boys' heights are equally scattered at this age and appear equally scattered by date. In the case of working-class boys and girls, the observations are quite numerous from about 1830 to the end of the period of interest in 1914. Heights of working-class girls scatter around 130–135 cm., and boys' heights appear to be slightly lower. In the case of girls, heights at the end of the period appear a little higher than those at the beginning of the period; for boys, the trend is a little less evident. The Galton urban artisans' average height at this age for boys is 133.30 cm. and 130.91 cm. for girls. The Tanner, Whitehouse, and Takaishi (1966) value is 141.90 cm. for boys and 142.70 cm. for girls.

At age thirteen, the heights of non-working-class youngsters in Table 4.9 tend to be evident after 1880, and the girls' heights are quite scattered. In the case of the more numerous boys, the range of heights is wide, around 145 cm., while that of the girls centers on 150 cm. in the earliest years and then scatters enormously. Boys' heights at age thirteen in the non-working-class stratum appear to fall with the passage of the decades. That outcome seems improbable, however, and

FIGURE 4.7   HEIGHTS OF WORKING-CLASS BOYS AND GIRLS AND NON-WORKING-CLASS BOYS AND GIRLS AT AGE NINE YEARS

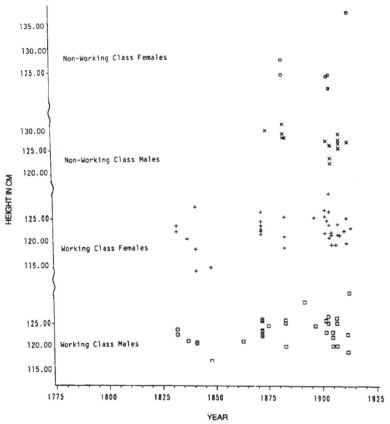

probably reflects accidents of sampling and reporting. In the case of working-class youngsters, there are mean heights for the earliest decades, although girls' heights are less evident in the third quarter of the nineteenth century. Centered on the range 140–145 cm., they show an evident trend to greater heights with the passage of time. With boys, the early scatter is wide, and a trend to greater heights at the end of the period is demonstrated. Galton's urban artisans' series provides a boys'

FIGURE 4.8 HEIGHTS OF WORKING-CLASS BOYS AND GIRLS AND
NON-WORKING-CLASS BOYS AND GIRLS AT AGE ELEVEN YEARS

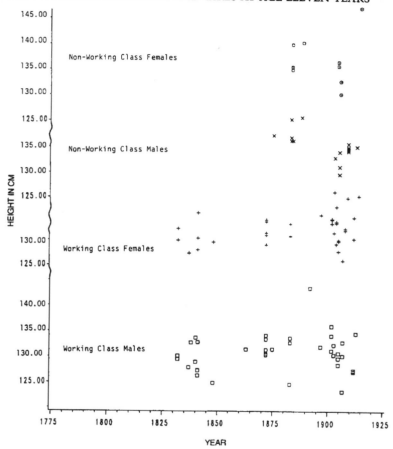

average height at this age of 141.75 cm. and for girls it is 142.79 cm.
The Tanner, Whitehouse, and Takaishi (1966) averages are 153.40 cm.
for boys and 155.50 cm. for girls.

At age fifteen, the number of mean heights begins to shrink,
as the level of personal maturity became less critical to nineteenth
century observers. Non-working-class boys' and girls' heights occur in

FIGURE 4.9 HEIGHTS OF WORKING-CLASS BOYS AND GIRLS AND NON-WORKING-CLASS BOYS AND GIRLS AT AGE THIRTEEN YEARS

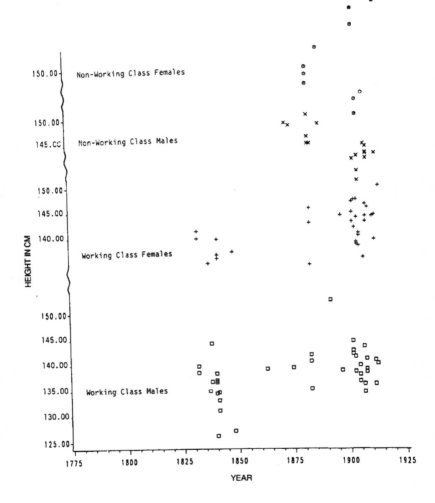

small numbers after 1880, approximately, and no trend is discernible. Much the same observation arises from working-class girls' mean heights, although the few later means are higher than the earliest. In Figure 4.10, there are several mean heights for working-class boys early in the period, centered on 145 cm., and the later means at age fifteen are higher. The Galton urban artisans' average height for boys, in 1884, was 155.85 cm., and 150.90 cm. was the mean for girls. The 1966 values (P_{50}) of Tanner, Whitehouse, and Takaishi were 167.30 cm. for boys, and 161.70 cm. for girls.

Finally, in this descriptive commentary on recorded mean heights, at age seventeen the numbers are still fewer. The non-working-class women in Table 4.11 are really too few to permit generalization, although the four around 1880 appear to range between 155 and 160 cm. Seventeen-year-old men's heights are few in number, and their mean heights also occur in the 1880s and centered on 170 cm. The Galton committee average heights at this age are 164.33 cm. for men and no height is given for women. The Tanner, Whitehouse, and Takaishi average height for men is 174.30 cm., and no mean value is available for females.

The contribution of the six age-centered bivariate plots in Figures 4.6–4.11, is most evident at ages seven to fifteen, and for working-class youth, if only because of the preponderance of mean heights established for them in greater numbers and across the decades of interest. The generalization from the means by gender, social class, and decade is that heights of children and adolescents increased a little in the century observed here. When numbers are sufficient, there is no evidence of decline in mean heights and therefore of degenerating stature, as a generalization. It should be noted that at all ages in all decades there is evident scatter. This reflects the demographic scatter and corresponding differences in social circumstances, a condition the anthropologist John Beddoe and the Galton committee phrased as *media.* Some working-class children were scarcely above the residuum, or depths of social distress, while others grew in families of skilled working men who constituted an elite within the working class.

Chapter Six augments this presentation of mean heights with a multivariate analysis of social-economic factors as influences on heights across the period of interest.

Estimating Rate of Change

Growth is a dynamic process in which the annual increments are uneven. To students of growth, increments represent velocity at

FIGURE 4.10   HEIGHTS OF WORKING-CLASS BOYS AND GIRLS AND
NON-WORKING-CLASS BOYS AND GIRLS AT AGE FIFTEEN YEARS

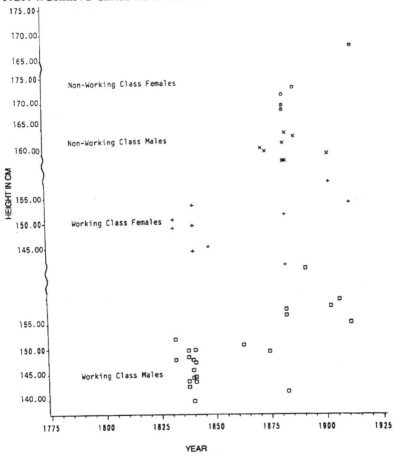

various ages. The maximum velocity is interesting because of the
questions of how fast growth is, and when in the cycle of development
it occurs most rapidly. It is a dynamic construct, and may or may not
affect the maximum height attained. In Morant's (1950) view, the maximum mean heights of British males remained 67.5 in. (171.45 cm.)

FIGURE 4.11   HEIGHTS OF WORKING-CLASS MEN AND WOMEN AND NON-WORKING-CLASS MEN AND WOMEN AT AGE SEVENTEEN YEARS

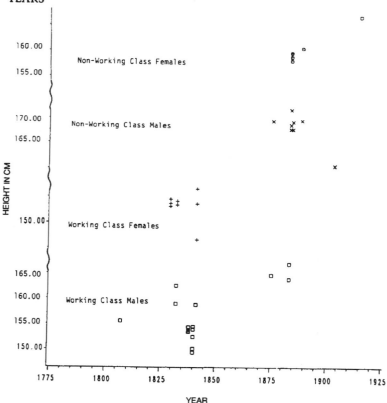

between 1845 and 1950, based on about 2 million records; 1.7 million were from the period 1860–1913. Morant concluded that the maximum mean height for a population is stable, but the growth rate is not. In the context of the Victorian era we are in a position to consider if the velocity of growth changed across the decades. We can do so by inspecting the increments in height by gender within and between social levels. However, a note of caution is necessary; data suitable for study of changes in the growth cycle are derived from repeated measures on the same subjects. However, the data available from the nineteenth century are cross sections of samples rather than repeated measures. Boulton (1880a) makes a fleeting reference to having ten-year data, composed of repeated measures, but it is not extant. The question of the process of growth and its velocity, however, is sufficiently important to require attention, although with acknowledgment of less than best data.

In Table 4.1 are mean increments in height for the combination of males and two social levels. There are nine sets for all, and for working class males there are five data sets. In the table, the Galton (Galton et al., 1884) and Tanner, Whitehouse, and Takaishi (1966) mean velocities are presented for comparison. The ten focal data sets in Table 4.1 begin with increments in height calculated from Horner's large compilation of heights gathered by certifying physicians in factory districts (Horner, 1837). A characteristic of the data sets is the comparatively narrow range of ages they record. Not until 1884 do we have a wide range of ages plus substantial numbers. Accordingly, it is necessary to examine the aggregations of calculated velocities separately to maximize the range of ages that structure the velocities. The data restrict this analysis to males.

Males, Middle Class

In Table 4.1 we see that the cross-sectional data, 1883–1908, indicate a maximum velocity in the age interval eleven to twelve years of 7.90 cm. This may be a population value, but it may also express a difference between the sampling of eleven and of twelve year olds in Health Exhibition data from 1888. In the 1908 data gathered by Mumford (1912) at the Manchester Grammar School, the period 16.5 to 17.5 years saw a peak velocity of growth of 7.92 cm. Elderton's 1905 data came from a superior district of Glasgow. While her data set has the merit of addressing growth in young middle-class boys, it ends before adolescence, apparently.

The mean increment in the four middle-class series 1883–1908 for the developmental span, ages ten to fourteen years, is interesting. For those ages, the data-specific mean increments or velocities beginning with the earliest series are as follows: 1883 = 4.68 cm., 1888 = 5.70 cm., 1905 = 4.31 cm., and 1908 = 5.17 cm. The mean of means is 4.84 cm. for the ages ten to fourteen years. It may be compared with the Galton mean increment for the years ten to fourteen of 4.75 cm.

TABLE 4.1 INCREMENTS (cm.) IN HEIGHT, 1837–1912: MALES

Author	Data year	5–6	6–7	7–8	8–9	9–10	10–11	11–12	12–13	13–14	14–15	15–16	16–17	17–18
Working Class														
Horner	1837				6.81	4.14	2.85	4.43	2.85	3.58	4.43	3.81	3.19	4.45
Bridge and Holmes	1873				2.89	4.83	3.25	5.92						
British Association	1883	3.97	4.88	4.44	4.65	3.73	5.28	7.90	4.50	4.57				
Royal Commission	1902		5.34	1.78	7.36	2.80	6.09	5.08	5.34	8.63				
Greenwood	1912	4.89	3.55	2.80	7.37	3.55	8.13	4.06	5.08	1.78				
Middle Class														
British Association	1883						4.14	6.02	4.11	4.45	3.37	1.10	.73	.03
Galton (Johnson 1987)	1888							7.90	5.46	3.74	1.80	-.33	1.73	2.21
Elderton (D)	1905	4.32	4.57	5.34	5.33	4.82	4.32	4.06	4.32	4.57				
Mumford	1908						5.21*	4.35	5.43	5.69	5.89	-.12	7.92	
British Association (all)	1884			2.74	6.73	5.44	4.22	3.78	4.87	6.15	7.39	5.26	4.90	1.83
Tanner et al.	1965	6.20	5.90	5.70	5.60	5.80	6.30	6.60	6.20	4.10	2.10	.90	.50	

*9.5 to 10.5 years et seq.

TABLE 4.2 MEAN HEIGHTS AT THE BEGINNING AND END OF TIME SPANS FOR HEIGHTS AT THREE AGES, SEVEN TO ELEVEN YEARS, 1832–1914

Age	Social Level	Data Span	N	Sex	Earliest Three Data Sets	Mean Height (cm)	Mid-Series		Last Three Data Sets	Mean Height
							Year[1]	M Height		
Seven	Working Class	1862–1913	19	Male	1848–1875	112.02	1883	110.59	1912–1913	112.87
		1841–1914	22	Female	1841–1883	112.92	1883	110.64	1912–1914	113.50
	Non-Working Class	1883–1913	13	Male	1883–1884	118.05	1903	112.36	1909–1913	114.56
		1883–1914	6	Female	1883–1904	113.66	1904	114.35	1905–1914	113.93
Nine	Working Class	1832–1913	34	Male	1832–1837	122.19	1875	123.69	1912–1913	123.26
		1832–1914	36	Female	1832–1837	121.72	1872	123.52	1912–1914	121.35
	Non-Working Class	1875–1913	15	Male	1875–1883	127.70	1903	125.32	1909–1913	124.71
		1883–1914	6	Female	1883–1904	124.54	1904	123.16	1905–1914	126.70
Eleven	Working Class	1832–1913	38	Male	1832–1837	129.22	1872	131.47	1912–1913	129.82
		1832–1914	35	Female	1832–1837	129.85	1872	131.47	1912–1914	134.59
	Non-Working Class	1875–1913	16	Male	1875–1883	137.16	1903	132.46	1909–1913	134.35
		1883–1914	9	Female	1883	136.70	1904	135.61	1905–1914	136.50

[1]Approximate.

Tanner, Whitehouse, and Takaishi's 1966 mean of 5.8 cm. is larger by about 1 cm. than the Galton and four data-set means.

Males, Working Class

The five data sets in Table 4.1 cover a span of seventy-five years, 1837–1912. The ages eight to fourteen are reasonably assessed in the five data sets that provide peak velocities as follows: 1837 for age 8–9, 1873 for age 9–10, 1883 for age 11–12, 1902 for age 8–9, and 1912 for age 10–11. Mean increments are as follows: 1837 = 4.11 cm., 1873 = 4.22 cm., 1883 = 5.10 cm., 1902 = 5.82 cm., and 1912 = 4.99 cm.; the mean of means is 4.85 cm., which is below Galton's mean and below that of Tanner for ages eight to fourteen.

Rate of Change

A rather different approach to the question of velocity of change narrows the age range to seven, nine and eleven years, but permits consideration of both genders. In Table 4.2 are twelve rows of mean heights drawn from three time periods. By inspecting mean heights across the twelve discrete series, at three ages, we can estimate roughly the rate or degree of change across the several decades of interest. In Table 4.2, our focus shifts from male heights by age and social class to heights by gender, social class and three ages—across a series of dates. The dates are constrained by the corpus of studies to a degree; this approach yields estimates which, while quite approximate, are data-based.

In Table 4.2, we see that the mean heights vary at three time points. At age seven, for example, the mean height of working class males in the earliest studies is 112.02 cm. (1848–75); at the end of the period, it is 112.87 cm. (1912–13), after a dip in mean to 110.59 cm. in 1883. There appears to be a slight overall increase across the period suggesting a modest rate of improvement. The other eleven rows of means across the era show fluctuations at each age by gender and social class.

The overall impression conveyed by Table 4.2 is that the rate of change in heights, viewed cross-sectionally, was not always positive, and was specific to sub-groups by age. This is an observation rather than a conclusion due to limitations in the amount and precision of data in Table 4.2. Caution is observed when drawing inferences from any corpus of data before the twentieth century, but modest data sets are better than none when an interesting question merits pursuit through empirical means; findings invite refinements in subsequent inquiries.

In general, the velocity calculated from cross-sectional data in Tables 4.1 and 4.2 suggest that growth had a lower velocity in the nineteenth century than in the twentieth. However, we lack comprehensive data on adolescent growth and consecutive statures culminating in adult height. The entire corpus leaves the impression that growth continued well into the twenties before beginning the inevitable but minor erosion of height associated with maturity and aging.

In general, this comparative analysis suggests that the empirical picture of heights across the Long Peace, as evident in the corpus of studies, tended to increase or remain stable in the great majority of cases. The evidence suggests that heights were not getting worse in the development period seven to seventeen years, and probably were getting better; that is, some youngsters were getting a little taller. Caution about this speculation is due, caused by the varying age ranges of samples, the limited time span of some aggregates, and the overall problem of coping with archival data frequently ill described and so open to misinterpretation. Also, the data, almost without exception, do not consist of repeated measures on the same subjects. Rather, people were sampled simultaneously at several ages at the same time. This approach is less desirable than repeated measures, but the latter, as I have discerned (Jordan, 1984, 1991), requires decades of commitment. Research in Victorian times was an amateur's business and rarely reached the level of organization required by longitudinal research using repeated measures. Even when pursued as "modified longitudinal research," compressing the time required by a degree of concurrent sampling at several ages, the technique is slow to yield data. We estimate that heights generally did not degenerate across the era and improved a little. An exception may arise in the case of nonworking class males, and females to a lesser extent, based on mean heights in Table 4.2. Non-working class data sets are far less numerous than those from the working class, and their mean heights probably should be viewed as an interesting anomaly.

Estimating Quetelet's Body Mass Index

Although weight is not unknown in Victorian data sets, it is comparatively scarce; in early studies, chest circumference follows height in reporting rather than weight. When available, it can be used with height to calculate an index of body mass. Such calculations are based on the height and weight of particular individuals, a requirement difficult to satisfy in nineteenth century archives. The requisite individual heights and weights are not available in quantities necessary to examine trends. Accordingly, this section estimates trends in body mass across the decades by use of means from massed data in archives.

In 1835, the Belgian anthropometrist, Lambert-Adolphe Quetelet wrote *Sur L'Homme, et le Développement de Ses Facultés*, published in Paris. As expressed in the Edinburgh edition of 1842 he observed that, "weight is in proportion to the square of the stature," a formulation he broadened a little in *Anthropométrie, ou Mésure des Différentes Facultes de L'Homme*, in 1871. To Stephenson (1888) placing h^2 as the numerator was preferable. However, the ratio w/h^2 to calculate body mass, has proven sturdy amid the infinity of calculable ratios of body measurements in Garrow's (1981) consideration. Florey (1970) endorsed Quetelet's index for study of male Britons, but found it less useful for females. In 1972, Newens and Goldstein analyzed data for seven year olds and reached a flexible position about anthropometric indices for children. Examining data from the British 1958 and 1970 birth cohorts Thomas et al. (1989) found Quetelet's index quite useful. More focally, Killeen, Vandenburg, and Harlan (1978) analyzed data from 6,768 subjects and concluded that, "Quetelet's index can be used as a measure of adiposity in juvenile populations." (It may be noted that Dugdale (1971) found that $w/h^{1.6}$ was useful with children in the first several years of life.)

The ratio of weight to height^2 is a simple matter to calculate and so describe the body. It may be compared briefly with Sheldon's somatypology of ecto-, meso- and endomorphy. Shephard (1991) pointed out Sheldon's reservations; Sheldon, according to Shephard, concluded that only a small percentage ($<12\%$) of the population fitted his typology, and seventy two percent had aspects of at least two of the types. In contrast, w/h^2 is a parameter which may be applied productively to describe most of the population, and at a variety of ages. The units of measurement are arbitrary, e.g. inches versus metres, but the ratio of numerator to denominator is central.

Body mass (w/h^2)is relevant to the study of stress in childhood; the reason is that it combines the discrete parameters height and weight into a representation of how they relate to each other at each stage of growth. When combined from metric components in kilogrammes and metres as k/m^2, values increase as children grow. Today, we use calipers to measure skinfold thickness to assess body composition. Fortunately, Quetelet's index correlates well with skin-fold measurement (Kelly, Stanton, Silva, and Jordan, 1991), so that we can use archival data to estimate body fat. Also, it is possible to assess changes in w/h^2 against increasing age year by year of individuals' growth and decade by decade at each age across an era.

Purpose

In this inquiry, the objectives are two: first, to describe estimated body mass of working-class boys ages nine to sixteen years across several decades of the period of interest, and second, to discern any trends in body mass in the eight decades between 1833 and 1911. Boys are used because combined height and weight data on girls are even more rare than those for boys. All data are cross sectional and means are employed. It is interesting to note that in some sets of individual measurements (e.g., S. S. Scriven's extensive listing of details about child colliery workers near Bradford in an appendix to the 1842 report to the commissioners on mines) the second measurement is "circumference" not weight, which is not given among ten variables.

Archives

The data sets begin with Samuel Stanway's (1833) report to the factory commissioners. Next is the 1850s (1853–1860) data set on boys attending the Friend's School in York presented in the 1884 report to the British Association by R. Clark. The comparative nutritive and social level of the York boys is a little problematic. Armstrong (1974) noted that York's economic base was narrow, so that "even craftsmen's families could easily find themselves below the poverty line," and barristers struggled for briefs (Neale, 1972). Rowntree (1901) and Finnegan (1976) noted York's low standard of living. Hennock (1987) concluded that York's incidence of poverty exceeded that of three of six comparable provincial towns.

Dr. John Yeats (1864) measured London boys at the Birkbeck School in Peckham. A few years later, in 1873 the indefatigable Dr. Charles Roberts provided data on young factory workers. Dr. William Farr's 1878 data came in an early report to the British Association's committee on anthropometry of boy postal workers. From the British Association (Galton et al.) report of 1884 we draw normatively, using a large data set from the sons of urban artisans. In the twentieth century, we turn to Thorne's (1904) study of London scholarship boys examined in the period 1898–1902. The last series of heights and weights is drawn from the large survey in 1910–1911 of Tuxford and Glegg; Tuxford, it may be noted, contributed his own anthropometric index. The totality is a set of eight indices using Quetelet's formula and presented in Table 4.3. There, in addition, is the Quetelet index expressed as a percentage of the index calculated from the Galton committee report of 1884; labeled the *Quetelet-Galton index*, its purpose is to provide a metric common to all eight data sets. We repeat the caution that indexes are calculated from group data, so they are offered as *estimates*, in the absence of a sufficient individual data.

In Table 4.3 are the Quetelet w/h^2 indexes calculated from mean data converted into meters and kilograms from the eight series between 1833 and 1910. Viewed horizontally the eight series show the maturing relationship between weight and height^2. In all instances the Quetelet index increases as the morphology of growing boys showed elongation and slimming. The series closest in mean value to Galton's normative 18.37 is the 1850s series of York Quaker boys studied by Clark. Most deviant are Yeats's Peckham schoolboys. When we examine the eight series from Stanway (c. 1832) to Tuxford and Glegg (1911) the mean indices rise, fall, and rise, and end at the Quetelet index at which they began, $M = 17.09$. Through a moving average based on three means we obtain four row means that, beginning with Clark in the 1850s, are 17.26, 17.69, 17.19, and 17.58.

With the exception of the third (1875–1883) moving average of 17.19, in the period from c. 1832 to c. 1900, the moving averages show a slight trend to increase from low to high. The exception is noteworthy since it comes from the Galton report of the British Association. Overall, the data vary modestly and suggest, informally, that body mass altered a little over the seven decades represented by the indexes estimated from group data. We surmise that slightly modified w/h^2 ratios across the decades indicate a trend to more height rather than altered weight. In the case of the Quetelet-Galton indices (indexes expressed as percentages of the Galton 1884 data midpoints and presented as the second row for each entry in Table 4.3) the apparent trend is to increase and decline across the decades, an ambiguous and contradictory process. When assessed against w/h^2 estimated from 1966 data of Tanner, Whitehouse, and Takaishi (1966) the Clark (1850s) and Galton (1884) w/h^2 values at ages nine to sixteen are a little over 100 (Jordan, 1991f).

When the Quetelet w/h^2 numbers in Table 4.3 are inspected by age and calendar year, that is, the row of mean indices at the bottom of each column, there is a slight change conveying the overall trend of

TABLE 4.3 ESTIMATED QUETELET'S INDEX AND QUETELET-GALTON INDEX FOR BOYS AGES TEN TO SIXTEEN

Data Set and Data Year	Index	Boys Ages				M
		10	12	14	16	
Stanway (c. 1832)	Quetelet	16.40	16.47	17.17	18.33	17.09
	Quetelet-Galton	93	92	96	90	
Clark (1850s)	Quetelet	17.59	18.14	19.31	20.19	18.80
	Quetelet-Galton	100.40	101.17	108.05	100.00	
Yeats (1860s)	Quetelet	14.81	15.07	17.84	15.88	15.90
	Quetelet-Galton	84	84	99	78	
Roberts (1872)	Quetelet	18.25	18.50			
	Quetelet-Galton	104.16	103.17			
Farr (1878)	Quetelet			18.12	19.34	
	Quetelet-Galton			101.39	.96	
Galton (1875–1883)	Quetelet	17.52	17.93	17.87	20.16	18.37
		100	100	100	100	
Thorne (1898–1902)	Quetelet	16.48	16.79	17.88	18.05	17.30
	Quetelet-Galton	94	93	100	95	
Tuxford and Glegg (1910)	Quetelet	16.51	17.12	17.66		17.09
	Quetelet-Galton	94	95	101.18		
All column entries	Quetelet M	16.79	17.11	17.98	18.65	17.63

the Quetelet indices to increase from 17.09 to 17.63. Those mean values combine calendar years and so mask the passage of decades. On the other hand, the bottom row of Table 4.3 documents the changing relation of weight and height^2 across the decades for the boys aged nine to sixteen. The grand mean Quetelet index of 17.63 shows the central tendency of all twenty-seven indices. For the period as a whole, the data series most resembling the bottom row is the 1910 series by Tuxford and Glegg (1912) followed by the 1884 Galton committee data. It is interesting to note that the previously noted reservation about the social (and hence nutritional) level of the York boys in the 1850s is borne out by the Quetelet indexes in Table 4.3; as for the percentages of the Galton urban artisans' sons, at no age are they below 100 percent. Values resemble those given for the series reported by Farr (1878) and Roberts (1872).

Discussion

The objective of this chapter has been to examine empirical data on the height and weight of young males and females. The topic has been approached by combining information from a variety of sources and regions. A future direction, data permitting, would be to push analyses further, into geographic units. Some are mere listings of young people by name in reports to givernment bodies requiring conversion into metric units and calculation of means and standard deviations. Others, especially toward the end of the period, have a modern flavor in the detail and mode of presentation, once the confusion of the mean and the mode is scrutinized in some reports. Although the number of data sets generally is satisfactory, we note that Quetelet's formula, w/h^2, could not be applied to parameters of individual patterns of growth because such data are scattered and rare. Rather, analyses treat mean values for lack of an alternative. It is for that reason we present them as *estimated* Quetelet indices.

The first topic of this chapter has been an exposition of heights from sources in the nineteenth and early twentieth centuries. The data are presented graphically in cm. in figures and show that social class and gender distinguished heights quite clearly. The times and social conditions were frequently contrary to the health and growth of the population in their years of maturing and beyond. When the data are examined across the decades of the period of interest we see a modest trend to better heights among the working class. In that regard, the evidence is similar to that observed by Brinkman, Drukker, and Slot (1988) in Dutch data. In that study, the authors cite Coronel's (1862) observation that children of factory workers had lowered stature, and that stature was still lower when the children themselves worked in factories.

The second topic was the trend of Quetelet indices of body mass across the period of interest. Data are far less extant and are formulated as estimates based on the central tendency of grouped heights and weights. By means of moving averages we detect a slight trend to rising Quetelet indices for the age range nine to sixteen years across the eight decades of interest.

Estimates of Quetelet's index from nineteenth century data are relatively free from a complication in the present-day study of body mass in the British population. Rona and Chinn (1987) reported significance in their assessment of adiposity due to ethnic differences in what now a multiethnic society. Rona and Chinn found the greatest deviation in the Afro-Caribbean group, for whom w/h^2 would measure density of lean body mass. The relative homogeneity of the Victorian population reduces the significance of geographic origin when drawing on studies from different English cities.

We close this chapter by noting that the data described emphasize the growth of young people. To deal with those recently matured and near mature, we turn in the next chapter to army data. There, we consider the condition of young men appraised by recruiting sergeants and by army physicians.

Mars and Hygeia

One of the enterprises of government in all epochs is war. When taken seriously, along with study of the wealth base to be taxed to support wars, managing armies called for estimates of manpower and development of records. In a version of swords into ploughshares we can draw on army archives to help explain changes *seriatim* in the welfare of populations from which recruits were drawn. A classic example of applying army data to social history is the use of Swedish archives by Sandberg and Steckel (1980). They examined 2,000 Uppland soldiers' heights from 1767 to 1881 in a study of height and nutrition. Spreading cultivation of the potato, but not wheat harvests, appeared to account for increments in height in the nineteenth century. Final height at maturity increased 2.5 inches (6.35 cm.) over 120 years. Studies of British army data are those of Morant (1950) and Clements and Pickett (1952). In press at the time of writing is Mokyr and O Grada's (1992) study of the height of 100,000 soldiers recruited over the course of a century by the East India Company; 40 percent of them were Irish, according to Mokyr (1988). A lower proportion, averaging about 13 percent, served in the army stationed at home, according to Skelley (1977). In the abstract, Mars can serve Hygeia as we apply army data to health questions. The earliest reference to the physical limitations of soldiers in the period is probably a comment about Napoleon's infantry. Marshall recorded in 1839 that Napoleon transported his youngest soldiers, "to distant stations by post carriages for preserving their health, strength and efficiency." In this anecdote is reflected the later age at which physical maturity was reached by men, and by women, in the early

155

nineteenth century, as well as the relative youth of Napoleon's conscripts. In the same year, 1839, the report of the commissioners addressing the circumstances of handloom weavers touched on their current and former condition. Then in his seventy-fifth year, a witness, Mr. Roques "recollects the Bethnal Green and Spitalfields' requirement of volunteers, during the war, as good looking bodies of men, but doubts if such men could be raised now." (Reports from the Assistant Hand-Loom Weavers' Commissioners, 1839). An empirical assessment of the quality of soldiers from factory and rural areas occurred in the United States conflict of 1861–1865. To President Theodore Roosevelt, commenting years later, it was very clear that New England regiments recruited from factory districts had been inferior to Southern regiments from rural areas (McKelway, 1906).

The Army as a Social System

For consideration of army data to be fully understood as shedding light on the health of the population from which it drew recruits we need to understand the military establishment. Armies are sources of energy and a potential threat to the state in all eras. For Victorian society, as today, the lessons of Cromwell's rule, the age of the Great Protector, was that never again should a standing army be larger than absolutely and minimally necessary. Wellington's army in 1815 consisted of just over 1 million men, according to Rostow (1948). Demobilization put virtually all of them back into the civilian economy, although a number were sent to colonial bases overseas. There, their numbers were further reduced by disease and death.

As a whole, the army was not called upon to engage in wars until mid-century in the Crimea (1854–1856). In that sorry episode amateurism and foolhardiness were revealed as poor substitutes for merit and organization. About the only people to emerge well were the bold Lord Cardigan who led the memorable cavalry charge into Russian guns, and Florence Nightingale whose persistence influenced both hospitals and the army.

Despite the long peace after Waterloo in 1815, the army was not immune to change. In the early peaceful decades punishment was minimized, and schooling was offered to both Thomas Atkins and his children. Subsequently, the length of enlistment was reduced, and the sale of commissions was abolished. Gilbert and Sullivan caught the changes at the upper levels in the patter song of "A Modern Major General." Regiments were rotated for service in outposts of empire

where ill-health and mortality were high. The changes can be reasonably described as radical and extensive (Skelley, 1977). However, balance requires that we point out the hazard to health posed by being a soldier. Setting aside the obvious threat of battle, there was the risk to health posed by living and sleeping in groups. In the 1850s, when reforms after the Crimean War were under way, a Royal Commission inquired into the sanitary condition of the army. Neison (1858) informed the British Association meeting in Leeds that soldiers in peacetime endured "a frightful rate of mortality." Tuberculosis was a major cause, and the death rate was three times that of agricultural workers of the same age.

Slowly, it became clear that the army should be viewed as a human complex to be managed prudently. Lecturing doctors entering the army's medical corps at Fort Pitt, Chatham, Dr. William Aitken (1862) addressed the examination of recruits and their training. Such "growing lads" required, "the exercise of a judgment in selecting him not less sound, and of a care in training him not less scientific, than the judgment and the care which a gentleman thinks judicious and proper to bestow upon a useful dog or a valuable horse."

Problems of Data

There are problems in the use of military heights to study trends across the nineteenth century. With the exception of the Marine Society boys studied by Floud and Wachter (1982) sets of heights across the decades are scanty; an exception is the set assembled by Floud, Wachter, and Gregory (1990) on the heights of officer cadets at Sandhurst. They would have been middle- to upper-class boys.

A second problem is that empirically observable changes in recruits' heights, even when evidently cyclic, might be anomalous within longer cycles of changing heights. At this stage, however, the hypothetical larger cycles are not really manageable for the population, although they can be examined in the long series studied by Floud, Wachter, and Gregory (1990), Komlos (1985; 1987), and Sutter, Izac, and Toan (1958).

A third problem with the army data is the geographical catchment area for British regiments. Then as now, counties supplied troops from, for example, Scotland and Wales, and elite units had their own minimum heights. In 1848, W. B. Brent reported height data as frequency distributions from 61 to 67 inches for four regiments plus the

British and French armies as a whole. The modal height of the Cold-stream Guards was 69 inches and for the Life Guards 72 inches—also the minimum; for the Scottish Militia the mode was 67 inches, and for the army as a whole and the Wiltshire Yeomanry it was 68 inches. This sampling problem was addressed in great detail using Italian data by Dr. R. Livi in 1892; he found tall soldiers averaging twenty-one years of age bound for service in India while aboard the ship *Clarence*. The Scottish were tallest at 66.61 inches, followed by the Irish at 65.75 inches and the English at 65.43 inches. For purposes of comparison, a set of nonmilitary passengers of the same age averaged 66.31 inches. In 1875, Dr. Leith-Adams reported average heights from a series of London recruiting districts. Several samples provided average heights of 67.1 inches to 67.7 inches for men between nineteen and thirty years of age. He also gave 69 inches as the mean height of police recruits in the city of London in 1872.

A fourth problem when using army data is that they represent a segment of the population above a minimum height qualification. Niceties such as minimum height tended to be set aside when the dogs of war had been unleashed, but were then observed once more in periods of peace. The Victorian journalist, George Augustus Sala (1857), described recruiting sergeants as *Fishers of Men* and gave a humorous account of how the minimum height was handled at a recruiting station. It was applied uniformly to volunteers for the cavalry, and set aside entirely for volunteers seeking to enter the infantry. The screening of volunteers was probably gravely compromised by the practice of awarding one guinea (£1.05) to the recruiting sergeant and five shillings (£.25) to the subdivisional officer. According to Thomson and Smith (1877), recruiting officers such as the highly effective sergeant Henry Cooper whose Westminster base was the "Mitre and Dove," also awarded ten shillings (£.50) to "bringers"; they persuaded men to share a moment of conviviality with the persuasive Sergeant Cooper in an atmosphere of good cheer.

A fifth problem with army data is that the pool of entrants varied across the decades. As we shall see in the next chapter, in Table 6.1, the economy waxed and waned across the century. The result was that the army as employer of last resort became salient in the lives of young men when other opportunities to earn a living shrank in an economic decline. At such periods, men who would not otherwise have joined up found the prospect less unpalatable. Conversely, when the Victorian economy was moving along in its somewhat haphazard evolution (Hoppit, 1990), men entering the work force had more than Hobson's choice to consider. The problem this presents is that the quality of potential entrants to whom admission standards were applied are not the same in all periods; that degree of uncertainty augments the uncertainty due to changes in the applicant pool caused by government fiscal and pension changes and by the martial call when the course of empire summoned men to the colors. The result is that our critique of military data begins with acknowledgment of a degree of ambiguity in the data due to a shifting pool of potential recruits.

In 1839, Henry Marshall, Deputy Inspector of Army Hospitals, wrote a treatise on recruiting and pensioning soldiers. He presented data on the heights, chest circumference, and acceptance rates of recruits in the London catchment area measured by Dr. Balfour. Heights were reported above 65 inches; and Table 5.1 abstracts the data, reporting relevant portions by midpoint heights. The estimated mean heights for town recruits is 171.35 cm. (67.46 inches), and for country recruits it is 164.61 cm. (64.81 inches). For all 1,434 applicants the estimated mean heights is 168.60 cm. (66.38 inches), these values exclude five men above 71.5 inches for whom heights were not given.

Caution is necessary concerning interpretation of heights estimated from Marshall's data, because Marshall's notations about measuring height without boots and stockings, begun in 1819, may not have been observed, and the presence of minimum height require

TABLE 5.1 PERCENT OF "LONDON DISTRICT" ARMY VOLUNTEERS ACCEPTED: HEIGHT AND ORIGIN (TOWN OR COUNTRY) OCTOBER 1838 TO JANUARY 1839

Inches	Centimeters	Town (N=979)		Country (N=460)	
		N	%	N	%
65.5	116.37	83	8.40	23	5.0
66.5	168.91	425	43.41	233	50.65
67.5	171.45	223	22.77	103	23.39
68.5	173.99	122	12.46	56	12.17
69.5	176.53	58	5.92	28	6.08
70.5	179.07	44	5.90	13	2.82
71.5	181.61	20	2.04	3	.06
>71.5		4	.04	1	.02

Source: Calculated from Marshall (1839).

ments truncates the left side of the height distribution. With those cautions in mind, however, we see that country recruits fell well below their city cousins in height, the difference being 2.74 cm. (1.08 inches) If this estimated difference is accepted, we conclude that country applicants were better physical specimens than town volunteers. The estimated mean height for Marshall's London pool, which was wider than the urban area, being one of nine recruiting districts, seems to coincide with other estimates at 168.60 cm.

It was in that era that the health of soldiers, publicized by Florence Nightingale's work in the Crimea, began to receive serious attention. Dr. William Aitken wrote *On the Growth of the Recruit and Young Soldier*, in 1862. Although derivative in some respects, it presented height data from the 1850s. In late 1854, 166.37 cm. (65.5 inches) was the minimum height for the cavalry. However, recruiting sergeants, those Fishers of Men, were expected to produce recruits; and Sala's observations undoubtedly apply to the scenario. A decade later, Aitken (1862) noted that years of service creditable toward a pension started at age eighteen, causing younger recruits to falsify their ages.

As a consequence of these considerations we view military data cautiously when seeking to use it to understand the population from which it was drawn. In particular, distributions of heights of volunteers accepted into military life do not present a Gaussian curve; rather, the distribution is truncated somewhat below its own mean as a regulation minimum height originates a distribution. In 1839, Marshall reported the minimum height for infantry as 65.5 inches (166.37 cm.), for light cavalry as 67 inches (170.18 cm.), and 68 inches (172.72 cm.) for heavy dragoons. Marshall also reported that "growing lads" are sometimes enlisted, although they are under the minimum height. Six years later, in 1845, the minimum height of British army recruits reported by Shee (1903) was 167.64 cm. (66 inches). In 1864–1865 the minimum height was reduced to 165.10 cm. (65 inches). In 1872 it was still at that height; and in 1901 it dropped to 152.4 cm. (60 inches), a standard for Bantam Battalions in 1914–1918. It can be seen that the distribution of heights in particular years would have been cut off at quite different points; no inferences are possible directly from those facts except that the decline in minimum acceptable height expressed a policy shift probably dictated by studying the effects of minimum standards that yielded less than the expected quota of recruits. On close inspection, recruits tended to be something less than Hector and Lysander. Dr. Henry Rumsey (1871) quoted a report in *The*

Standard of September 7, 1871, whose reporter observed the arrival at Aldershot of the militia and noted,

> Today there was a better opportunity of observing the general physique of the men. The youthfulness and want of bone and muscle was greater than I had thought. Many of them looked no more than sixteen or seventeen years of age, and were conspicuous for their narrow shoulders and shallow chests; their arms and knapsacks seemed quite as much as they could carry, and more than was good for them. How they will bear the fatigues before them remains to be seen . . . their stragglers and sick list will be painfully apparent.

Military data can be used in several ways. Records of height are a valuable description of a particular male population. Komlos (1985; 1986; 1989) used military archives in Vienna to study the heights of soldiers and cadets in the eighteenth century and West Point cadets in the nineteenth century (Komlos, 1987; Cuff, 1989). Stein, Susser, Saenger, and Marolla (1975) used Dutch data to study the effects of malnutrition in 1945 on the subsequent development of young males. Another use of army data is to study mortality rates; an example is the effect of overcrowding in army barracks as an influence on mortality rates for lung diseases. The 1858 Report of the Royal Commission on the Sanitary Condition of the Army compared mortality rates from four groups of soldiers in 1837–1846 and 1864–1870 (Sykes, 1901). The least drop in the rate of mortality was for the infantry, and the greatest decline in the rate of mortality for lung disease (presumably tuberculosis, for the most part) was in the Household Cavalry who lived in the least crowded housing in 1864–1870. In 1858, F. G. P. Neison's report of the royal commission studied the health of soldiers and found that, "a frightful rate of mortality takes place in the ranks of the army while stationed in the United Kingdom." The infantry were particularly affected, exhibiting 2,823 deaths in one peacetime year. Of those nearly 3,000 deaths, 50 percent came from tuberculosis of the lungs, *phthisis pulmonalis*. Neison compared the rate with those observed in various segments of the population and found that the army exhibited an excessive rate of mortality, apart from tuberculosis, with the communicable ("zymotic") diseases expressing the consequences of overcrowding among civilians and soldiers alike. Rosenbaum (1990) pointed out that in the 1840s there was only a 6-inch space between soldiers' cots in barracks; such crowding would expedite the spread of communicable diseases. Rosenbaum also reported that the army dressed soldiers in a flannel cummerbund, a "cholera belt," as a prophylaxis.

Recruits

An early picture of heights developed by Wachter and Trussell (1982a,b) comes from data on Marines at Chatham. They estimate that the average Bullock (Marine) toward the end of the Napoleonic wars stood 64 inches (162.56 cm.) tall. In part, that may have been due to recruiters' willingness to accept young boys. For example, in 1804, "a premium of £2 2s. was allowed to parents who brought a boy under 16 years, but who was then five feet two inches in height" (Aitken, 1862). According to Tanner, Whitehouse, and Takaishi's (1966) norms, 157.48 cm. is the height of a thirteen and a half-year old boy, or the ninety-seventh percentile for 11.5 years. For the year 1817 we have the heights of Scottish militia gathered by a supplier of recruits. An anonymous informant refers to him as, "a gentleman of great observation and singular accuracy" (Army Contractor, 1817). The data were presented as frequency charts, particularly addressing chest size, from eleven regiments totaling 3,849 men. For the 2nd Edinburgh Regiment of Militia, presumably an urban population, I calculate the mean height at 68.18 inches (173.17 cm.). For the Lanark Highland Local Militia the mean height is 67.15 inches (171.45 cm.). Those are good heights and above those of the Marines by about 10 centimeters, or 4 inches. For comparative purposes American Revolutionary War soldiers average 5 feet 8 inches, according to Wachter and Trussell (1982a,b). In the years before Princess Victoria came to the throne in 1837 British Marines' average height was probably 2 inches shorter, at 66 inches (167.64 cm.).

With the end of the inglorious Crimean war we pick up our next lead. Staff-Surgeon MacGrigor (1857) reported to the Army Medical and Surgical Society that the minimum height for recruits was 64 inches (162.56 cm.). During the Crimean war it appears that half the recruits—the interquartile range, as we would express it—were between 64 and 66 inches; presumably 65 inches (165.10 cm.) would have been the average height. A work of great significance for the study of army data is that of Dr. Benjamin A. Gould (1869), who analyzed height, weight, and respiration of American Civil War soldiers fighting for the North. For comparative purposes in his study of 1,232,256 men Gould cited British army data from 40,049 recruits. They were twenty-one years old, typically, and the 1860 recruits averaged 66.2 inches

(168.15 cm.), and the 1861 recruits averaged 66.8 inches (169.17 cm.). Gould offered a cautionary observation against overdrawing comparisons as recruiting standards differed in the two countries. We turn, once more, to Shee (1903) to learn that the minimum height was dropped, in 1872, to 65 inches (165.10 cm.). In 1883 it was reduced an additional 2 inches to 63 inches (160.02 cm.). Finally, in 1900 the minimum came down to 5 feet even (152.40 cm.). This last height approximates that of a boy thirteen years old in Tanner Whitehouse, and Takaishi's (1966) norms.

It appears that we can document a picture of minimum heights for recruits dropping across the nineteenth century, and it seems reasonable to construe it as indicating that men could not be obtained in sufficient numbers at higher minimum heights. It was not until 1867 that Cardwell's reforms dropped the enlistment period from twenty-one years to six years plus six years in the reserve that the flow of manpower was seriously addressed (Bond, 1962).

What we have indicated so far is the matter of who got into the army; equally significant is the matter of who did not. The warnings came early in the century. Three years after Waterloo, in an 1818 debate on the Factory Bill, the elder Robert Peel noted that, "Manchester, which used to furnish numerous recruits of the army . . . now chiefly underproductive in that respect" ("Debates in the House of Commons on the Factory Bill," 1959).

Rejection Rates

Rates

The first date for which we have data on the proportion of volunteers rejected by the army is the biennium 1835–1837. Rumsey (1871) reported data supplied by Dr. Gordon; the rejection rate for volunteers in England in that period was 32.7 percent, or one in three men. In 1843, the rejection rate in Birmingham was 39 percent (Children's Employment Commission, 1842). In 1857 Staff-Surgeon Mac-Grigor summarized the rejection rates from 1832 to 1841, based on Dr. Balfour's analyses, as 30 percent. In 1845, it appears that the number of men under the prevailing minimum height was 10.5 percent (Shee, 1903). In that year, the average recruit seventeen years of age was distinctly superior to those who took the Queen's shilling forty years later, according to Surgeon-Major Leith-Adams (Gattie, 1890). A decade later the rejection rate was 24.9 percent for the period 1845–1849 (Rumsey, 1871). In the period 1860–1864 the rejection rate was 37.16

percent (Crawford, 1887). For the recruiting area around Leeds Dr. J. I. Ikin acted as physician for the militia. He personally rejected 45 percent of the volunteers, he reported to the National Association for the Promotion of Social Science (Ikin, 1864). Dr. Ikin also presented data gathered by Staff Surgeon-Major Donald from "the Northern recruiting district" for 1862–1863; in that analysis the rejection rate was 30.52 percent, or one man in three. For 1865, we return to Dr. Henry Rumsey's (1871) report of Dr. Morgan's paper on "The Deterioration of Race in Great Cities," read at Sheffield, There, Dr. Morgan had summarized recruiting examinations "in some of the manufacturing districts" as rejecting four out of every five (80 percent) volunteers. For 1869, we have the report of Dr. Ord that 79 percent of a series of young volunteers were rejected, "as under the standard of width of chest and height" (Smyth, 1904). For 1882–1886, Crawford (1887) placed the rejection rate at 41.55 percent. For 1887, Shee (1903) reported the 52.80 percent of would-be recruits were rejected as under the minimum height. At the Manchester depot in 1899, 8,000 of 12,000 men (66 percent) were "rejected as virtual invalids" (Gilbert, 1965). At the opening of the new century, 1900, Shee (1903) placed the overall rejection rate at 56.50 percent. On a positive note, Roberts (1900) concluded that the general rise in health since 1860 had rendered 108 men per thousand of use to the army as acceptable recruits.

Height Standard

The percentages in Table 5.2 show that rejection rates based on physical disability changed across the period. Unfortunately, those figures tell only part of the story, and we need to know against what criteria men were rejected. The data are not extensive, however. It appears that in 1817 the minimum height was 64 inches in Scotland (Army Contractor, 1817). In 1845 it was 66 inches and was reduced by 1 inch subsequently, so that the minimum height in 1854 was 61 inches with the higher minimum for the cavalry cited earlier from Aitken (1862) at 61½ inches. In 1872 it was 65 inches (Shee, 1903). By 1874 it had been reduced to 64½ inches but was raised back to 65 inches in that year (Lowe, 1983). In 1897, it was down to 62 inches, and dropped to 60 inches in 1900 (Shee, 1903).

Causes for Rejection

It seems probable that very little beyond minimum height was required of volunteers in the early decades of the nineteenth century.

TABLE 5.2   CAUSES OF REJECTION PER THOUSAND FOR MILITARY SERVICE: 1860–1864, 1882–1886, AND 1891–1902

Cause of Rejection	1860–1864	1882–1886	1891	1892	1893	1894	1895	1896	1897	1898	1899	1900	1901	1902
Under chest measurement	33.17	120.00	93.03	95.90	108.55	110.27	126.38	139.64	89.44	73.88	65.84	59.84	49.88	56.72
Defective vision	—	39.06	40.35	42.35	41.51	42.90	39.88	40.72	41.15	42.64	41.99	36.42	35.84	39.23
Under weight	33.30	46.07	32.47	27.62	39.99	39.61	36.58	35.95	45.58	34.82	33.84	28.52	25.15	21.72
Under height	.21	28.70	26.76	32.71	33.24	28.67	28.72	28.77	24.86	21.79	20.21	15.18	13.56	11.59
Imperfect constitution and debility	23.48	6.82	18.40	9.87	9.47	5.00	3.57	4.44	4.45	5.49	5.82	4.94	3.36	3.91
Disease of veins	38.65	17.19	16.39	16.24	17.11	15.84	15.85	15.72	15.42	15.74	14.22	11.69	13.98	12.30
Disease of heart	16.67	18.76	16.06	13.87	17.74	19.62	20.71	18.76	17.67	17.26	15.69	13.15	16.74	17.33
Defects of lower extremities	34.85	12.81	15.57	17.09	14.40	17.44	18.16	18.14	18.12	17.72	13.98	10.53	10.35	12.27
Varicocele	25.61	17.12	12.93	11.85	12.85	14.25	12.28	13.07	13.07	12.29	12.16	11.21	13.89	12.59
Flat feet	—	9.31	11.04	9.83	12.45	14.71	13.16	17.81	16.79	12.24	12.31	9.02	11.66	12.44
Loss or decay of teeth	13.11	9.33	10.88	14.56	15.33	16.26	17.95	19.75	24.16	26.34	25.29	20.02	26.70	49.26

Sources: 1860–1864 and 1882–1886, Crawford (1887); 1891–1902, Memorandum by the Director General, Army Medical Service, On the Physical Unfitness of Men Offering Themselves for Enlistment in the Army [1903].

Such information would give us an insight into the range of health problems. In 1857 Staff Surgeon MacGrigor reported weights and chest measurements. He noted that in the Crimea the smaller French soldiers could carry heavier loads than British infantrymen. In 1869, *Lancet* struck an informative note; implicitly, the poor health of the town population was the subject when degeneration was discussed. Country life had never been very easy and had been the occasion for people to seek work in the cities. An example is the Cotswold farmer's son William Tayler, who left the family farm and did quite well as butler in London. The Norfolk laborer James Clarke moved to Leeds in 1836 and was happy to report in a letter that he and his family were much better off (Springall, 1936) in Yorkshire than they had been down in East Anglia. Illustrating the point that rural life was stressful, *Lancet* reported that many men rejected by the army presented "curvature of the spine and malformations of the chest." Even so, agricultural workers provided two-thirds of the men recruited in Dublin (Marshall, 1839).

The first detailed look at reasons for rejection comes six years later in 1864. Dr. Ikin's paper presented to the Social Science Association contained information in tables from his personal inspections of young factory workers. Malformation of the limbs, that is, defects of trunk, limbs, or fingers, was the most frequent cause; 6.57 percent of 51.86 rejections were for that reason. Heart and lung problems rejected a further 2.62 percent. That condition was followed by varicose veins. Dr. Ikin reported that, for the army as a whole in 1861, the greatest number of rejections was for "small or deformed chests and curvature of the spine". This same condition was reported in *Lancet* ("Employment of Children Agriculture," 1869) as the chief cause for rejection by the army of volunteers from agricultural districts. The cause, in the opinion of the editorial writer commenting on the Second Report of the Commission on Employment of Children, Young Persons, and Women in Agriculture (1869), was "premature exertion in the fields."

In 1875, we gain further insight into the complex of criteria for acceptance from Colonel Lane-Fox's paper read to the Royal Anthropological Institute. Lane-Fox, to be known later as Pitt Rivers, gave a detailed presentation on how to measure men's chests. Two years later, in 1877, Lane-Fox reported his measurements of arm strength and vision.

In 1887, the director-general of the army's Army Medical Department, Sir Thomas Crawford, made a detailed presentation to the British Medical Association meeting in Dublin. In his speech, later printed in the association's journal (Crawford, 1887) he presented comparative data on rejection rates and conditions for 1860–1864 and 1882–1886, for forty-two conditions. These frequencies and percentages over two decades are interesting separately and comparatively. In 1860–1864, the rejection rate for all causes was 37.67 percent, or one man in three. For the period 1882–1886 it had risen to 41.58 percent. In the 1860–1864 period, as Table 5.2 indicates, the three most frequent reasons were diseases of the eye, defects of the lower extremities, and being under the minimum chest measurement. Two decades later, 1882–1886, the three chief reasons were being under the minimum chest measurement, defective vision, and heart conditions. Dr. Crawford summarized his results saying that "the lower classes, from which the recruits for the army are chiefly taken, are of an inferior physique now to what they were twenty-five years ago." The same data were presented to the Interdepartmental Committee on Physical Deterioration in 1903 by Sir William Taylor for the years 1892–1902 (Taylor, 1903). For that last year, 1902, a small chest was the prime basis for rejection of recruits followed by bad health and defective vision. When we compare the 1860–1864 data with those for 1902, four decades later, we see that small chest size was still an important factor, but bad teeth had risen dramatically as a problem. By occupation, the highest rejection rate in 1902 was 307 per thousand, from indoor workers such as clerks. In that same year the Royal Navy and the Royal Marines rejected 27.3 percent of all their volunteers (Smyth, 1904).

Skelley's (1977) data in Table 5.3 shows that the rejection rate in the four decades, 1860–1899, was never below 25 percent, was around 40 percent on five occasions, starting in 1860 at virtually 50 percent. The trend of the rejection rate overall, however, was a decline in rejections across the last forty years of the nineteenth century, culminating in the Boer War.

TABLE 5.3   PERCENT OF RECRUITS REJECTED AS UNFIT FOR MILITARY SERVICE, 1860–1899

Year	Percent	Year	Percent
1860	47.9	1885	40.0
		1885–1888	47.17[2]
1865	42.6	1890	39.7
1870	33.7	1895	41.4
1880	40.8	1899	33.1

Source: Skelley (1977). [1]London recruits, Don (1889).

In Figure 5.1 several indices of health in the nineteenth century illustrate changes over time. The health indices per thousand are presented against a backdrop of gross national production in pounds (£GNP) per capita for the years 1835 to 1914. £GNP per capita illustrates how national wealth (per person) changed, and so provides a *general* background of society's condition. Figure 5.1 is illustrative rather than evidential, and it attempts to show how health indices change across several decades. We see that tuberculosis fell as a proportion of all deaths in men fifteen to thirty-four years. The next highest percentage is overall rejection rates for army volunteers in a narrower time span of the nineteenth century. It is followed by the mortality rate per thousand of the population. Below is the army rejection rate for "imperfect constitution." The bottom line is the frequency rate (%) for decayed teeth. For approximately the last eighty years before 1915, income, broadly speaking, rose. Health appears to have improved at a moderate rate, although the army data are less clear due to variations in recruiting standards and practices; additional influences to be recognized are the influence of rising wages, which made the army less attractive to the healthy young working man, and its corollary, a deteriorating pool of volunteers among whom even the best might appear quite puny. As the health of a pool of volunteers in any year fluctuated from previous expectations, so the indicators of health would decline.

The interpretation of historical information, even when apparently in empirical form, may be understood in the terms used by Hoppit (1990) when discussing Victorian econometric data; namely, "too often meagre and mutilated." To put rejection rate in perspective we can turn to twentieth century data: Rosenbaum (1990). In 1921, the rejection rate was 38 percent, in 1934 it was 36 percent. In 1952, a year in which all men were eligible for service, the rejection rate was 20 percent, to which a further 10 percent may be added for men in grade II. Obviously, standards differed from those of the nineteenth century, but the level of nutrition and health was also higher. Even so, we see that mid-twentieth century rejection rates were substantial.

The Boer War

After years of mounting political tension between British immigrants and Boers, South African farmers who speak a dialect of Dutch that has evolved into a separate language, conflict broke out in October 1899. The conflict ended with a treaty signed at Vereeniging, which is south of Johannesburg, in May 1902. In two and a half years less than

170

FIGURE 5.1 £GNP PER CAPITA, ARMY REJECTION RATES AND MALE TB DEATHS (1835-1914)

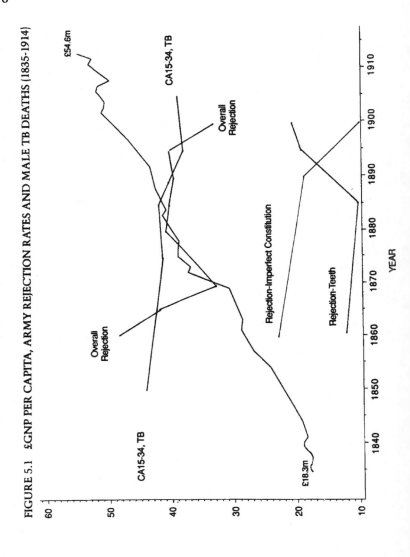

100,000 Boers fought effectively against four times that number of young Brits (Bond, 1962). In the end they lost, but did so aided by spectacularly incompetent generals on the British side. A British population of unhealthy young men was revealed by inquiries into the quality of recruits anxious to fight in South Africa. Writing as "Miles" (Soldier) Sir Frederick Maurice (1903) reported that, "out of every five men who are willing to enlist only two are fit to be effective soldiers." In 1903, writing under his own name he reiterated his theme as the proposition, "5–2." In 1904, the Earl of Meath extended the indictment of the people's health by reporting information from Manchester on recruiting. "out of every 11,000 men who offered themselves from Manchester for the army, only 3,000 could be accepted as recruits owning to physical defects, and that, of these 3,000, only 1,000 were found fit to be sent abroad . . . " At a more analytic level, it turned out that among the invalids sent back from South Africa were men who had not been touched by the small, lethal bullets used by the Boers; they had been laid low by illness, which was traceable to weakened health caused by poor eating habits. The ultimate cause in the long chain was said to be bad teeth or few teeth (Miles, 1902), an observation not possible to evaluate empirically.

The significance of the Boer War from the point of view of health was that it brought the problem of health of the bulk of the population into focus. What was the point to an imperial empire without an imperial race to run it, ran the observation attributed to Lord Rosebery. In 1865, Dr. J. E. Morgan had anticipated Lord Rosebery in an address to the Social Science Association, asking, "May not nations, like individuals, curtail their day of power in the world . . . by overtaxing the physical and mental energies at their disposal, thus prematurely consuming that national life blood on which permanent greatness depends?" The evolving race for military and economic hegemony in Europe revealed a nation at risk. Comparative data from continental powers showed that the problem yielded identifiable causes and evident hints for remedies, given time. In the new, post-Boer War era, at the end of Victoria's long reign, the quest for national efficiency, a kind of sociopolitical Darwinism, required Benthamite facts. However, the facts were not available to undertake a thorough appraisal of national health as a backdrop to the challenge of fielding an imperial army in which Private Thomas Atkins was as strong as his continental cousins. In 1903, the Royal College of Surgeons sent a purse-lipped statement to the Home Secretary about the report of the director-general of the Army Medical Service, pointing out that it was difficult to express a decided opinion upon the question of whether there is, or is not, a necessity for an inquiry into the causes of the physical deficiency of those offering themselves as recruits for the army.

The College is in possession of no means for comparing the condition of the population from whom recruits are drawn at the present time with that which obtained in former years. The figures given in the Director-General's statement show that there has been no increase in the proportion of rejections, and although the numbers of those discharged from the service in 1901–2 are proportionately larger than those in former years, no details are given as to the circumstances under which the increase has taken place; and, indeed, the figures may not be strictly comparable. (*Report of the Royal College of Surgeons of England, 1903*)

Later, in the same year, the medical establishment returned to the topic of recruits' health ("Physical Degeneration," 1903). In an article prepared by Amelia Watt Smith, the *British Medical Journal* drew on army data to observe that in the decade 1891–1902 the rate for rejection of recruits fell from 42 to 34 percent. The presentation did not address the stability of army recruiting standards and observed that, "it would appear that chest measurements, weight and height have all improved in recent years." The article went on to note the occupational level of recruits ("labourers, servants, husbandmen, etc."). It should be noted that there had been no comprehensive study of the population since the Galton committee in 1883, and in the area of financial policy no new data had been gathered between 1886 and the second decade of the twentieth century (Bowley, 1910).

The question of generating the necessary information had been raised nearly twenty years before by Lord Brabazon in 1887. At that time he expatiated on the lack of stamina in young men. Many recruits in training at Aldershot were unable to raise their chins to a horizontal bar through arm strength-chin ups. Brabazon called for a, "Royal Commission to inquire into the physical condition of our people." In 1903, some sixteen years later, and after the ignominious victory over the Boers, the Duke of Devonshire conceded something less for the Unionist government, an interdepartmental committee. The committee ended its inquiry on a classic bureaucratic note; it could find no concrete evidence of continuing degeneration, but it could not avoid the self-evident fact that the health of young people was bad. Dr. Eichholz's report from the Johanna Street School in Southwark was discouraging. Practically all the children had a defect of one kind or another. The committee temporized by saying that there were insufficient facts, a position evident in other fields of public affairs at the turn of the century (Bowley, 1902). From 1900 to the outbreak of war in 1914 there was a spate of studies of child health, including a massive national study by Tuxford and Glegg (1911) in 1909.

However, the problems of poor health among the young were not easily relieved. After 1916, when the search for recruits brooked no artifice, "of every nine conscripts medically examined . . . four were totally discarded and only three were found fit for active military service" (Birch, 1974). For the period November 1917 to November 1918, Soloway (1982) summarized the army's evaluation of 2,425,184 conscripts. Only one-third (36 percent) were entirely fit, and one-tenth (10 percent) were wholly unfit. The remaining, middle one-half (46 percent) were evaluated as fit only for clerical duties (32 percent) or partially fit, that is, with some disability (23 percent). Of course, this summary covers an unspecified age span; we do not know how low the standards sank in that last year of a terrible war of attrition in which young men were devoured as so much cannon fodder. Even so, it is evident that the second decade of the twentieth century found the health of British males far from perfect.

So far, we have addressed recruits into the ranks, brothers in arms to Pvt. Tommy Atkins; Floud (1989) and colleagues assembled a file of heights from young men entering the Sandhurst Military Academy as would-be officers in the nineteenth century. Table 5.4 lists mean heights at ages thirteen to fifteen, with means in 1854 for ages seventeen and eighteen. Those data have the additional value of augmenting the data on non-working-class males in Chapter Four. In Table 5.4, we see that the heights of teenage boys measured from 1805 to 1854 at ages thirteen to fifteen increased considerably. At the risk of over-interpreting these data segmented by age, rather than by repeated measures, we note that the inter-age mean differences also increase, that is, the velocity of growth; of course, this is a reasonable corollary to the changes in mean heights. From the Sandhurst data we observe that the probability of increasing heights across the first half of the nineteenth century was considerable; it is certainly more pronounced than the trend to greater heights in working-class youth.

Commentary

We have presented data on heights from Chatham Marines in 1805–1809 to army conscripts in 1917–1918. We conclude that army data, although gross, deficient, and insensitive in some respects,

TABLE 5.4 CROSS-SECTIONAL HEIGHTS (cm.) AND HEIGHT INCREMENTS OF SANDHURST ARMY CADETS BY AGE AND YEAR OF BIRTH

Birth year	Date	Age 13	Increment	Age 14	Increment	Age 15	Increment	Age 16	Increment	Age 17	Increment	Age 18	Increment
1792	1805	144.09	5.93	150.02	5.87	155.89							
1802	1815	148.23	9.38	157.61	4.10	161.71							
1812.5	1825	149.52	6.70	156.22	7.30	163.52							
1822	1835	153.54	2.85	156.39	4.48	160.87							
1831	1844	153.11	5.05	158.16	2.95	161.11							
1841.5	1854	150.50	8.51	159.01	6.09	165.10					171.86	2.35	174.21	

Source: Personal communication from Professor Roderick Floud; see Floud, Wachter, and Gregory, A. (1990).

document the observation that the health of many men was poor. Specific medical criteria such as chest circumference and unacceptably low weight and height partially document the case, despite fluctuations in recruiting standards and their probable avoidance in many settings.

The explanations given in the nineteenth century were many. Urbanization, overcrowding, and bad family life had a cumulatively stressful effect. Ill-nourished women reared ill-nourished children in a downward spiral of social disorganization. Abuse of alcohol and early entry into the work force were the lot of children who displaced adult workers at lower wages. Baby and childrearing practices contributed, and a commentator told of a mother feeding cabbage to a six-month infant and gin to her other children. Excessive use of sugar led to poor teeth, a phenomenon that, in the Boer War led to malnutrition and lowered resistance to disease, according to contemporary accounts. Ironically, poor teeth were more prevalent, in the late nineteenth century, among the middle than the lower class; a possible explanation is the greater proportion of discretionary income—pocket money.

Our consideration of things military need not be wholly negative. The army was not without thoughtful men, and there were spasmodic attempts to increase the fitness of recruits by means of physical exercise.

In 1823, *The Times* noted with approval that the would-be soldiers in the school of the Woolwich Military Asylum "leap, run, climb ropes and poles and go through a variety of exercises." A lesson had been learned from the unsatisfactory condition of men "enlisted chiefly from . . . the manufacturing classes," who lacked "that alacrity of body which would have been inherent in men bred to more active employments." However, *The Thunderer* spoke in an era before that of a Modern Major General. An ameliorative regimen, as opposed to drills for parades rather than the battlefield, depended on the rare instances of enlightened leadership at the regimental level. Not until the appointment of P. D. Clias, the Swiss-born physical education expert in 1822 (Hearle, 1983) did army cadets at Woolwich and Sandhurst receive rational exercise. Prior to that innovation, drill—"square bashing"—was the extent of physical activity. Skelley (1977) reported that a school of gymnastics was established at Aldershot in the early 1860s, and in 1865, recruits were required to undergo extensive physical training. Skelley cites an 1864 report that many rejected volunteers could have been brought to acceptable level of fitness by such training. In the work of Colonel Lane-Fox in the 1870s we see an enlightened regimental commander whose excursions into anthropometry contributed data on the physical condition of his troops. In 1889, Deputy Surgeon-General W. G. Don reported the effects of fifty-six days' basic training on the physique of fifty recruits at St. George's Barracks. Height increased by 3/16 inches, weight by 5½ lbs., and minimum chest circumference by 3/4 inch, on the average. Dr. Don also reported, "a marked improvement in general smartness and intelligence, as well as in sense of cleanliness and self-respect." At the turn of the new century army data was the best data available to the Interdepartmental Committee on Physical Degeneration; the British Association data, Galton's committee, was twenty years old, but it would be the benchmark for years to come.

The military data sets we have described cover the period from Trafalgar to the 1914–1918 war. They deal only with men and only those young enough to be recruits—usually men under twenty. However, such people are generally on the brink of physical maturity and are approaching the peak of their strength. Their heights were not those of the entire Victorian population, for they were drawn from the ranks of the poor and unskilled. In contrast, the middle and tiny upper classes were usually several inches taller (and heavier, proportionately) across the years of Victoria's long reign. The military population shared with the general population the impact of the industrial revolution in the form of child labor and damaged health. Soldiers and civilians ran the gauntlet of infectious diseases such as typhoid, which spread at the pace of a man walking across a city. Like civilians, soldiers were always at the mercy of the water supply; Prince Albert's death, for example, was probably due to the bad drains at Windsor.

On the basis of army data we can conclude that the health of the population of young men, especially those in urban centers, was poor. Many were too small, thin, or narrow chested to soldier. We cannot conclude that heights were in decline across the nineteenth century; that is, that degeneracy of health was progressive. Army data do not lend themselves to conclusions about chronic poor health as an hereditary phenomenon.

At both Waterloo and Mafeking young Britons rose to the occasion. Their deficiencies scared the Duke of Wellington, but when well lead, as fortuitously occurred, they showed their mettle. Stressful living circumstances rather than inherent defect lead to Private Tommy Atkins's vulnerabilities. This formulation transferred itself into public opinion after the Boer war. It took the form of realizing that it was the milieu, not the de-armified man, which required attention. The lately returned, ex Boer fighter, who had been a laborer before enlisting in two-thirds of the instances, (Skelley, 1977), had responded well to the "total institution," in Goffman's phrase (1962) of the army that fed, housed, and doctored him. Society, it was reasoned, should do no less for those who might yet be called to the colors in the increasingly troubled climate of European relationships. By 1914, the efficacy of the proposition would be put to the test.

The single most important observation which emerges from army data about the degeneracy question is the comparatively high rates of rejection in all decades. The population for which volunteers were at best a rough sample, was, disproportionately, short, thin, and weak and burdened with small chests, flat feet, skin problems, and visual disorders. In that sense, degeneracy was confirmed as a significant problem. However, its putative acceleration and hereditary transmission are not demonstrable within army data. Further, we cannot rule out the possibility that the health of recruits sagged because they were the best of a labor pool which deteriorated. The economy expanded and created jobs for those more physically fit, and improving wages in the private sector made the army less attractive to them.

The second supportable inference is that the data demonstrate that the poor young men's health and habitus was greatly below that of their middle class counterparts. From Table 5.2 we recall "imperfect constitution and debility" dropped from 23.28 percent to 3.91 percent in the same period. This difference, allowing for evolving standards and economic and social changes, suggests improvement in the health of volunteers in the last half of the century, rather than further deterioration or degeneration.

Despite substantial reservations about the data, including the possibility of cyclic trends within secular series, Victoria's thin red line can provide some insights into the physique, health, and welfare of the young male population of Great Britain in the nineteenth century. Mars, the God of War, can be of service to Hygeia, the Goddess of Health, in the study of physique, stress, and degeneracy in Victorian days.

The reader's attention is called to the paper, Rosenbaum, S. and Crowdy, J.P. (1992) British Army Recruits: 100 Years of Heights and Weights. *Journal of the Royal Army Medical Corps. 138*, 81-86, which presents data on heights and on Quetelet's index.

Social-Economic Circumstances and Height

*T*he major phenomena of nineteenth century Britain were the industrial revolution completed in the early decades and a subsequent degree of international hegemony in the latter decades. To observers of that period, social stresses affected and probably distorted the lives of ordinary people in both the nineteenth and early twentieth centuries. Even regional unemployment patterns in the post-1945 period appear to be foreseeable consequences of the structure of the Victorian economy according to Southall (1988). I have shown in *Victorian Childhood* (Jordan, 1987), that children, a protected group in our day, were major victims of rapid social change and stress. Early in that era, Peter Gaskell (1833) recorded that "children from nine to twelve years of age are now become part of the staple hands." Out of 800 weavers in a Manchester factory engaged in piecework, the highest earnings, according to Gaskell, went to a "girl of sixteen years of age—a stunted, pale and unhealthy looking creature, apparently unfit for work of any sort"; such children had obvious economic value in factory life as poorly paid, docile workers. One can, in temporal sequence, point to the rise of factories and factory towns, the Hungry Forties, and subsequent economic growth. Parallel to that we can cite the reports of various commissions studying health and welfare. We can then connect the events and report in narrative form the social process they represent. Cunningham (1991) has described how the story of childhood, i.e., its representations, evolved from the seventeenth century.

A more vigorous, analytic approach would be to formulate the state of the economy in quantitative terms and in narrow temporal segments of decades or, possibly, years. We can try to formulate the "Condition of England" topic, the Two Nations of Disraeli, in terms of the actual, physical condition of individuals. This chapter addresses the relationship between economic and human data in the period 1805–1914, and draws conclusions about the course of physical development across the century.

The Industrial Revolution

The state of the economy in that period can be summarized in five ways. First, Table 6.1 lists aspects of economic life across the nineteenth century; also, later Figure 6.3 will present a series of economic indexes. Second, Rostow (1948) summarized the economy across the century as, "The rise in prices during the French wars; the falling trend to the late forties; the rise to 1873; the fall to the late nineties; and the rise to the outbreak of the first World War." It should be noted that the clarity of business cycles may be authoritative but often impressionistic; the analyses of cycles of growth, 1700–1913, by Newbold and Agiakloglou (1991) suggested that cycles in the British economy were far from clear-cut.

Third, decade by decade, Deane and Cole (1969) saw the century as follows:

- 1801   Depression : revival
- 1811   Deep depression
- 1821   Slow revival
- 1831   Recession : depression
- 1841   Depression
- 1851   Prosperity
- 1861   Uneven prosperity
- 1871   Prosperity
- 1881   Mild prosperity
- 1891   Industrial recession
- 1901   Mild depression

Fourth, Crafts, Leybourne and Mills (1989) summarized growth of the industrial economy by rate as, 1818–1835 = 3–4 percent, 1856–1876 = 2–3 percent, and 1877–1935 = 0–2 percent.

Fifth, in a more restricted range Gazely (1989) reported the view of Hobsbawm that the best economic news came in the years 1880–1895; he also cited Hall's observation from Teesside that workers' cost

TABLE 6.1 ASPECTS OF THE BRITISH ECONOMY IN THE NINETEENTH CENTURY

Year	Business Activity By Year	Peak Period	Peak Years	Year
1781				1781
1791				1791
1801	Depression			1801
		1802–1815 Peak years for enclosure (740k acres)[5]	1810 Peak years<1860 for money wages[5]	
1811	Deep depression	1811–1821 Peak decade of population growth (+16%)[5]	1811 Peak year for agricultural contribution to GNP (35.7%)[5]	1811
	Slow revival		1812 Peak year for price of a quartern loaf of bread (4d. per lb)[4]	
		1820–1830 Peak years for handloom weavers (240k)		
1821	Depression			1821
1831	Depression			1831
	Depression			
1841	Depression	1840–1860 Peak period for importing raw and unfinished materials[3]	1847 Peak year railway track laying (6.4k miles)[5]	1841

TABLE 6.1 (cont.)

Year	Business Activity By Year	Peak Period	Peak Years	Peak Years	Year
1851	Uneven prosperity			1851 Lowest Rousseaux price index[4]	1851
–			1854 First year railway passengers >100 millions[4]		–
–					–
1861		1861–1891 Peak period of real national income[5]		1860 >5,000 tons of U.S. wheat imported[4]	1861
–			1866 UK Coal output > 100 million tons[4]		–
–				1868 Coal to London rail>ships[4]	–
1871	Prosperity		1871 N agricultural workers <50% of 1801 (15.1%)[5]	1871 Peak year of iron's contributions to GNP (11.5%)	1871
–	Mild prosperity		1874 Peak year employment <CA 14 years in cotton mfr. (13.9%)[5]		–
–				1875	–
1881	Recession		1881 Peak year for housing's contribution to GNP[3]	1881 Peak year of ship bldg. (£17.9 millions)[5]	1881
–					–
–					–
1891	Depression		1893 Lowest retail price index[4]	1891 Peak year for mfr. contribution to GNP[3]	1891
–					–
–					–
1901					1901
–					–
–					–
1911					1911

1 Hohenberg (1968).
2 Gayer, Rostow, and Schwarz (1953).
3 Deane and Cole (1975).
4 Deane and Cole (1962).
5 Deane and Cole (1967).

of living fell one-quarter in the years 1872–1895. In another inquiry, Gazely (1989) concluded that in the years 1886–1912 the cost of living evolved a little in favor of the poor. In summary, the nineteenth century saw the British economy expand, especially in overseas trade, across the years. There were bad periods but the overall trend was positive, leading Irwin (1991) to conclude that expansion was not at the price of immiseration of the people.

Understanding the course of physical development and health of the British population during the nineteenth and early twentieth centuries is possible only when placed in the context of the Industrial Revolution. There is a tendency to think that it began one day in 1780 and ended with equal precision on another day, presumably December 31, 1850; however, the process of technological change had been afoot for centuries. More focal is the application of power in the form of water tumbling down both sides of the Pennine Chain and, later as steam, vitalizing the spinning mills of Lancashire and Yorkshire. Power defines the first phase of the Industrial Revolution, and capital invested in factories, machines, and railways was the next phase. In the last half of the century, Britain became the chief industrial nation, but was pursued with energy and increasing efficiency by German technology and science (e.g., dyes) and by the competitive price of North American wheat and manufactured goods.

Within the economy were the men, women, and increasingly, children who minded machines and executed tasks of narrow scope. Each increment in specifying subtasks opened the way to displace male heads of households and replace them with women and, eventually, children at lower wages. Huddled in rapidly growing towns the population worked long hours and, in the earliest decades, were worn out or deformed by excessive demands on their energy. Out of their misery the economy roared through the century making Britain the workshop of the world. Crouzet (1982) estimated the gross national product in 1802 as £138 millions, at £394 millions in 1841, and at £1948 millions in 1901. In 1860, he reported, Great Britain's workers turned out 53 percent of the world's iron and consumed, for the purpose of manufacturing, 49 percent of the world's cotton; one merchant ship in three was British and flew the red duster. O'Brien and Keydar (1978) showed that industrial output expressed in pounds sterling tripled in the hundred years beginning in 1803.

The relationship of economic growth to the question of physical degeneration is, hypothetically, closer up to 1850 in the traditional formulations of economy history (Lindert and Williamson, 1985; Crafts,

1983; Mokyr, 1988), due to the stress of the earliest period in which the most egregious conditions prevailed. For the remaining decades to 1914 the hypothetical antecedent to the physical condition of the population is the social "condition of England" question of the 1830s writ large; that is, the circumstances of life which formed the social residue of slums, polluted water and air, and a population by then largely urbanized and constituting the stock from which successive generations would be formed (Brown, 1990; Hoppit, 1990). In that respect we note in passing that mis-nutrition, as well as the simpler deprivation of malnutrition, played a role. A girl overworked, and so subjected prematurely to stresses on growing bones, was prone to develop a small, possibly abnormal pelvis from which deliver babies in her later years. Those infants, subject to insult at delivery, were the heirs of mothers' early malnutrition. We do not need the elaborate explanation of an inchoate genetics, as did the Victorians, when parsimony is satisfied by mechanical explanation.

In consequence, our formulation of industrial growth takes two consecutive forms. The first is the nature of the Industrial Revolution in the period we begin to address in 1805. In the period 1780–1850, the Industrial Revolution assumed its original, technological form of inventions, evolving subsequently, into the human form of standardized tasks increasingly simplified; the human side was workers' loss of choice about how to structure the tasks of the working day as the "manufactory" whistle marked the start and the end of the shift, summoning children and women, as well as men, to the workplace.

Of theoretical interest is the question of contemporary influences on life that augmented or modulated the stressful effects of industrialization. The most abstract is the corollary of modernism, the process by which people became more conscious of time and acquired a secular view of life and its valuation. That process is partly a consequence of urbanization and the evolution of *gesellschaft*, the ordered form of life in which status determined that the worker at the mill touched his cap to t'gaffer. In contrast, the country squire might have been all-powerful in "Sweet Auburn" (Williamson, 1982) but he, at his best, acknowledged obligations to his tenants. Exceptionally enlightened paternalists early in the Industrial Revolution were the Brothers Grant of Oldham and Robert Owen of New Lanark; in Cheshire, Henry Ashworth of Mellor and the Greggs of Styal brought a sense of conscience and charity to their factories.

A second influence in the early period was the French War, which ran in two phases between 1793 and 1815 and was interrupted by "Old

Boney's" temporary incarceration on Elba. The relevance lies in the powerful effect of war on the process of industrialization and its equally powerful effect on the economy; Baines (1873) recorded that silver coins were rubbed so smooth by circulation during the war years that no marks could be seen on either side. When a military force swelled to over 1 million men was cut back in 1815 to its traditional peacetime size, a surplus labor force was created.

At the same time, a third process, that of the migration from country to town, was under way (Williamson, 1990). The rural population was deprived of its traditional relationship with the agricultural economy. The balance was destroyed by "improvements" in agriculture such as enclosing common land and eviction of tenant farmers. In that context, sons had to look at the army or the town for work.

Accordingly, we see that several processes were under way as the nineteenth century began. They all interacted to create the workshop of the world in the last fifty years of the century.

In the period from 1850 to Sarajevo, the Industrial Revolution affected the human condition in a less direct way. In its consolidated form within Victorian society "The Mighty Moloch of Steam," as Andrew Ure had styled it in 1835, expressed itself. The new economy was a manufacturing phenomenon; raw materials flowed into the British Isles and flowed out as finished goods to all corners of the globe. Great wealth accumulated in the manufacturing towns of the North, the Midlands, and lowland Scotland. However, the wealth flowed to the southeast as manufacturing families, landed families, and financial interests vitalized the establishment. The workers were left behind, except as the rising tide lifted all bottoms—in twentieth century terms, the "trickle-down" theory of progress.

The period saw the second and third generation of industrial workers contributing their labor. In many respects a lumpen proletariat, factory workers had seen their lives protected a little by fragmentary legislation governing hours of work and conditions. Labor was unionized and enfranchised, but it was also acculturated as a working-class stratum (Thompson, 1980), emphasizing solidarity, drinking to excess, and prizing its rough and tumble ways. In 1870, Forster's Education Act gave local authorities the power to make education compulsory, but Smout (1986) reported that half-time child workers were evident in Scotland as late as 1936. The new industrial economy, through the discipline of the factory, shaped lives into means to achieve business ends. Working-class people lived near the factory, and usually in houses put up by speculators. Sporadically, factory owners built model houses, and a minority were able to live at Saltaire, between Leeds and Bradford, and later, at Bourneville and Port Sunlight. At the latter site near the Mersey, Dr. Mackenzie (Arkle, 1907) was able to demonstrate the improved heights of ordinary children attending the lower schools in planned neighborhoods.

Apart from work, there was the effect of factory life on wages and the standard of living. That topic has kept economic historians busy exchanging views about the standard of living enjoyed by workers across the nineteenth century (Tucker, 1936; Hartwell, 1959; Williamson, 1982; Lindert and Williamson, 1985; Crafts, 1983; Mokyr and O Grada, 1988). Volumes have been filled about a rising or not-rising standard of living. Much of the shot and shell has been exchanged over technical formulation of data such as that organized by A. L. Bowley (1937) and, to a lesser extent, by von Thyszka (1914). Williamson's (1985) cost of living, indexed to the year 1900, covers the period 1846–1914. In 1846 the cost of living was 140.31 and rose to 161.81 in 1855. It then fell more or less steadily down to 137.96 in 1866, only to soar to 155.02 in 1867. It then fell until it bottomed out at 91.62 in 1856 and climbed to 111.08 in the year of Sarajevo, 1914. From 1886 to 1899, Williamson's cost of living index was below 100, a period of thirteen to fourteen years. The general conclusion appears to be that, in the long run, the standard of living rose, but there were occupations and regions that fared better than others.

It should be noted, however, that the peak of British economic, if not geopolitical, hegemony had probably been reached two or three decades before the end of the century. By that time, the link between locally grown food and population had ended. The Malthusian threat of a growing population impaled on soaring prices (Schofield, 1983) had been mediated by industrialization. As the last half of the twentieth century showed, however, unemployment returned to the Northern mills, the Midlands, and the South Wales steel industries due to technical obsolescence locally, and lower wages in the lately industrialized Third World.

The question of a progressive degeneration in the health and physique of the British population in the nineteenth century is quite broad. The major source of change was the economy, which expressed its nature in the form of rising and falling prices, the symbol at which people faced the industrial complex as a highly personal experience. It tends to be the case in many contexts of want that it is not goods which are absent, but prices which are beyond people's resources and create problems for families. Economic development creates desirable goods, clothing, food, and rent, for example; but the price of those items may not be compatible with another variable, the resources of individuals working within the economy, across the nineteenth century.

Social Indicators

There are many indices of the quality of life, and elsewhere (Jordan, 1983) I have reported on the condition of childhood around the world. The NICQL index is based on several aspects of childhood, and it was possible to contrive it because there are fairly good statistics available on most countries. In contrast, early Victorian Britain barely emerges from the mists of traditional society, in terms of the requisite statistics. We see, in the spirit of Jeremy Bentham, the statistical societies of London, Manchester, and Leeds providing the first quantitative descriptions of life. In Hare's (1839) paper, a program for quantitative studies was set forth, and it has a ring of modernity. In the following decades the statists aggregated data from censuses, blue books, and other sources to provide a picture of factory wages, physical data, and the scope of the economy. There were still gaps as the new century progressed; in 1910, A. L. Bowley pointed out that Whitehall was still using wage data gathered a quarter-century before, in 1885, for fiscal planning.

"Tabular standard of value," as index numbers were first called, was introduced early in the Victorian era by G. P. Scrope (1833). After the first World War, economists began to unearth and aggregate quantitative information. Kondratieff (1926) calculated several economic indices covering the long period 1780 to 1922. Rostow (1948) created an index of social tension through "imaginative construction," to use his term, of data on unemployment and prices for the period 1790–1850. Economic historians continue to devise indexes of the cost of living, prices, and wages based on archival and similar sources. Those innovations generate technical criticism (e.g., Lindert and Williamson, 1985), and recent indices tend to cover only part of the period 1807 to 1914; for example, Lindert and Williamson (1983), Greasely (1989), and Gazely (1989). Some economic and demographic analysts add mortality rates and life expectancy (Williamson, 1982) to the list of sources for contriving indexes.

Although many valuable indexes exist to connote annual prices, wages, and the cost of living (Williamson, 1985), offsetting annual variables for (e.g.) deflating those indexes are not extant. It turns out that social indicators are subject to short-term variations due to weather, temperature, and cycles of disease (Wrigley and Schofield, 1981). The winter of 1837 saw an epidemic of influenza (Wise, 1962), and sociopolitical events, such as repeal of the Corn Laws in 1846 and the loss of raw cotton for Manchester mills during the U.S. Civil War, affected populations at risk. There does not seem to be an index summarizing a broad set of social influences on the full life-span that experts agree on, and the number of years that recent indices cover is frequently brief (see Jordan, 1992 a.b.c.)

VICY Index. In an attempt to synthesize a number of social indicators across the period of interest I developed the Victorian Index of Children and Youth—the VICY index. It is a simple, descriptive index derived from twelve items in three domains. They are health, economic and social variables, and they were listed in Table 3.11. Accounts of the VICY index for children, and a parallel version for adults, may be found in Jordan (1992a and b).

The general picture revealed is that children began the period well behind adults with reference to the 1914 numbers (Jordan, 1992c). The curve of VICY index numbers across the one hundred years inflected into a sharper rate of change about 1860, and still more steeply about 1890. Figure 6.3 will present the VICY index in relation to two economic variables, £GNP per capita and a cost-of-living index, and Quetelet's body mass index at two dates in the nineteenth century.

Nutrition

In periods of malnutrition, health and growth can be seriously depressed. In Ireland, the Famine brought starvation and death in the 1840s. For malnourished adolescents, attainment of predicted height is retarded during the period when bone epiphyses are flexible. Norwegian data analyzed by Forsdahl (1977) show that childhood malnutrition, even when followed by adequate diet, leads to arteriosclerotic heart disease. In Victorian Britain, the inhibition of growth in response to deprivation was due to working conditions, poor housing, malnutrition, and the prevalence of communicable diseases such as tuberculosis and cholera. These elements, in turn, were mechanisms that worked out the condition of the economy in families. Families constitute a culture that determines how resources are applied and therefore, determines the level of nutrition received by members of the family. In the case of the gifted children of the Reverend Mr. Bronte of Haworth, a rich inner life sustained them in the presence of their father's penurious style of living. The girls, Charlotte, Anne, and Emily, were small; their brother Branwell stood 63 inches tall, and Charlotte had poor teeth, according to her friend and biographer, the novelist Mrs. Elizabeth Gaskell of Manchester.

At the extreme, the phenomenon was similar to that experienced by twentieth century populations in wartime. During the period 1919–1920 German infants endured malnutrition whose sequelae were evident in diminished height at school entry six years later (Wolff, 1935). Relevant reports about delayed growth from the 1939–1945 war came from Paris (LaPorte, 1946) and Greece (Valoaras, 1946). During 1942, the siege of Leningrad led to heightened infant mortality and lowered birth weights (Antonov, 1947). Of lesser duration but considerable intensity were the periods of semi-starvation in Belgium in 1944–1945 (Ellis, 1946) and in western Holland in 1945 (Stein, Susser, Saenger, and Marolla, 1975). Two findings of significance are reports on the health of American children interned in the Philippines in 1942 for three years (Butler, Ruffin, Sniffen, and Wickson, 1945), and on the health of Parisian children (LaPorte, 1946) during five years of deprivation. In both cases investigators reported that girls were affected less than boys by poor diet; this finding was also reported by Hiernaux from Rwanda in 1964. Ironically, war, in the form of the U.S. Civil War (1861–1865) and the Franco-Prussian War (1870) saw declines in infant mortality in Manchester and Paris. Unemployed mothers stayed at home and breast-fed infants who, otherwise, would have received unsuitable food.

The trend of heights to increase over the years since 1870 has been observed in Japan. Asahina (1975) reported that adult heights at the end of the Edo period, 1870, probably averaged 156 cm. (61 in.), rising to 162 cm. in 1900, 164 cm. in 1940, and 170 cm. (67 in.) in 1970. Nukada (1975) addressed industrialization and urbanization in the period, 1920–1970. In 1920, 82 percent of the population lived in rural areas; by 1970, the proportion was down to 28 percent. Nukada thought that industrialization led to urban living which increased outbreeding ("hybrid vigor") as a contributing mechanism.

Economic Variables and Height

The general question is the relationship of social-economic stress to the health of the population represented by height. This last measure is an index of nutrition and, unlike weight, is not subject to fluctuations due to transient influences. Prior studies (Jordan, 1990a) sought to optimize the relationship between economic circumstances and heights of adults and children across the nineteenth century. Outcomes of those inquiries (e.g., Jordan, 1990a) are incorporated into this chapter.

Predictor Variables

The goal of this chapter is to attempt an understanding of the course of growth in working-class males and females in terms of the impact of economic change on their lives. In that regard, health represented by height is the outcome or dependent measure, indexed to the Galton committee's data for urban artisans presented to the 1883 meeting of the British Association for the Advancement of Science at Southport. The choice of predictor variables, the hypothetical influences, is less obvious, however.

The general framework is the dialogue, now several decades old, among economic historians about the course of Britain's nineteenth century economy. In recent decades, analysts have drawn on data series developed in the nineteenth and early twentieth centuries for wages, prices, and other indices. Studies by William Neild, Leon Levi, A. L. Bowley, and G. H. Wood are examples.

From these data and additional, original sources, specialists have constructed a series of sophisticated indexes. Examples of them are Cook and Keith (1975), Mitchell (1975), Williamson (1985), Gazeley (1989), and Greasley (1989). There are technical difficulties in the development of such indicators; for example, the range of local economic conditions, the scarcity of individual family budgets, the absence of regional data on unemployment or specificity of occupations, radical differences in rent and costs between London and the provinces, an understanding of the psychology of consumerism including abuse of alcohol, and a grasp of the interaction of health, weather, and unemployment on the incomes of working people.

To the would-be user of such indexes, secondary to data on height, there is the problem of the span of years covered by indexes. Gazeley's (1989) index addresses the years 1886 to 1912. Greasley's (1989) index runs from 1856 to 1913. Williamson's (1985) index covers the years 1846 to 1914. These three indexes, all of which correlate highly with each other, fall short of the height data in the range 1805 to 1914. Kondratieff's (1926) index of commodity prices, employed by Gayer, Rostow, and Schwartz (1953) in their study of the British economy, spans the years from 1780 to 1922. Mitchell's (1975) index is used to summarize gross national product from 1809 to 1914. Figure 6.1 illustrates the comparability of Kondratieff's (1926) index of commodity prices and Williamson's (1985) cost of living index, together with Galton-indexed heights of all young males and females.

FIGURE 6.1   KONDRATIEFF'S (1926) COMMODITY INDEX, WILLIAMSON'S (1985) COST OF LIVING INDEX, AND THE HEIGHTS OF ALL MALES AND ALL FEMALES

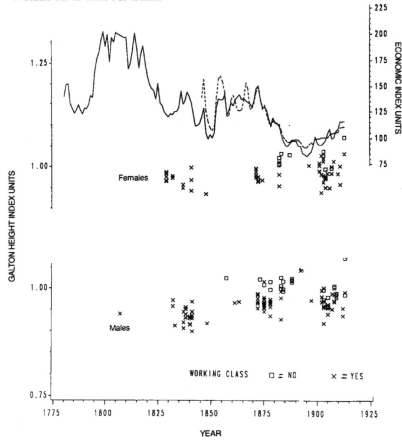

A Descriptive Consideration of Heights

For a preliminary consideration of height data, Figure 6.2 displays Williamson's more recent (1985) cost of living index for the years 1846 to 1914. It is evident that the cost of living rose and fell until about 1875, when it fell steadily, rising slightly from about 1895. In Figure 6.3 the remarkable growth of wealth, expressed as £GNP per capita is presented. Against these two economic indicators we show an index of growth. It's the Quetelet index, w/h^2, for two groups of boys seventy years apart.

Williamson's Cost of Living Index and Galton-Indexed Heights

The prime data in this work are the heights of young male and female Britons 1805–1914; this valuation is placed on them because diverse sets of heights have not been aggregated on the scale of this inquiry. Quantification based on the ages and decades involved has obvious value when attempting to survey health across the nineteenth century and into the twentieth. Once that assertion has been set forth, it is appropriate to consider influences on the course of heights across the period, and I have employed several social-economic indicators. The years 1846–1914, the years of Williamson's cost of living index, enfold many of the data sets of height. By examining heights in the presence of Williamson's index we generate a preliminary sketch both quantitative and comprehensive in terms of the cost of living trend and the bulk of the height data.

In Figure 6.2 are Galton-indexed heights for males and females, working class and non-working class. At the bottom of Figure 6.2 are Galton-indexed mean heights without specification of social class, plus the distribution of the Williamson cost of living index. In general, height indexes are flat across the decades. In the middle portion of the figure the impression is that there is a slight upward trend toward the right, the later decades. In the top portion, the observer discerns a flat, or possibly declining, level of Galton indexes in the later decades. For all three social groups, there are two clusters of height indexes on either side of the year 1890.

Comparing the two data sets in the critical data on the working class we see heights rising as the cost of living, initially, fell. Heights are heterogeneous in the later clustering, but slightly higher than

194

FIGURE 6.2   WILLIAMSON'S (1985) COST OF LIVING INDEX AND THE
HEIGHTS OF MALES AND FEMALES

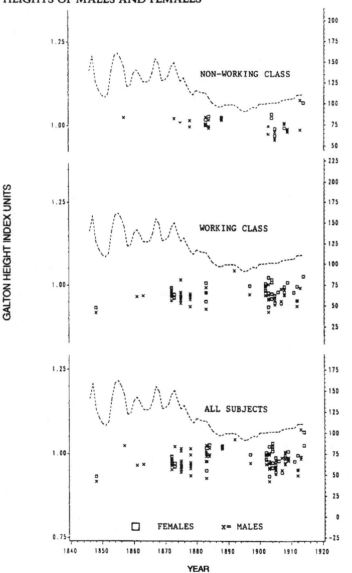

the earlier cluster, even as the cost of living began an upward turn in the 1890s.

By way of commenting on these last observations it seems likely that personal wealth had outstripped the secular trend of the cost of living; also, many working-class families probably were behaving with greater economic rationality than their early and mid-nineteenth century forbears. We know that the gross national product per capita (£GNP), a measure of the total of goods and services, rose sharply in the nineteenth century (see Figure 6.3), a topic approached analytically in this chapter. A comparative advantage lay with families in their contest with economic forces; in the matter of wages, apart from wage indexes, A. L. Bowley, in *Wages in the United Kingdom in the Nineteenth Century* (1900), showed that London artisans' wages rose from 22/- per week in 1793 to 38/- in 1894; Manchester carpenters earned 18/- in 1793 and 35/- in 1894. Macclesfield artisans' wages rose from 18/- in 1793 to 33/- in 1894. Glasgow printers' wages rose from 15/- per week in 1791 (midpoint of Bowley's range) to 34/- in 1899. In these four geographically dispersed sites wages doubled in a century, generally speaking, while commodity prices fell. By 1860, wages were 75 percent of their level in the final years of the nineteenth century.

As a final descriptive commentary on Williamson's (1985) cost of living index and heights in the years 1846 to 1914, I report statistically insignificant correlations in the population groups, all males, working-class males, non-working-class males, working-class females, and non-working-class females. In the case of working-class females, there is a significant r of $-.30$ ($df = 50$, $p = .05$); that is, as the cost of living rose and fell, heights varied in the opposite direction. In such instances, the connection is finely drawn and ignores a variety of covariants such as disease, the genetic endowment for height, and the accumulated impact of all social factors in the preceding years. Chapter Six moves from a descriptive to an analytic, multivariate approach to height and associated factors.

Social-Economic Indexes and Estimated Quetelet Indexes

The trend of physique against a background of economic changes can be examined by taking the earliest and latest Quetelet indexes that have complete data at all ages, and plotting them against several indexes. In Figure 6.3, economic changes plotted across the years 1800 to 1920; also there, are estimated Quetelet indexes from the data of Sam-

196

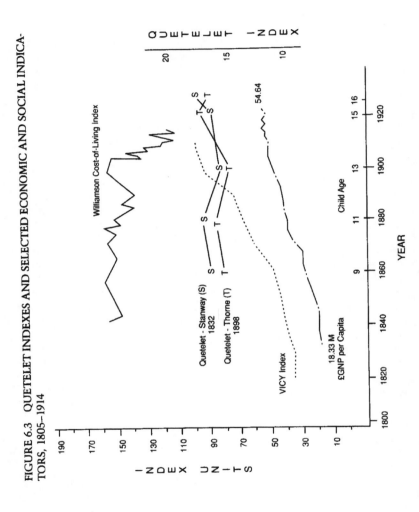

FIGURE 6.3 QUETELET INDEXES AND SELECTED ECONOMIC AND SOCIAL INDICATORS, 1805–1914

uel Stanway in 1832 and L. T. Thorne in the years 1898–1902. This presentation is pictorial because the Quetelet indexes are insufficient for a statistical analysis.

In Figure 6.3, we see that £GNP per capita rose rapidly across the period of interest, a span of 120 years. A briefer span, seventy years, separates the two lines for estimated Quetelet indexes at ages nine, eleven, thirteen, and fifteen years. Both lines have the same value at age nine, but the course of development from that age into the teens diverges immediately. The 1898–1902 heights and weights which Thorne took from London schoolboys drop more rapidly than those of working boys measured by Stanway seven decades before.

Of course, it would be ideal if the two samples were drawn from the same catchment area across the decades. However, both are working-class youth, although the connotations of the descriptive phrase they both share were probably different in several respects. However, Figures 6.2 and 6.3 illustrate the attitude that we should try to discuss nineteenth century growth patterns by drawing on data, acknowledging that it can take a quite derivative form, eventually.

In the case of Thorne's data, the change in estimated Quetelet index is from 16.05 at age nine to 18.71 at age fifteen. In the case of Stanway's data, the proportions of w/h^2 are parallel. At age thirteen, Quetelet's index for both sets of boys declines, and that of Stanway's 1833 factory boys falls below that of Thorne's (1904) London boys but recovers at age sixteen.

A Multivariate Analysis

In this attempt at an empirical rather than impressionistic appraisal of influences on heights across the nineteenth century, we employ several indexes. This approach allows several benefits. It permits focus on indexes with particular merits; it allows concentration on abbreviated periods within the overall range 1805–1914; and it incorporates several concepts of economic forces. Williamson's (1985) index addresses the cost of living; Mitchell's (1975) index describes gross national product in millions of pounds (GNP), and Kondratieff's index (1926) considers commodity prices across the entire period, unlike recent indexes. (Employment of this index does not imply subscription to the long-wave theory of Kondratieff.) These economic factors are grafted onto the three ecological predictors employed in Chapter Three: mean winter temperature, population, and infant mortality.

That height and social-economic forces, apart from ecology, should, hypothetically, relate is evident in Dutch studies of the nineteenth century. Van Wieringen's (1979) analysis showed a linkage in the years 1850–1978 by drawing on data from thousands of army recruits. Brinkman, Drukker, and Slot (1988) reviewed the significant Dutch literature on the nineteenth century and emphasized the first forty years of the twentieth century in the study of heights and the state of the economy. On a broader scale is Steckel's (1983) demonstration from worldwide data that per capita income influences height, using twentieth century data.

In this chapter, we address the heights of immature Britons, male and female, in the years 1805–1914; Table 6.2 displays the economic indices employed, and Figure 4.1 schematized the data sets of working class heights by year of publication. Figure 4.2 displayed the data sets by gender. We repeat the three ecological variables from Chapter Three: the mean winter temperature, the mortality rate for children below one year, and the size of the population, using annual data. To those we add social-economic variables. The first is GNP per capita expressed as millions of pounds. The second is Kondratieff's (1926) commodity price index, and the third is Williamson's (1985) cost of living index. It may be noted, in passing, that the VICY index is not used

TABLE 6.2   DESCRIPTIONS OF THE VARIABLES

Variable	Dates of Application	Index Date	Source
Population	1805–1901		C. Cook and B. Keith, (1975) (interpolated)
Mean winter temperature	1805–1914		A. J. Drummond (1943)
Mortality rate 12 mos., per K	1839–1914		B. Mitchell (1975)
GNP per capita	1805–1914	1900	B. R. Mitchell (1975) and C. Cook and B. Keith (1975)
Williamson cost of living index	1846–1914	1900	J. Williamson (1985)
Kondratieff commodity price index	1805–1914	1901–1910	N. Kondratieff (1926)
Galton heights	1850–1914	1883	British Association, Galton et al. (1884)

as a predictor or covariate since there exists linear dependance between the index and the chosen variables. To employ the VICY index would have contributed additional collinearity to the analysis.

In prior research, I ruled out lagged effects and autocorrelation; I also examined the relevance of the observation by Brinkman, Drukker, and Slot (1988) from nineteenth century Dutch data that curvilinearity may be a better explanation than linearity of the relationship of economic factors to heights, using five economic indexes (Jordan, 1991d). In that study, economic predictors were applied to the height-index data used in this chapter, with subjects grouped by gender and social class. It emerged that linearity generally sufficed; in the case of the three predictors to be reported here, nonlinearity was statistically significant, for two groups: all males, when the predictor is GNP in millions of pounds per capita; and all females, when Williamson's cost of living index is employed.

Table 6.3 presents descriptive data for the analyses of three economic variables, covering three time periods with differing starting dates, grouped by gender with a subgroup of working-class subjects; non-working-class groups were small and lacked sufficient subjects/variables ratio to avoid overfitting regression lines. Generally speaking, the means and standard deviations are quite similar.

Table 6.4 presents the regression analyses where each of the three economic indexes is included in the particular series with annual data for mean winter temperature, child mortality before the first birthday, and the size of the population; those three variables function as covariates. In Table 6.4, we see the first economic variable examined by social class and gender is GNP per capita; for all subjects, a significant influence on Galton-indexed heights is evident in all males ($F = 7.35$, $p = .008$), but not all females. In the case of working-class males, deletion of the GNP per capita predictor variable lowered the R^2 from .30 to .23 ($F = 5.45$, $p = .02$); for females, the outcome was statistically insignificant. GNP per capita did not influence heights of non-working-class males or females.

In the case of the Williamson cost of living index statistically significant effects were evident in all males ($F = 6.83$, $p = .01$) and all females ($F = 8.23$, $p = .006$). No significant reduction in R^2 due to deleting the cost of living variables was observed in the working-class or middle-class data sets. One of six data sets employing the Kondratieff commodity price index produced a significant result. In the case of all females deletion of the variable of interest dropped the R^2 from .18 to .06 ($F = 6.94$, $p = .01$).

200

TABLE 6.3 DESCRIPTION OF THE VARIABLES—REGRESSION ANALYSIS

	Population (millions)	Mean Winter Temperature	Child Mortality Per K	GNP Per Capita	Galton Height Index
All Males (N = 96)					
Mean	36.37	40.08	139.60	40.70	.97
Standard Deviation	6.08	2.07	16.57	10.26	.03
Working-Class Males (N = 64)					
Mean	35.41	39.96	142.70	39.31	.95
Standard Deviation	6.10	2.17	15.80	10.82	.02
All Females (N = 52)					
Mean	38.22	40.46	137.15	43.91	.98
Standard Deviation	5.68	1.76	14.02	8.74	.02
Working-Class Females (N = 42)					
Mean	37.95	40.43	137.42	43.45	.97
Standard Deviation	6.04	1.84	15.09	9.42	.02
				Kondratieff index	
All Males (N = 95)					
Mean	36.35	40.09	139.51	116.94	.97
Standard Deviation	6.11	2.08	16.63	18.23	.03
Working-Class Males (N = 63)					
Mean	35.36	39.97	142.61	121.00	.96
Standard Deviation	6.14	2.18	15.92	18.53	.02
All Females (N = 52)					
Mean	38.22	40.46	137.15	115.09	.98
Standard Deviation	5.68	1.76	14.02	22.39	.02
Working-Class Females (N = 42)					
Mean	37.95	40.43	137.42	118.11	.97
Standard Deviation	6.04	1.84	15.09	23.74	.02

TABLE 6.3 (cont.)

	Population (millions)	MeanWinter Temperature	Child Mortality Per K	GNPPer Capita	Galton Height Index
All Males (N = 84)				Williamson index	
Mean	37.63	40.32	138.22	115.16	.98
Standard Deviation	5.29	1.91	17.21	15.38	.02
Working-Class Males (N = 53)					
Mean	37.02	40.33	141.32	117.43	.96
Standard Deviation	5.23	1.93	16.95	15.17	.02
All Females (N = 49)					
Mean	38.93	40.76	136.67	115.56	.98
Standard Deviation	5.06	1.33	14.31	19.54	.02
Working-Class Females (N = 39)					
Mean	38.81	40.80	136.84	118.07	.97
Standard Deviation	5.36	1.31	15.52	21.00	.02

TABLE 6.4 REGRESSION ANALYSIS OF ECONOMIC FACTORS AND GALTON-INDEXED HEIGHTS

		Males						Females					
Predictor	Subjects	N^{**}	R^2_F	P^*	R^2_R	F	P	N^{**}	R^2_F	P^*	R_R	F	P
£ GNP per capita	All	$96^2(-)$	.17	.005	.09	7.35	.008	52	.06	.54	.06	.00	1.00
	Working Class	64	.30	.0002	.23	5.45	.02	42	.06	.63	.06	.08	.77
	Non-Working class	32	.38	.02	.38	.11	.73	10	.86	.06	.86	.08	.78
Williamson Cost of Living Index²	All	$84(-)$	.13	.04	.06	6.83	.01	49	.19	.04	.04	8.23	.006
	Working Class	53	.02	.84	.02	<.01	.93	39	.07	.64	.05	.53	.46
	Non-working class	32	.33	.06	.32	.10	.75	10	.75	.20	.75	.00	1.00
Kondratieff Commodity Price Index²	All	95^2	.07	.14	.05	1.58	.21	$52(-)$	.18	.04	.06	6.94	.01
	Working class	63	.27	.001	.25	1.19	.28	42	.08	.49	.06	.94	.33
	Non-working class	32	.39	.02	.38	.15	.69	10	.73	.22	.73	.00	1.00

*Significance of the difference from zero.

$(-)$ = Negative regression weight.

² = Predictor squared.

**N data sets

Discussion

The results of the three multiple linear regression analyses are diverse. First, there is a small gender difference; three analyses of males and two of females were statistically significant. Second, social class makes a little difference, and then only in the case of GNP per capita, as the three results for males involved working-class people while the sole result for females did not. The most effective model of prediction, beyond the three ecological variables, involved GNP per capita whose R^2 based on the four variables was .30 (p = .0002), which is not large, although statistically significant, for working-class youths. It was followed by the predictor set involving the Kondratieff index and employing all female subjects: its R^2 was .19 (p = .006). The pattern of statistical significance for the three variables by gender and social level are quite distinct. For GNP per capita, statistically significant influence on Galton-indexed heights involves males and both specifications of social class. For Williamson's cost of living index it involves males and females, but only when social level is not specified. The Kondratieff index affected heights of females when social level is unspecified. The three variables have quite unique roles as influences on Galton-indexed heights.

Not surprisingly, none of the three social-economic influences produced effects in the non-working-class sets of young males and females. These, essentially middle-class subjects were well nurtured and, by virtue of their niche in the economic strata, probably were at minimal risk for the poverty-related diseases.

Finally, there is the matter of linearity of regression for the three economic predictor variables. As Table 6.4 indicates, for aggregates of nineteenth century males and females linearity is occasionally and not exclusively observed. Nonlinearity created by squaring the value of a predictor significantly increases the fit of the regression model in selected instances. In Table 6.4, the two instances determined in a previous study are £GNP per capita with all males, and Kondratieff's index with all males.

For males, increments in the economic predictor score uniformly range from minus one standard deviation below to one standard deviation above the mean. The typical increment in the Galton height index across that range is +.10. In the case of the two regression lines for females, the change in the criterion Galton height index differs in two ways; it is a negative change, criterion scores drop as the economic predictor score rises, and the change is slight, −.03 Galton height

FIGURE 6.4 REGRESSION LINES FOR SIGNIFICANT ECONOMIC PREDICTORS OF GALTON-INDEXED HEIGHTS

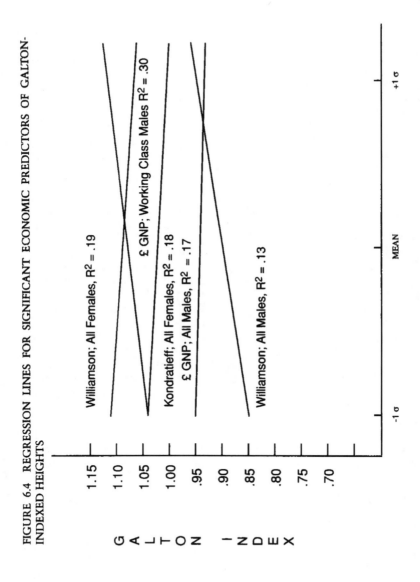

index units, in both instances. This gender effect is evident in the case of two economic predictors, Williamson's cost of living index and Kondratieff's commodity price index. Table 6.4 demonstrates numerically a small but significant impact of economic forces in the periods of time addressed by the three economic indicators. In absolute terms, the changes in criterion scores are not great, suggesting that the radical change in British heights achieved by 1965 and documented in the norms of Tanner, Whitehouse, and Takaishi (1966; 1976), are best explained after our period of interest closed in 1914; Morant's (1950) study suggests that conclusion. Boyne, Aitken, and Leitch (1957) reviewed height and weight changes since 1911. The London portion of the studies reviewed "Showed a pronounced secular trend of increasing heights and weights of children in the 40 years up to 1954."

For the topic of this book as a whole, the empirical evidence suggests that heights did not decline, but also did not improve radically. This conclusion is attenuated to a degree by the qualitative limitations of the original corpus of height data.

When we relate this multivariate analysis to the general topic of the state of the nineteenth century economy and heights, we see that, in general, a relationship between the two domains exists and, in instances of gender and social class, (e.g.) working-class males and all females, it is quite specific. Of no less interest is the observation that relationships are less discernible in females and are quite absent in females of working-class status. This last observation may relate to the findings from the 1939–1945 war by Butler, Ruffin, Sniffen, and Wickson (1945) and LaPorte (1946) that girls were affected less than boys by poor diets. In the case of non-working-class youngsters, none of the three economic variables affected the Galton-indexed heights across the period of interest, as might be expected.

Commentary

The overall picture of the contribution of auxological data to study of the degeneracy question is blurred slightly by the nature of the original materials and by its indexing in order to maximize utility through a common metric. With those reservations offset to a degree by a multivariate analysis of heights, we estimate that there was an improvement across the decades in the habitus of young people. It was not dramatic and, consistent with the overall conclusion of comparative and persisting disadvantage of childhood (Jordan, 1987b, 1992c), the improvement was far less than it might have been. The reasons might be found in the economic value of children and young persons as compliant, cheap labor, and in families' standard of living and concomitant patterns of nutrition and hygiene. Whatever the causes the mechanisms take the form of differential rates of social change for age groups. As an example, children worked as part-timers well into the later decades, with Scotland's children suffering, perhaps, more than those of Lancashire (Smout, 1986). Finally, we note the limitations posed by reality, in the form of sources developed in the period of interest, to an empirical-statistical approach to period-specific questions about human development. Such an approach exceeds the value of relying on impressions formed at the time, suggesting that physical deterioration was progressive among the poor. The corpus of studies formulated and analyzed here suggest otherwise, although the data are far from systematic in representativeness by year, chronological age, gender, and social class. At that point we encounter the limitations to study of auxology by empirical means implicit in examination of an earlier era. Even so, the data tell us that the trend of heights was not down, even if not sharply up, as progressive degeneracy would have demonstrated.

The distinctive contribution of this chapter to understanding the course of physical maturation by social level and gender has been the attempt to relate several social-economic indices to mean height indices from group data stratified by age. In Table 6.4 are the outcomes of regression analyses that assess by multivariate means the impact of £GNP per capita, commodity prices, and the cost of living on heights indexed to the central tendency of the Galton Committee data of 1883. Where appropriate, according to prior research (Jordan, 1990a), the squared value was employed as the form of the economic variable.

From the pattern of results in Table 6.4, it is evident that the three social-economic predictors had quite different mechanisms. £GNP per capita influenced heights of males with and without specification of social level, but not those of females. In contrast, the cost of living affected the indexed heights of both males and females, but did not explicate further when subjects were specified as working class. Commodity prices affected indexed heights only of females and then only when social level was unspecified. Thus, the mechanism by which the economy of the period 1815–1914 affected the development of young people appears to be a series of discrete processes. Accordingly, it is not enough to speak of an impact of social and economic change on health. It is necessary to view it as a complex of processes in which gender and social class respond discretely to social-economic forces. Only £GNP per capita is sensitive in the analyses of Table 6.4 to further specification of young people by social class; only Williamson's cost of living index affects boys and girls; and neither responds to gender and working class membership simultaneously. Most narrow of all three is the impact of commodity price indexes on females, and only when not further specified by social class.

It may be helpful to recall that non-working-class data sets are not addressed here; the reason is that only ten female data sets were not working class. The male, non-working-class groups were not numerous either. Only specification of social level as working class provided consistently substantial numbers of data sets dispersed broadly across the century under scrutiny.

From height and economic data presented in this and preceding chapters (see Figure 3.6 and Table 6.4) some trends are evident. First, social-economic circumstances impinging on the welfare of families and their children improved, despite occasional setbacks. More narrowly, the quality of children's lives increased through its several components. At a more rarified level, society's values also evolved in the form of laws restricting child labor, promoting education, and protecting families from hazards in the world of work. The second trend was the comparatively modest progress in the heights of ordinary people's children toward the standards of the present day. When we compare the rate of change in these two domains a discrepancy is evident, even after allowing for a lagged effect in measurement. The discrepancy is that heights failed to increase at anything like the rate of change observed for general social indicators; indeed, even the children's social indicators improved less quickly than those of the population in general, a conclusion demonstrated elsewhere (Jordan, 1987b, 1992c). In the case of heights, it was not until the twentieth century, post-1914, that heights of young Britons began to improve rapidly. In this regard, the data of this inquiry resemble, in their failure to show much improvement across most of the nineteenth century, the data summarized by Floud, Wachter, and Gregory (1990, Figure 7.2).

Although no explanation about the discrepancy between modest improvement in heights and more positive improvements in social indicators is self-evident in the data, it may be that a takeoff in physique—in this case, the height of the common man's children as a population at risk—like a high rate of economic growth, presupposes a set of necessary conditions. Apparently, those circumstances had not reached a critical mass by the turn of the century, and it took the earliest decades of the twentieth century to establish the necessary base. Innovations in social policy in the decade after 1900, including meals and medical attention at school, were followed after the war of 1914–1918 with establishment by municipal governments of urban and suburban housing estates. Consideration of those events is beyond the scope of this work, but may be pursued in (e.g.) Winter (1979, 1982) and Acheson (1991).

We now turn to a consideration of other phenomena that describe the status of people in the period of the Long Peace. Throughout the period under scrutiny thoughtful people had looked at the state of British society. Led originally by the Benthamite sociomedical observers thoughtful, analytic people began to describe the human problems they saw in quantitative terms. In that respect they were not alone. In France, Villermé (1829, 1840) and Benoiton de Chateauneuf (1830) surveyed the condition of the poor and documented their lowered life expectancy and greater risk for survival at birth; in the same period Lambert Adolphe Quetelet quantified height and weight in various social settings. In the next chapter we augment the picture of height and the factors influencing it by turning to the evolution of public policy in British society and through government actions across the period of interest.

7

Public Policy and Reform

Ideology

$\mathcal{T}$ he nineteenth century was an era of great change; the scourge of Bonapartism had been eliminated at Waterloo and with it the threat of social ideology as extreme as Jacobinism or as mild as evangelism. Insularity contained the ideological evolution of the population which lacked the vital element of disaffected intellectuals. As a result, political thought evolved slowly from the corresponding societies of the turn of the century into the damp squib of Chartism at mid-century. In the years that followed, Karl Marx read and wrote in the British Museum developing a corpus of thought in which the economic basis of society would be challenged in the twentieth century. In these same decades, as Table 7.1 shows, laws were enacted to improve social conditions in a stream of increasing quality. By the end of the century ideology, or the public philosophy in Walter Lipmann's phrase, had evolved to a recognizable level of maturity. The end of our period saw the great liberal reforms of 1906–1914 and introduction of pensions and similar provisions from German social welfare. The degree of change from Trafalgar to Sarajevo was enormous. The ideological position of the poor, the thinkers, and the politicians began to come together as the twentieth century opened. Farsighted legislation was suddenly possible and the resources of society were focused on improving child health, while also protecting the elderly and unemployed. Just how far sensibilities had evolved by the turn of the century may be illustrated by a quotation from Bulwer in 1836 about children of the

TABLE 7.1 REPRESENTATIVE NINETEENTH AND EARLY TWENTIETH CENTURY REFORMS

Year	Child Welfare	Education	Social Welfare	Health	Work
1802	Health and Morals of Apprentice Act				
1808		Lancastrian Society			
1811		National Society (Anglican)			
1814		British and Foreign School Society			
1816		Owen's New Lanark School			
1819					Cotton Mills and Factories
1833	Althorp's Factory Children's Act				
1834			Poor Law Amendment		
1840	Chimney Sweeps Act				
1842					Women and Children–Mines
1846			Repeal of the Corn Laws		
1847					Ten Hours Act
1848				Public Health Act	
1861		Newcastle Commission Report		Food Adulteration Act	Lace Works Act
1862		Lowe's Payment for Results			
1864					Chimney Sweeps Act
1867					Work Gangs Act
1868			Torrens' Dwellings Act		
1870		Forster's Education Act			Chimney Sweeps Act
1875			Cross' Dwellings Improvement Act		
1880		Mundella's Attendance Act Cross Commission Report			
1884			Housing Commission Report		
1895		Secondary Education Report			
1903			Interdepartmental Physical Degeneration Committee Report		
1905			Interdepartmental Medical and Feeding Committee Report		
1906			Education–Meals Act		
1911	Children's Act		National Health Insurance Act		
1913			Mental Deficiency Act		

wealthy, impoverished by the inheritance law of primogeniture: "A sense of their inferiority in younger children will excite them to make extraordinary exertions."

Tracing the process of evolution in ideology is not easy, but it is necessary in order to understand the beginning of the end of the degeneracy scare. It does not consist of a single nuclear thought expanding across the decades nor of several themes coalescing into an overarching leitmotif; rather, it consists of a number of themes early and late supported by increasingly better information affecting the interests of special groups.

In the sociopolitical arena, the days of George III and leadership shared among factions of the elite merged into those of William IV, uncle to Princess Victoria. Subsequently, manufacturers in the Midlands and the North allied themselves with City men, despite a tension between chapel and church. Money was made by the elder Peel in Lancashire and advanced the career of young Robert Peel in Westminster. The ennobled haute bourgeoisie absorbed the newest men of money into a functional alliance. An English God resembling a propertied country set with City connections sanctioned the unquestioned power of a privileged, shrewd minority through the established church.

And then there were the evangelists; ranging from the followers of Joanna Southcott, and even a few Muggletonians, to the followers of John Wesley. This wing of Christianity was moved by conscience to implement the social mission of the Gospel. Methodism is the best example of this movement and has been well described by E. P. Thompson (1980). Rather than a conscientious observation of ritual, this radical Christianity required scrupulous examination of the inner self and conformity to the demands of conscience. A religion accessible to ordinary folk the evangelical movement required literacy, an ideology institutionalized in the New World through the "Old Deluder Satan Act" of the Plymouth Colony in 1647. Evangelicals faced their Maker and found confidence in their power of self-analysis. When applied to other working men and women, frequently abusers of drink and neglectful of their bairns, it took no leap of the imagination to perceive that life was as easy for some as it was hard for others. There were few of the former, and life appeared to consist of laws and customs which favored the few at the expense of the many. This imbalance permeated popular thinking and expressed itself in repeal of the Corn Laws in 1847.

In Himmelfarb's (1968) view, the years of Victoria's long reign demonstrated a pattern of evolving values. Methodism and analogous values affecting social problems were the engine of change, and spread from the middle class to the social strata above and below. On the other hand, Thompson (1980) also viewed Methodism as central to the values and actions of the Victorians; in contrast to Himmelfarb, Thompson saw Wesleyism as the ideology by which such industrialists as chose to engage in niceties of justification could live with the exploitation of working people. In both views of the central role of Wesley's Methodism is the idea that it appealed to all social levels. Lacking the core of doctrinal certitude advanced by a Calvin or a Knox, Methodism could tolerate a variety of personal adaptations by master and workers, reformed and unemployed. All were caught up in a shared identity, and those who stressed good works sought to assist their fellow pilgrims.

Journeymen wondered about the cycles of unemployment that sent them on the tramp looking for work. In their associations, slowly to evolve into unions and at great pain, they recognized their lack of power. They resented their lack of representation by anyone but the Squire, or his protegé occupying a safe seat in a rotten borough until the first Reform Bill of 1832. The second Reform Bill of 1867 extended the franchise in a classic, defensive move of cooption by the middle class and the more enlightened of the establishment. With extension of the £10 franchise came parallel evolution; Robert Lowe, the archconservative described by Asa Briggs (1955), saw that the upper classes must educate their new masters, albeit in a niggardly fashion. With extended literacy came powers of analysis and extraction of concessions from the powerful to the relatively powerless. However, it was not until 1892 that James Keir Hardy took his seat as a representative of the Labour Party, himself a working man.

Public Policy

It should be borne in mind that there was little by way of bureaucracy in local and national government in the early decades of the nineteenth century. A state of affairs hard to grasp in our day is that people looked to private philanthropy or the parish vestry to relieve the poor of their burdens. Society at this early stage of the nineteenth century was a matter of *gesellschaft*, in Tonnies' term; that is, theirs was an ordered society with deference from the lower orders to the higher, and a sense of formality between the classes was the norm acknowledged by all. This unquestioned view may be illustrated in the content of a sermon preached at St. Sepulchre's church in London in the preceding century. The Bishop of Gloucester warned of the danger of educating the lower orders of society beyond the ability to read the Bible and to write a few lines: "So little instruction as this, so low degree of learning, might, one would think, be safely taught without danger of its inspiring any undue elevation of mind" (Slater, 1930). Public policy on economic and social matters reflected this attitude. In the form of the old Poor Law, there was a little government aid for the destitute, but private charity by public subscription was a viable mode of relief. Government's job was to do as little as possible, to defer, postpone, avoid, and—in the end—to do nothing for the lower orders of society.

The quality of laws enacted to help children and the poor was low. The 1802 act to protect apprentices had no enforcement procedures beyond a theoretical inspection. There was no bureaucracy to compile data, evaluate it, and propose refinements. In the case of the 1834 law on chimney sweeps—"climbing boys" and occasionally girls—a part of the regulations consisted of requiring a, "leathern cap, with a brass plate on which was inscribed the names of the master and the apprentice." Not until 1842 was use of children to clean chimneys of soot by having a small child climb up from the fireplace totally forbidden; but boys were to climb chimneys for decades due to lack of an apparatus for enforcement of the law. Even at mid-century the entrepreneur Isambard Kingdom Brunel was driven to distraction by the inefficiency of what little national bureaucracy existed in Whitehall. In Brunel's case, Admiralty indifference to his screw propeller for ships incensed him (Rolt, 1957). To be sure, Edwin Chadwick's great report on the health of towns had galvanized the government into sanitary reforms, but Chadwick was no ordinary man. Few people thought about the nation as a collective, and few used the idiom as an abstraction similar to Britannia or John Bull.

However, there were people thinking about the public affairs, a tradition having its modern antecedents in Edmund Burke and Sir Frederick Morton Eden's 1796 report on the poor. In Jeremy Bentham and his philosophy of Utilitarianism the nineteenth century began to enunciate critical propositions. They would be expressed in the second quarter-century in the search for facts and for the guides to action that reasonable, rational men might deduce in order to act prudently. Bentham's philosophy of government postulated action as opposed to inertia. It elevated rationalism to a level a little below its status among the Jacobins, and it slighted traditional morality as a guide to action. It fell to Bentham's disciplines, Edwin Chadwick and Thomas Southwood Smith for example, to express utilitarianism at the level of sanitation and clean water. As a movement influencing public policy, Utilitarianism emphasized the marshaling of facts. It used select committees as platforms to denounce half-naked women working in coal mines and other abuses judged to be beyond toleration in a civilized, modern state. As propagandists the Utilitarians combined with the medical reformers to create a new public agenda. Facts were carefully assembled and legitimated in the pages of the *Journal of the Statistical Society*. They refuted the denials of the privileged who found no evils in female and child mineworkers, or in the scarred bodies of factory workers old before their time.

However, even sanitary reform was not consolidated without retrograde episodes. One of the great nineteenth century anecdotes about sanitary reform is Snow's demonstration that disease was spread across the Golden Square area of London from one contaminated source, the Broad Street pump. Prompt removal of the handle, an elegantly simple remedy, ended the spread of cholera. However, it is not generally known that in 1866 the Vestry proposed to install a handle on the Broad Street pump in the week in which two people died of cholera in the neighborhood in a hot July (The Broad Street Pump, 1866). An editorial in *Lancet* interdicted a foolish mistake and so prevented further spread of cholera. Two years before, in 1864, the St. James vestry had opposed closing down street pumps, to the chagrin of the well-known Coroner, Mr. Lankester (1864).

Shapers of Public Policy

Jeremy Bentham (1748–1832)

Bentham shaped the evolution of policy indirectly and lived in an era before the problems of urbanization and degenerating collective health were apparent. Bentham's contribution was the philosophy of Utilitarianism bequeathed as refinement of empiricism to Edwin Chadwick and the statistical-medical reformers. Gathering facts and debating them in the meetings of the British Association for the Advancement of Science, local statistical societies and, eventually the National Association for the Promotion of Social Science, Bentham's heirs provided unambiguous descriptions of the social ills they sought to remedy.

Sir James Kay-Shuttleworth (1804–1877)

One of Edinburgh's medical graduates, James Kay of Rochdale, returned to his native Lancashire to practice in 1827. Kay experienced the cholera outbreak of 1832 in Manchester and saw firsthand the sufferings of the afflicted from the swift, usually fatal disease. Kay's outlook was broader than the clinical, and he appreciated the complexity and intensity of the life of the poor. Areas such as Deansgate, then called *Devilsgate* by some, gave evidence of a terrible way of life, one to which the term *degeneracy* would have seemed quite appropriate, in view of the incidence of overcrowding, communicable diseases, malnutrition, and mortality. In 1832, Dr. Kay wrote *The Moral and Physical Condition of the Working Classes Employed in the Cotton Manufacture in Manchester.* This work provides an excellent account by a sympathetic but detached analyst. It was drawn on, a decade later, by Friedrich Engels for his polemic on the condition of the working class in England. Two years later, in 1834, Kay became an assistant commissioner of the poor law and spent several years in East Anglia. There, he expanded his grasp of the hard life of the poor. In 1839, he began the major theme of the remaining years of his public life, the development of education, including the preparation of teachers (Jordan, 1987b). Retiring in 1848, he became a baronet. It was at Gawthorpe Hall, near Bolton, the seat of his wife's family, the Shuttleworths, that he entertained two writers who included the poor in their works, Elizabeth Gaskell and Charlotte Bronte. During the cotton famine, 1861–1865, Kay-Shuttleworth was involved in relief of the poor. During his busy life Kay-Shuttleworth associated with Dr. William Farr, a fellow graduate of Edinburgh, and other reformers. He was active in the Social Science Association and, in his years with the Office of the Privy Council, joined forces with many other prominent people of the period engaged in reform.

Edwin Chadwick (1800–1890)

In study of the health of the British population in Victorian days Edwin Chadwick and his 1842 report on the health of the working population of towns was a major event. It defined a problem and proposed solutions in the form of clean water and effective sewage. Chadwick's life work was in the Benthamite tradition of empirical description and prescriptive solution. Chadwick's effectiveness was limited by his testy relationship with those who did not agree with him, and frequently they were people in important positions. Chadwick is associated with the early "statist" tradition of describing the nature and scope of problems with statistics and using the numbers in effective propaganda. In relation to the degeneracy question, Chadwick is remembered for his grasp of the importance of sanitation to preservation of life and health. His role was that of groundbreaker and tactless reformer.

Thomas Southwood Smith (1788–1861)

Relatively unknown to the general public of Queen Victoria's early years, who would have recognized and applauded Lord Shaftesbury, Southwood Smith's life covered the early years of the Industrial Revolution. Like James Kay a graduate in medicine of Edinburgh, Southwood Smith combined religious motives with reform. Eight years after qualifying in medicine he entered the literary and intellectual life of London while practicing his profession.

Southwood Smith began writing in the 1820s and, by 1830, was recognized for his demonstration of the linkage between poverty and disease. Jeremy Bentham authorized Southwood Smith to perform his autopsy in 1832, the year in which Southwood Smith joined the commission studying factory conditions of child workers. Over the next three decades, he wrote treatises on health and participated in philanthropic ventures such as model housing, the Board of Health, and several sanitary studies.

In some respects, a transitional figure, Southwood Smith was trained before Victorian public health assumed its mature form (recalling the Salerno school and other ventures). He was contemporary to Villermé in Paris, to James Kay, and to Chadwick. He represents the Benthamite impulse modulated by professional training. He set a standard for the medicosocial reformers who followed him.

Dr. William Farr (1807–1883)

Reformers tend to strike us, at a distance, as strong personalities who impose their vision of reform on a reluctant generation by a combination of persuasiveness, moral certainty, and visibility. The latter is certainly not apparent in the career of Dr. William Farr whose name would also have been recognized by few Victorians.

William Farr contributed to the degeneracy problem through a career in public health that culminated five years before his retirement in the 1875 Public Health Act. Farr was one of the medicosocial reformers who sought collective action through laws to protect and advance the welfare of individuals. He based his actions on statistics of a simple sort, although not embracing them as self-divining. Farr believed that urbanization and population density disposed a population to degeneracy.

Farr advanced the comparatively backward state of census data in Britain, introducing occupational categories (Eyler, 1979). Farr also worked on life tables, an enterprise that shed light on the disparity of life among various social groups; he also contributed to the theory of disease, then designated as *zymotic* and due to pernicious vapors and gases. Working from time to time with persons of the period such as Florence Nightingale and Sir James Kay-Shuttleworth, William Farr attacked the complex of ill health and degeneracy through a life of scholarship and effective administration.

Mary Carpenter (1807–1877)

Mary Carpenter spent most of her life in the west of England and was buried in Bristol, the site of her Red Lodge school. Her career was that of thinker and reformer addressing the problems of delinquency and education. By 1851, she was recognized as an influential thinker and associated with James Kay-Shuttleworth and his brother Joseph on educational matters. In the area of delinquency, her views were well received in the Social Science Association, and she cooperated with Mathew Davenport Hill. Like Kay-Shuttleworth, religious ideas were at the core of her practical steps, and she was conservative in her goals for the betterment of the poor. With regard to the degeneracy question, Mary Carpenter is not a central figure, but her efforts to deal with crime and education, aspects of the central problem of social disorganization, make her relevant. All cities of the time had children living on the streets, a situation evident today in Latin America. Their welfare was the central topic of her life, and her impact on practice and law in the treatment of children ineluctably drawn into conflict with property and middle-class expectations was considerable. She can be viewed as a person who made a difference through her personal example, and also through the keen mind and occasionally sharp tongue she brought to discussions of public policy affecting Victorian youth. Up to the year before her death she was active in promoting the welfare of poor children through education and correlated free meals.

Thomas Barnardo (1845–1909)

We now turn to a reformer addressing street children and those whose nominal family life was destroyed by alcohol abuse and violence. Working later in the century than Mary Carpenter, William Farr, and James Kay-Shuttleworth, Barnardo's influence is still evident today.

Barnardo, born in Dublin, saw degeneracy evident in the prevalence of crime and in the persistence of crime in the children of criminals, according to Fishman (1988). Trained as a physician and intending to become a missionary in China, Barnardo shared with earlier reformers a religious zeal and a bent for practical improvements. Buoyed by his creed and a Victorian sense of self-assurance, Barnardo gathered children from the streets, fed them, and clothed them. He frequently dispatched children abroad consistent with the theme of the times that a fresh start in Canada and Australia was the best solution. Elsewhere (Jordan, 1987b) I have discussed that enterprise.

For the purpose of our consideration of degeneracy, Barnardo, like Mary Carpenter, saw individual children, rather than social problems. He dealt with children and faced directly the plight of children on the streets. London was Bristol many times over, so that his task of attacking the degenerated population of starving, abandoned, and abused youngsters in the East End of Jack the Ripper was endless. At his most practical, Barnardo fed, bathed, dressed, and schooled children of the streets; Fishman (1988) states that in the 1880s he was receiving four children every day. Barnardo became an excellent fund raiser and was adept at boarding out children. Through his efforts, which are not beyond criticism, especially in the case of some highhanded practices, many children were salvaged by an organization that has persisted a century beyond its founding.

John Simon (1816–1904)

With the entry of John Simon (who maintained the French pronunciation of his name brought from Orleans by his grandfather in 1775) into government at the Privy Council, reform acquired the trappings of bureaucracy within the national government. In the late 1850s, John Simon developed a team of skilled sanitary investigators who created a series of annual reports on health problems. From 8 Richmond Terrace, John Simon worked up an effective relationship with the redoubtable Robert Lowe and the cabinet; at the same time, he alienated the formidable Florence Nightingale and other influential people. The result of Simon's career was that public health was institutionalized on the public agenda as a responsibility of government. In this process the initiative in health matters left the chaos of multiple, uncoordinated boards of local government and migrated to the state. In that process, Simon and his group used the power of law to force local government to attend to public health in the form of vaccination, sewage, and housing. One of Simon's proteges was Edward Smith, whose study of nutrition was cited in Chapter Three. Lambert (1963) credits Simon with establishment of the first lectureship in public health at St. Thomas's Hospital in 1856. The Public Health Act of 1875 was Simon's major contribution to public health. It updated and consolidated previous legislation and was not fully replaced until 1936.

Margaret McMillan (1860–1931)

In an era replete with reformers whose character provided the impetus to reform, Margaret McMillan is distinctive. Raised in Scotland after her birth in Westchester County, New York, Margaret McMillan spent her seventy-one years striving to improve society by advancing the cause of children, especially those of preschool age.

Until her late twenties, Margaret McMillan earned her living as a governess, on several occasions, and broadened her ideology from Scottish christianity to include socialism. Her public life began in the 1890s in Bradford, the Yorkshire town that had seen Richard Oastler campaign on behalf of factory children six decades before. There, she worked within the agenda of the Independent Labour Party and was elected to the School Board. In a style acceptable to her world of middle-class initiative, but contrary to today's distinction between setting and implementing policy, McMillan learned firsthand of the problems of working-class children and of the struggle for even minimal hygiene faced by the poor. Dirt and the attendant problem of sickness struck her forcibly. At the same time, her role as an instructor in adult education increased her skills as an effective speaker.

In 1902, Margaret McMillan moved to London where she worked in the impoverished district of Deptford for nearly two decades. There, she opened a clinic and expanded communication of her ideas on education and socialism by writing both fiction and nonfiction; the two modalities would achieve a sort of apotheosis in a curious biography of her late sister Rachel.

In her writings, the value of children and the importance of their health and welfare were paramount. At Deptford, McMillan arranged for poor children to live in the fresh air. She reunited her earlier insistence on health with a public demonstration of education that attracted many visitors and admirers. Not the least of the elements in this complex was the importance of providing medical inspections and meals for the children of the poor (McMillan, 1906), and she contributed to the establishment of the school medical service. Living until

1931 Margaret McMillan was a link to the twentieth century, and her voluminous writings have acquired a hagiographic quality. Steedman (1990) recorded this aspect in the phrase, "the legend of Margaret McMillan." Yet, beneath the legend there was a core of reality in which practical suggestions for reform and an intellectual formulation of childhood within society are evident. Like other figures of the era she demonstrated certainty and self-assurance that were matched by the degree of authority on education matters ascribed to her by influential people.

28

There emerged a cadre of like-minded people conscious, despite differing backgrounds and ideologies, of the need to meet and discuss. For example, the heights of school children were on the general agenda of Rochdale by the early 1890s. The recently appointed vicar, Archdeacon Wilson, stimulated the school board and the *Rochdale Observer* to assess the health of school children. Archdeacon Wilson noted the poor habitus of boys at his Sparrow Hill school in 1891 and compared their heights and weights with Dr. Charles Roberts's data from sons of artisans ("The Physical Condition of Rochdale Children," 1892), a norm we have employed elsewhere. Wilson stimulated the School Board to undertake inquiries, leading the *Rochdale Observer* (May 7, 1892) to denote the communitywide attention as follows: "So far as we know, Rochdale is the only town in England where . . . information has been obtained in such a systematic and comprehensive way. . . . We may soon be in possession of a body of facts of great value to social reformers and all who can do anything to improve the health of the people."

Rochdale would have been quite typical of textile towns in Lancashire and Yorkshire. Blackburn, Lancashire, twenty years later, had its half-timers, but Gradgrindian facts assembled by medical offices had not translated into the positive changes nearby Rochdale had hoped for in 1892. Karn's (1937) analysis of typical Blackburn boys and girls from the years 1908–1911 showed that they were still quite short. Table 7.2 shows the heights of Blackburn's twelve- and thirteen-year-old boys and girls at the end of the period of interest, in 1908–1911. In Karn's paper, age given is for the last birthday; here, I have construed that to be approximately the midpoint between two birthdays, for purposes of comparison with the data of Tanner, Whitehouse and Takaishi (1966). In Table 7.2, we see that Blackburn's youngsters, including half-timers whose number or identity was not quoted by Karn, were quite short. The Galton (1884) indexes for the heights of boys at

TABLE 7.2 MEAN HEIGHTS AND WEIGHTS OF BLACKBURN (LANCASHIRE) TWELVE AND THIRTEEN YEAR OLDS, 1908–1911

Age	N	Height		Weight		Galton (1884) Height Index	Tanner (1966)[2] Height Index	Body[1] Mass
		Inches	cm.	lb.	kg.			
Boys								
12.5	343	53.70	136.40	71.50	32.50	.99	.91	17.66
13.5	68	55.70	140.20	77.90	35.41	.99	.89	17.61
Girls								
12.5	279	54.30	137.92	72.70	33.04	1.05	.90	17.39
13.5	108	56.20	142.74	80.00	36.36	.99	.90	18.08

Source: Means from Karns (1937).
[1]Kilograms/meters[2]
[2]Percentage of P50 value for height from Tanner, Whitehead, and Takaishi (1966).

twelve and thirteen years are both .99. For girls the indexes at twelve and thirteen years old are 1.05 and .99. By 1966 standards (Tanner, Whitehouse, and Takaishi, 1966), their index values are, at twelve years, boys = .91, and girls = .90. A short distance to the east, in Batley, Yorkshire ("where the crows fly back'ards to keep t'muck out of their eyes") thirteen-year-old boys at Park Road School had a mean height of 52.25 inches (132.71 cm.) (Finnegan and Sigsworth, 1978), which is a Galton (1884) index of .97, and a Tanner (1966) index of .84; the discrepancy in this last instance is 24.1 cm. (9.48 inches).

For the pre-1914 years, Addison (1983) credits young Winston Churchill with a vision of a benign if socially stratified view of society, early in his long career. The discontent of wage earners with the price of food and other essentials required remedies ensured by collective action, in Churchill's version of Lord Randolph Churchill's vision of British society.

Across the nineteenth century, individual reformers had begun to coalesce, and they formed associations in which proposals for public action were debated. Among the major agencies for reform were the Royal Statistical Society, the National Association for the Promotion of Social Science, the Salvation Army, and the Society for the Prevention of Cruelty to Children. Frequently, the major voices in these societies were the same people.

The Royal Statistical Society

An amalgam of local societies, the society began as a coterie of the British Association for the Advancement of Science. The London Statistical Society was the central group, and the societies in Bristol, Manchester, Leeds, and other places slowly yielded place to London. After several decades, the society received the royal assent.

In the early years, members engaged in descriptive studies of poverty, literacy, and other topics of public concern. Their Bentham-like preoccupation with numbers pre-empted the opportunity to develop a rationale of society as the republicans in France had tried and as Karl Marx would do subsequently. In the later decades of the nineteenth century, the statists saw their society evolve from a forum for public health issues, much like the sanitary journal of later decades, into a technical journal for mathematicians. In some respects that step was possible because public discourse accommodated public health questions; even Parliament eventually mounted significant inquires, such as the studies of child health in 1902 and 1904, and explicit attention appeared in popular literature; for example, Gorst, 1905a.

National Association for the Promotion of Social Science (NAPSS)

As the nation's thinkers, if not its politicians, began to address the complex that included widespread ill-health it became apparent that a forum was needed. In such a setting, reformers associated with a variety of social problems, who therefore would be unlikely to meet in the ordinary course of events, would exchange views and refine agendas. By midcentury, the British Association and the Statistical Society were jointed by the Social Science Association. Founded in 1856, under the patronage of Lord Brougham, the society began three decades of annual meetings (Rodgers, 1952). In relation to the degeneracy question in all its aspects, NAPSS functioned as a reformers' assembly in which proto-legislation was enunciated. Many pieces of parliamentary legislation were at least adumbrated in the sessions of the association. The *NAPSS Transactions* are a source for this discussion of the degeneracy question. In 1886, the association ended its formal sessions, having been addressed by the reformers of the preceding thirty years. By that time, different, more specialized societies were emerging and public discussion of ideas about social problems continued in those contents. Experts on crime and sanitation conferred with like-minded brethren. They saw enlargement of government's functions through law as the obvious way to institute reforms. Topics addressed included public health, women's legal rights, possible reintroduction of transportation for prisoners (which they opposed), protection of children, legal rights of accused persons, and registration of all births including the stillborn.

Charity Organization Society

In Victorian Britain, relief of social problems fell to the inefficient vestry or parish system of aid in the early days and was succeeded by more comprehensive systems of public relief through the revised Poor Law in the later decades. At all times, private philanthropy was a major force operating through charitable individuals and organizations. In London, about two-thirds of the way through the century, the need to coordinate charitable relief became evident. There were the organizational problems of overlapping and duplication of services, but at a more critical level, there was the question of how to aid the deserving without destroying initiative. In some respects a precious question, as today we tend to emphasize need not mere entitlement, the policy complex illustrated the discrepancy between the need to help individuals and its implementation—a gap also illustrated by public discourse about the degeneracy question.

Organized in 1869, the Charity Organization Society was led initially by Charles Bosanquet. Six years later, he was succeeded by Charles S. Loch who served for nearly forty years. A man of strong opinions and scholarly bent that complemented his organizational skills (Mowat, 1957), Loch was an excellent spokesman for a philosophy of social work distinguished by a less value-biased approach to the poor. The society survived in the postwar years as the Family Welfare Association. It adapted to the change in casework values exemplified in social legislation of the twentieth century and demonstrates that continuity is possible in human agencies by adapting procedures and, more important, values, to the inevitable evolution of ideology.

National Society for the Prevention of Cruelty to Children

The tenor of organized attention to disorganization and abuse in the nineteenth century is exemplified by the comparatively late date at which cruelty to animals was followed by recognition of cruelty to children as a public evil. In 1883, the society was founded, and royal patronage followed seven years later. The object of the society was to end child abuse, and it pursued that end by casework and vigorous prosecution of offenders. It takes no great imagination to see that child abusers would also neglect nourishment of children, placing them at more than the high degree of risk for illness other children faced routinely. The society exists today, its earliest years having been structured by the redoubtable Benjamin Waugh from a number of parallel, local societies.

The Salvation Army

In the work of the Salvation Army's founder, William Booth (1829–1912) of Birmingham, we see several aspects of the evolution of public thought. There is continuity with the evangelical tradition in religion, and there is concrete action on the streets in the form of direct assistance. For our purposes here, a third, ideological element is significant.

In 1890, General Booth wrote *In Darkest England, and the Way Out*. The fundamental value, in retrospect, was not the proposal to establish centers of employment, farms, and emigration schemes but the assertion of a novel theory of personal disorganization. The nineteenth century saw poverty as the direct consequence of "moral" failure—a broad concept including acceptance of personal responsibility for one's fate regardless of circumstances. To Booth, who dealt with the poor on the streetcorner, the algorithm was backwards. In his clinical, as opposed to metaphysical, approach social circumstances, such as unemployment, set the stage for failure and shortcomings, not the reverse. Booth rejected the conventional wisdom that moral failure led to poverty, an ideology that made it convenient to blame the victim. At the concrete level Booth fed children and fought alcoholism. Children benefitted indirectly, also, as he salvaged parents and so preserved family life among the poor. In Booth we see the combination of a reformer and a radical contribution to the evolution of social ideology. A useful summary of Booth's work may be found in Bailey (1984).

The Anthropometric Committee
of the British Association

Given the importance of height to consideration of the degeneracy question, the work of the Anthropometric Committee between 1875 and 1883 merits consideration. At its meeting in Bristol, the British Association for the Advancement of Science appointed a committee chaired by Dr. John Beddoe. Among the other twelve members were Dr. William Farr, Francis Galton, Col. Lane-Fox (later Pitt Rivers), Sir Rawson Rawson, and Professor Leone Levi. On the basis of a grant of £100, they proposed "the collection of heights, weights of human beings in the British Empire, and the publication of photographs of the typical races of the Empire." In 1877, four more members were added, and the first file of data from the 2nd Royal Surrey Militia was provided by Col. Lane-Fox. Those measurements joined others taken by Dr. Farr and Mr. Redgrave, and the committee refined its spirometer for measuring lung capacity. By the third report in 1878, the committee had refined its instructions for field workers, reported a balance of £16 on hand, and requested funds to return their balance to £100.

The forty-ninth meeting of the British association in 1879 was held at Plymouth. The Farr committee reported acquisition of 12,000 measurements plus a further 50,000 measurements gathered by Dr. Charles Roberts. The fifth report in 1880 saw the retirement of Dr. Farr and the accession of Francis Galton for the remainder of the life of the committee. In the 1880 report are figures tracing the growth of individuals based on twice the 12,000 measurements at hand one year before. The 1880 report provided data on color of hair and eyes. It also includes a data set of consecutive measurements on twelve boys and thirteen girls in Massachusetts developed by Dr. William Bowditch. The committee thought that the cephalic index would be useful in the future, and reported receiving photographs from various parts of the United Kingdom.

The 1881 report of the Anthropometric Committee at York reported that 80,000 measurements were recorded, and that their "scientific arrangement by skilled computers" was beyond their financial resources of £30. In the matter of detail, they had expended ad hoc £143 15s., or about £40 per year of operations. The report gave heights for 38,953 people and discussed the relative claims of the mode and the arithmetic mean; Dr. Roberts used the mode, but named it the average in his appendix to the sixty-page report. In 1881, the committee decided that color-blindness was important, and concluded that "it is exceedingly desirable that more complete details should be obtained with regard to the earlier ages from birth to ten years." The 1882 report to the fifty-second meeting of the British Association was quite brief, but promised a map of comparative heights developed by Dr. Roberts for the following year. The members thought that stature could be understood by taking into account ethnology formulated as Saxon, Iberian, Caledonian, and Anglian races, for example. Additional influences were geology, climate, and sanitation.

The 1883 Report of the Anthropometric Committee

This was the final, comprehensive document presented to the British association at Southport. The heading credits Sir Rawson Rawson and Dr. Charles Roberts with drawing up the report. The statement of objectives was reworded to define the scope of the study as the population of the British "Isles" rather than Empire. Data were presented from 53,000 individuals, and the mean-mode distinction was addressed once more. The report is significant in many ways. It presented a great deal of data and cited international studies. In the matter of children, the report indicated that between the extremes of the social scale at age eleven there were height differences of 5 inches, and 3½ inches for adults.

On the topic of degeneracy, the 1883 Galton committee report (p. 298) observed that data taken in 1833 and 1873 showed "a slight but uniform increase in stature, and a very large increase in weight. . . . A child of 9 years of age in 1873 weighed as much as one of 10 years in 1883." A series of tables, figures and maps provided comparative data on stature by occupation and by region. Setting aside "Idiots and Imbeciles," the report (p. 271) listed the tallest people as the agricultural population of Galloway, Scotland, with mean height of 70.5 in. (129.07 cm.), and the shortest was Hertfordshire laborers at 65.35 in. (161.20 cm.).

All things considered, Francis Galton, Charles Roberts, and their colleagues performed a prodigious task of gathering data and tabulating it for analysis in an era in which "skilled computers" were people. The data obtained established a norm for several decades and provided a quantitative base for discussion of questions leading to the formulation of public policy.

Documents and Inquiries

From the onset of the Industrial Revolution, there were inquires through which observers of British society sought to appraise contemporary society and its problems. Just before our period, Sir Frederick Morton Eden wrote *On the State of the Poor*, in 1797. Relevant to the physical growth and welfare of the young was his observation that the poor had eaten meat twice a week before the French war, but now ate barley bread and a lot of potatoes. In 1830, William Cobbett wrote *Rural Rides*, in which he recorded the living conditions of the poor several years before.

In 1845, the future prime minister, Benjamin Disraeli, wrote *Sybil, or the Two Nations*, in which he described poverty and privilege sundered by the evolving economy and social structure to the detriment of the poor. In 1850, the Rev. Thomas Beames reported his investigation of slums, *The Rookeries of London: Past, Present and Prospective*. One year later, in 1851, a Medical Gentleman wrote *An Enquiry into Destitution, Prostitution and Crime in Edinburgh*. By midcentury, investigative reporting culminated in a series of articles in the *Morning Chronicle* in 1851. A group of reporters analyzed social conditions around the country attending to housing and work in agricultural and industrialized counties. In 1859, G. Godwin wrote *Town Swamps and Social Bridges*.

A little later, Thomas Wright began to publish a series of books describing the lives of the poor to middle class audiences. Using the name, Journeyman Engineer (1867), initially, he reported the lives and customs of the working class for the edification of their betters. More serious, were *The Bitter Cry of Outcast London*, in 1883, by the Rev. Andrew Mearns. William Booth's (1890) *In Darkest England and the*

Way Out, offered the Salvation Army's prescription for improving the health and welfare of the poor. Beginning in 1889, Charles Booth began to write the seventeen volumes composing the *Life and Labour of the People in London*. In 1898, Frank Hird, who in 1912 edited an edition of the mid-nineteenth century work by Porter, *The Progress of the Nation*, turned his reporting skills toward children working in the East End of London. Hird thought that five trades employed children iniquitously: box making, belt and umbrella making (whose vendors were known as mush[-room] men), paper bag making, and furniture polishing. Hird added a sixth group of children subject to great stress and fatigue, canal-boat children. In that respect, he echoed the work of Smith of Coalville (1878), twenty years before. Finally, in this brief overview of nongovernmental studies, there was Seebohm Rowntree's (1901) study of the poor in York, *Poverty: A Study of Town Life*.

In the case of Hird's (1898) exploration of child workers in the East End we have a glimpse of how the poor received social investigators and reformers. Meg Martyr, an unmarried woman in her thirties, attending night school after the day's work to learn to read and write, told Hird:

> "I thought at fust as 'ow you was one o' them folks as comes darn 'ere to look at us, just as they go an' look at fat cattle in a show. Only Gawd knows," she added bitterly, "we ain't fat most of us, we don't get enough to eat for that. It makes me reg'ler sick, that it do, when these fine ladies an' gents come to me and ask me to show 'em rarnd. 'What for?' I always ses. 'O, because we are *so* interested in the poor people, and we want to see how they really live down here in the East End!' " (Meg's imitation of what she herself called "torf talk" was inimitable.) " 'We have heard of you through some ladies interested in the Women's Union, and they told us you could take us to all sorts of places that we could never find by ourselves.' 'They're right there,' I says, 'cos I do know more even that the school inspectors; but if I take yer to some of the worst places, what are you goin' to do for these pore people?' And then most of them look a bit silly. Do? Why they ain't a-goin' to do anythink, except stare, an say, 'O, my!' So I just up and tells people of that kidney that workin' men and workin' wimmen abart 'ere ain't like figures at Madam Tusseyside's wax works, even if they do live like pigs becors wages is so low." Meg paused for breath, and regarding me severely, asked abruptly:
>
> "You're a torf, ain't yer?"
>
> I meekly supposed that I was.

Resistance

In a consideration of physical degeneracy in the period 1805–1914 there is reason to discern an improvement in the health and habitus of the British population. However, one should be alert to the tendency to report events as moving teleologically toward their current status. As an illustration that conditions were not always constructive for the health and welfare of children we may consider some of the forces and persons shaping events in the middle of the nineteenth century. In particular, is the emerging theme of Victorian childhood, which brought children together and crystallized people's thinking about them, and schooling. On that topic, there is, for example, the clash of Christians over the role of religion and the force of personality within the Whitehall apparatus for administering state funds for educating children.

Social Conflict

Central to child welfare, from the point of view of large-scale interventions, is the fact that children come together in schools. There, they are traditionally organized by age, in manageable groups, and for a considerable portion of their waking hours. On that premise, the development of schooling becomes an opportunity to pursue instruction beyond literacy and numeracy. The early Victorians were not slow to discern the opportunities that state support for schools would present. However, they were not of one mind and split along religious lines. The interests of the established church clashed with those of the nonconformist protestant sects, against a background of previous, myopic legislation requiring education for factory children (e.g., the Factory Act of 1833). In the private sector, Sunday Schools and ragged schools were the innovations of the age; proprietary schools and the occasional endowed school also contributed.

Parallel to the deadlock between the religious sectarians there was a generalized opposition to schooling in many quarters. In the earliest decades of the nineteenth century, the reformer Hannah More, who was quite conservative except for her insistence on literacy as a vehicle for christianity, encountered opposition to schools because they disturbed the social order. Silver (1977) quoted Bertrand Russell's recollection of 1891 as the year in which his grandfather established a village school in Petersham. The gentry were distressed at the destruction or "the hitherto aristocratic character of the neighbourhood."

To the resistance of the comfortable classes must be added that of the poor. Frequently, they saw schooling as an intrusion into the sphere of authority exercised by parents. They had come to no harm without schooling, and what was good enough for them was good enough for their children. In general, many sectors of the population were at a great distance, in terms of value systems, from today's unquestioned acceptance of schooling as a necessary and helpful opportunity.

For a variety of reasons, quite diffuse and unrelated, the organization of children in schools was resisted, and the aggregation of children in accessible units was delayed, in pursuit of theological advantage.

Andrew Ure (1778–1857)

An M.D. and Fellow of the Royal Society, Ure worked as a physician, chemist, and lecturer. Of his two studies of manufacturing, the lesser known is his 1856 book, *The Cotton Manufacturers of Great Britain* (P.J.H., 1960). Ure represents an early Victorianism determined to be progressive in keeping with the advance of technology driven by steam. That sensibility was expressed forthrightly in *The Philosophy of Manufacture* (1835). Concerning labor in cotton mills, Ure noted that,

> all the hard work is done by the steam-engine, which leaves for the attendant no hard labor at all, and literally nothing to do in general. . . . These remarks certainly apply more especially to the labor of children in factories. . . . Consequently, if a child remains at this business twelve hours daily, he has nine hours of inaction. (pp. 309–310) So much nonsense has been uttered about the deformities and disease of factory children. (p. 350)

In the face of the blue books on the evils of factory work, Ure's own acknowledgment of a twelve-hour working day for children without a murmur of criticism seems Dickensian, or more exactly Gradgrindian. However, Ure's words were written before Dickens and show that reality anticipated fiction in the nineteenth century. Child welfare ran a poor second to profit in the early decades.

Robert Lowe (1811–1892)

At the end of a long and pugnacious life in public affairs this son of a Nottinghamshire person became Viscount Sherbrooke in 1880. A brilliant man who thrived on contentiousness, Lowe brought to his influential role in public affairs the view that government should play only a modest role in people's lives. He also brought the presumption that the poor were not reliable or trustworthy, a view not much better than his withering opinion of all but the most intelligent of his contemporaries (Sylvester, 1974). Although generally insensitive to the plight of the downtrodden, Lowe adopted the children of a murdered woman in whose legal procedures Lowe participated during his Australian years, 1842–1850. Lowe's effectiveness as a combatant in public affairs makes him noteworthy, beyond his brilliance, insufferability, and appearance (he was an albino).

Like the leaders of his era Robert Lowe subscribed to a rationalism he hoped to see prevail in public affairs, a desire to see the quality of human life improved without resorting to government as the means, and an aversion to public expenditures beyond the minimum. In the latter instance, Lowe's impact on the lives of other people's children was considerable; an insistence on "payment for results" led to poor schooling becoming poorer, and teachers and pupils suffered a degree of constriction in their respective roles. Inspectors (HMIs) begun a century or more of visits and evaluation that, initially, brought educational progress to a standstill and encouraged mindless memorization far into the twentieth century. Finally, some of the blame for delay in developing secondary education can be laid at Lowe's door, according Sylvester (1974).

In relation to the degeneracy scare and the health of children in primary schools, Lowe's influence delayed evolution of public policy and the eventual use of schooling as an opportunity to improve health and nutrition. Not until the turn of the century would the collection of children in classrooms be seen and an opportunity to address major health problems through constructive legislation. Even then, clinical attention required creative use of the statutes. Accordingly, the process of moving to public acceptance of children's health as a self-evident matter of collective welfare may be seen as one in which reactionary values were episodically altered by innovations. The legislative initiatives of the early twentieth century were by no means prefigured in the public dialogue of the Victorian years.

Ralph Lingen (1819–1905)

Paralleling Robert Lowe's career, but perhaps more narrowly focused on the bureaucratic machinery of mid-nineteenth century government, was the role of Ralph Lingen. Entering government after Oxford and Lincoln's Inn he succeeded Dr. James Kay-Shuttleworth, who resigned in 1849. For twenty years Lingen affected the processes by which Kay-Shuttleworth had sought to broaden support for public education. His actions were, according to Bishop (1968), excessively influenced by a legalistic propensity to follow principle whatever the impractical consequences. As a consequence, grants to schools were shrunk by overzealous interpretation of the principle of payment for results. Teachers and headmasters were kept at a distance, and inspectors of schools (HMIs) were required to be parsimonious and pettifogging in their search for compliance with performance criteria. The inspectors also suffered; their initial lack of personal experience with elementary school children was compounded by Lingen's abandonment of the gatherings of inspectors at which they had previously compared notes. Whitehall bureaucrats were held to rather less rigorous standards than those in the field, inspectors and teachers, for example. Bishop (1968) cites memoirs indicating a very brief attendance and frequent absence by those who dealt with requests for payment. Inquiries from inspectors and school people were thought impertinent and intrusive. As a result, the welfare and instruction of the young, and the opportunity for practical experience to inform government policy, shriveled during the twenty years of Lingen's tenure, 1849–1869. After his period as secretary to the Committee of Council Lingen moved on to the Treasury and was, subsequently, knighted.

Private Philanthropy

The social complex of piety, sympathy, and organization described by Prochaska (1988) as "the voluntary impulse," did much to set the tone of philanthropy (Prochaska, 1970). In many ways it set the values recognized more formally in public philosophy and in the rationalizing of services to poor families. In the decades before the period addressed in this work, Jonas Hanway had founded the Marine Society (whose records contributed to the study of heights by Floud, Gregory, and Wachter in 1990), and Thomas Bernard and others established the Society for Bettering the Condition and Increasing the Comforts of the Poor. In addition, there were unrecorded acts of charity in the form of gifts of food and clothing at the kitchen door. Prochaska (1990) describes the range of charitable acts as ranging from reactions to cholera outbreaks to assistance for thirsty horses and adds that the poor were charitable to each other. It should be noted that not every voluntary impulse led to a happy outcome. Elsewhere (Jordan, 1987b), I have described the disgrace of Captain Edward Brenton whose Children's Friend Society became a public scandal in 1841. Similarly, the originally high motives of later Victorian philanthropists who pioneered emigration to Canada and Australia for children were besmirched by public outcry over high-handed practices. Even so, the call for reform of child welfare led to eventual expansion of philanthropy from a personal to the societal level of organization and regulation. School meals and medical examinations in the twentieth century did a great deal to restore the health of children and may be traced to personal, charitable impulses in preceding generations, pioneered in many cases by women (Prochaska, 1980).

Government Action

The Victorian era is distinguished, in part, by the effective employment of government resources to inquire into social problems. Commissions formed by Parliament and by the executive held hearings and recommended action to legislators and ministers. In 1816, Robert Peel's factory inquiry began a sequence of studies. The year of the first reform law, 1832, also saw establishment of the commission examining the poor law. Based on a statute developed in the age of Elizabeth, this Tudor legislation, amended from time to time, provided a theory and a practice for welfare. Over-strained in the excesses of the early Industrial Revolution it received fundamental reform in its theory and became known as the new poor law. The change was an ideological emphasis on encouraging self-reliance. The workhouse became an instrument of the new policy in which external relief was deemphasized, and relief of low wages was superseded by relief of destitution among paupers.

Edwin Chadwick's Health of Towns report in 1842 addressed the infrastructure of urban life on which the health of young and old depended. Communicable diseases, overcrowding, and the value of accessible clean water and sewage were stressed. At the time, disease was thought to be due to miasma, a combination of foul smells and vapors, which generated disease. Interacting with the health complex was the primitive state of local government; for example, many industrial towns were dependent on the parish vestry of former times to address the problems caused by rapid growth of population.

A series of inquires into factory work, of which Althorpe's 1833 act was an early product, improved working conditions. In 1847, the

Ten Hours Act set some limits, and subsequent factory acts, like that of 1867, extended the reforms. In the case of the Ten Hours Bill, Thomas Babington Macauley, in 1846, eloquently connected health and national survival. Speaking in support of Fielden's bill he said, "Your overworked boys will become a feeble and ignoble race of men, the parents of a more feeble progeny . . . if we are forced to yield the foremost place among commercial nations we shall yield it to some people preeminently vigorous in body and mind." In connection with the theme of this essay, attending to growth of the young, "half-time" work by children continued into the twentieth century to the detriment of education and health. On this latter topic, in this brief and selective overview, there was the Public Health Act of 1848 and the more effective acts of 1866 and 1872 which gave explicit responsibility corresponding authority and obligation to local health authorities.

In 1887, alarmed at the conditions he observed in the general population, Lord Brabazon had called for a Royal Commission to study of the public's health. In the magazine, *Nineteenth Century,* Brabazon asserted that,

> If the results of the Commission be to show that all our fears are unfounded, and that our town population is the equal of the country, we shall have every cause to rejoice; but if, on the other hand, it be shown, as I firmly believe it will, that large numbers of the inhabitants of our cities are physically unfitted, though in the prime of life, to defend the country in time of war, or to carry on her work in peace.

Brabazon thought that a first step "towards reform of an evil which would ultimately lead to a degeneration of the race and to national effacement." Brabazon's 1887 request, following the recent success of the British association's 1884 study of stature and health, usually associated with the leadership of Francis Galton, was not unreasonable. Other surveys on a large scale included Porter's (1894) survey of 50,000 children in St. Louis during the winter months. Porter's study is interesting and prodigious, but it was denounced by Karl Pearson (1894) on the hitherto unprecedented grounds that it lacked a theoretical component. Pearson was no less critical of British "statistical dilettanti," as he termed them. Such criticism might have emerged from the activities of the British Association's anthropometric committee whose enthusiasm for measuring led them to span their own members attending the Nottingham meeting in 1893. Warner (1896) had examined 50,000 children in London in the period 1892–1894 (Galton et al.,

1894): 30 percent of boys and 16 percent of girls were considered to be free of defects, and upper-class children were not exempted from health problems. However, Brabazon's call in 1887 for a study of physique was repeated years later by Karl Pearson in 1900 (Pearson, 1907) and then by Bray seven years after that. The closest Britain has come to an anthropometric survey has lain in the analyses of data from the 1945, 1958, and 1970 national birth cohorts; however, their objectives have been primarily social, and physical data has been a secondary matter. The 1966 report of Tanner, Whitehouse, and Takaishi has been a vital source of information on physical development, as have the 1980 survey of Rosenbaum et al. (1985) and Rona and Chinn (1987).

The tenor of the times was less a matter of viewing the condition of the residuum as "moral" failure than it had been. Also, it was no longer the style that facts should be piled upon facts in the tradition of the early medico-social reformers. The National Association for the Promotion of Social Science had run its course as the think-tank for reformers. It had been replaced by specialized professional groups, the bureaucracy of the Charity Organization Society, and by the writings of people who were analytic and not merely descriptive. The tradition of philanthropy in the formation of public policy as an extragovernmental function persisted. Helen Bosanquet (1898) asserted three principles to guide charity. They were all phrased negatively as the avoidance of encouraging bad habits, interfering with the free movement of labor, and raising unrealistic expectations. Across the preceding decades, public affairs had absorbed Disraeli's style and Gladstone's approach to public affairs and personal philanthropy. Bureaucracy was now manned by shrewd and sophisticated men who ran complex offices with international agendas. As a result, government was averse to undertaking study of pressing problems; with a wary eye on the electorate politicians opposed new legislation and the possibility of higher local taxes ("rates").

With the debate on the Boer War an unceasing stream of articles came from Sir Frederick Maurice, Sir John E. Gorst, Frances Duchess of Warwickshire, Sidney Webb, and the Earl of Meath.

The Royal Commission on Physical Training (Scotland, 1902)

In 1902, the government of Arthur Balfour appointed a royal commission ostensibly to study physical training; in fact, it did something quite different, commissioning Matthew Hay and Leslie Mackenzie to do a survey of the physical condition of schoolchildren in Edinburgh and Aberdeen. The description of 600 Edinburgh children and 600 Aberdeen children, the testimony of 127 witnesses, and visits by the commissioners to Edinburgh, Aberdeen, Glasgow, and Portsmouth provided the evidence for the 1902 report. In general, the commission concluded that the health of children depended on nutrition, environment, and heredity and that attention to physical exercise in the absence of sufficient nutrition would be unproductive. Edinburgh children were found to have deteriorated health. Rippon-Seymour (1903) calculated from the data that one-third to one-fourth of the children needed immediate medical attention, with almost all of the Edinburgh girls examined showed "defect of the ear and throat." More critical was J. H. Vines (1903), in contrast, pointing out that the report drew faulty comparisons with other data sets some of which were gathered in 1877. He also noted the banality of reporting, "undeniable degeneration of individuals of the classes where food and environment are defective . . . gymnastic exercises will hardly benefit a half-starved child." To A. R. Hunt (1903) it was clear that good minds and healthy bodies were generated in the country and that, "the evolution of the human race will obviously not be promoted by the growth of cities, but will be impeded thereby."

Despite over-aged comparative data and samples perhaps misdrawn by social class level in Aberdeen and Edinburgh, the physical training report of 1902 placed emphasis on data and documented that poor health in schoolchildren was widespread; a report on the situation in England was called for.

The Interdepartmental Committee on Physical Deterioration

In 1903, the Royal College of Surgeons advised the Unionist government through the Secretary of State on the necessity for an inquiry. Their position was that "there is no need for a large inquiry into the national health" (*Report of the Interdepartmental Committee on Physical Deterioration,* 1903); however, should the government decide to conduct a study the college would nominate members for the study group. In consequence of the public debate, the Balfour government, in 1903, reluctantly named a mere committee, although the calls had been for a royal commission. In his memoirs the chairman, Sir Almeric Fitzroy (1925), recalled the interest expressed by Edward VII in the matter. However, Unionist attitudes prevailed, and the Duke of

Devonshire appointed the Interdepartmental Committee on Physical Degeneration. The membership consisted of civil servants and the Duke's protege at the Privy Council, Almeric Fitzroy; there were no physicians or representatives of local health bodies (Gilbert, 1965). In addition to Fitzroy (chair), the members were Colonel Fox, J. G. Legge (of whom Fitzroy formed a high opinion), H. M. Lindsell, Colonel Onslow, J. Struthers, Dr. J. F. W. Tatham, and Mr. E. H. Poole (secretary). The committee held hearings and sixty-eight witnesses provided data on children's health, some of which were employed in Chapter Four's figures on comparative heights. Not all the witnesses were useful: Mrs. Close spoke to the committee and droned on about her reminiscences of forty years before. The committee rendered its report in spring 1904 and, significantly, drew no conclusions about progressivism of poor health; rather, they moved on to advise remedial steps.

The work of the interdepartmental committee was followed by that of the interdepartmental committee on medical examinations and school meals in 1905. Later that year, the committee completed its work. In 1906, after a public campaign led by Sir John E. Gorst, an act permitted local school authorities to provide milk and meals to schoolchildren. This was a radical step brought about by consensus among politicians and the populace. It was not an act of progressive legislation motivated by constructive policy, however. It expressed the victory of determined people over the resistance of a fading liberal tradition exemplified by a reluctant administration. In 1908, laws affecting children were codified once more and extended to protect children from neglect, in legislation sometimes referred to as the *Children's Charter.*

With the passage of time and the progress of public debate, it had become apparent that poor health was a serious problem; but mortality rates had declined and fewer babies died. From the combination of statistics it appeared that people started life less at risk and lived longer. Thoughtful people inferred, correctly, that people started life with fair prospects, but failed to realize them for circumstantial rather than genetic reasons. The environment, not defective "germ plasm" or "cachexia Londoniensis," explained the health of the population. Tranter (1973) has contrasted the life expectancy of those born sixty years later. In the earlier period males had a life expectancy of 39.9 years; for the birth cohort 1901–1912 it had risen to 51.5 years. In the case of females the rise was from 41.9 years to 55.4 years.

Popular opinion saw the inefficiency of affairs in the conduct of the Boer War. Both radicals and conservatives saw that the domestic agenda of the nation required attention if national as well as individual interests were to flourish. To conservatives the need was a healthy generation to rule the waves and police an empire. To radicals the challenge was to develop a healthy generation not devoured by Ure's (1835) "Mighty Moloch of Steam." To reach that goal, the prevailing inefficiency of affairs needed to be replaced by efficiency. The Fabians prescribed reforms and provided grandiose schemes for the prevailing political parties. The Fabians had hopes for a political party based on national efficiency. Sidney and Beatrice Webb, George Bernard Shaw, Bertrand Russell and H. G. Wells would provide the policy. The plan expired when, bubblelike, it touched reality. To the present-day observer, one of the interesting aspects was the nascent totalitarianism in the cult of efficiency, eugenics, and political leadership unimpeded by democratic attitudes (Rose, 1986). In that value complex may be glimpsed the immanent excesses of the 1930s and 1940s.

The Royal Commission on the Poor Laws and Relief of Distress

In the period, 1905–1909, a distinguished group of commissioners worked for thirty-eight months beginning December 4, 1905, to create one of the more voluminous blue books. Originated by the Balfour administration, its charge was to look into the working of laws governing "the relief of poor persons in the United Kingdom," and into "the means outside the Poor Laws for meeting distress arising from want of employment particularly during periods of severe industrial depression."

The commission consisted of people from a wide variety of backgrounds and was chaired by Lord George Hamilton. Among the members were Charles Booth, Dr. Arthur H. Downes, George Lansbury, Helen Bosanquet, Beatrice Webb, and Octavia Hill. The report of the majority of the committee ran to 1,200 pages, and that of the minority of 400–500 pages.

The majority report contained many proposals. Those relevant to youth included

1. Raising the school-leaving age for boys to fifteen.
2. Encouragement of a "continuous system of physical drill."
3. Promotion of career and vocational guidance.
4. Modification of the elementary curriculum to reduce its literary and diffuse character and to encourage manual training.
5. Elimination of workhouse placement of children.

Other aspects of the majority report included

1. Better classification of the unemployed leading to "segregation of the loafer" in a "course of severe discipline and training."
2. Promotion of emigration.
3. Public works schemes developed by local authorities to be subvented not by government grants but by government loans, a system employed during the 1863 Cotton Famine.
4. More precise qualifications for Poor Law officers.
5. Classification of the indoor (workhouse) poor by age, gender, and disability.
6. Improved health care for Poor Law recipients.
7. Establishment of labor exchanges following the German model.
8. Resistance to unemployment insurance as a "universal compulsory system."
9. Advocacy of "labor colonies," on a "guarded" basis.

Eras of Progressivism

Bureaucracy

The scope of government in the early nineteenth century was narrow. A small bureaucracy had much in common with the earliest departures from government as an extended form of the king's household. The monarch would grant pensions, and parliament would vote budgets based on modest incursions into John Bull's pocket, usually through excise taxes. Bureaucracy consisted of a few appointees, in the early days, men of means who would devote a few hours a day to public service aided by a few well-chosen clerks. McGregor (1957) considered the appointment of naval Captain Fitzroy to open a meteorological service in 1855 to be a major step. It followed by eighteen years establishment of the geological survey in 1837. In the case of the assistant commissioners appointed to study working conditions in factories and mines about that time, the public interest was well served at midcentury by Hugh Seymour Tremenheere, Leonard Horner, Thomas Southwood Smith, William Farr, and the brothers John and James Kay (Shuttleworth). Quite invisible, in contrast, were the half-pay naval officers who, according to MacDonagh (1955), reformed the laws which protected emigrants at sea in the period 1833–1850.

At a more detailed level of analysis have been phases of thought and action across the nineteenth century. In Hennock's (1976) view, there had been two periods of progressive social thought that presaged the reforms affecting the poor: the 1860s and the 1880s. He added the observation that such conceptual progress need not coincide with periods of progressive legislation. To MacDonagh (1958) there were five stages of legislative-administrative progressivism. The first stage was exposure of a social evil, followed by realization that earlier legislation had failed. In the third stage executive officers empowered to enforce statutes came on to the scene in a focused, centralized bureau. With experience, they came to see remediation of problems as a continuing process of adjustments. In the final stage, observed MacDonagh, they undertook to develop information from which policy could be deduced or induced. In MacDonagh's view his model applied particularly to the period 1825–1875. Nine years before, Greaves (1947) perceived three stages of public philosophy. Originating in the eighteenth century was the phase of "oligarchic administration and interfering paternalism." With the nineteenth century came the "regulatory state," which was followed by the social service democracy of the twentieth century.

Both MacDonagh's and Greaves' formulations followed the formulation of the relationship between "popular opinion" and the formulation of laws in the nineteenth century set forth by A. V. Dicey (1905). In a series of lectures at Harvard University Dicey set forth the view that the relationship between evolution of new legislation and the mind of the public had been approximate, at best, over the course of the nineteenth century. The chief reason was that British law had been the accretion of juridical solutions based on equity to practical problems. Blackstone's works codified reactive court opinions and legal deductions about private and public interests. There had been no process of working-out or formulations of a philosophy of law beyond the scope of presented problems. In Dicey's view, Jeremy Bentham (1748–1832) was the first philosopher of British law. His entry into the forum of public philosophy ended, in Dicey's view, a period of negative conservatism precipitated by the fear of Jacobinism, and frozen juridically by the views of Lord Eldon. Dicey credited Bentham with ending "legislative timidity," "stagnation," and "reactionary legislation." He formulated the first three decades of the nineteenth century as "the Period of Old Toryism or Legislative Quiescence." It was followed by a half-century of "Benthamism or Individualism" from 1825 to 1870. The last three decades to 1900 Dicey characterized as a "Period of Collectivism." It is interesting to note that the three periods are approximately the same length, and the initial and final years are tidy but arbitrary.

The ethos, or prevailing value, of the first period was the appearance of humanitarianism whose object was the relief of pain, suffering, and oppression. Through that community-shared value men of otherwise irreconcilable beliefs in (e.g.) religion worked together.

In the second phase, underlying Bentham's utilitarian view, was the idea that the formulation of legislation could be scientific. A second notion was that there was one overriding end to society, the greatest good for the greatest number of people. A third conviction was that every person is the best judge of his or her interests. It may well be that this last point was the influential element because it led to a kind of collective individualism acceptable to Victorian men of influence.

In the third, collective period the prime values emerged from a more self-conscious view of society as a whole. It may well be that the brief but seminal affairs of the National Association for the Promotion of Social Science infused a broader view of the life of Victoria's Britain into public affairs. The working class were to be educated, a process leading to greater self-awareness and powers of analysis. Robert Lowe is credited with the aphorism that society had better educate its new masters—a process institutionalized by Forster's 1870 Elementary Education Act and by the Second Reform Act of 1867 extending the franchise.

The informality and duplication of private philanthropy had led to formation of the Charity Organization Society. Its view of poverty as the moral failure of individuals led to casework and a degree of bureaucraticism of private philanthropy and so to a view of the larger whole. Centralization is an apparently inescapable aspect of evolving bureaucracies, and so the collectivization of life became an implicit component of the late nineteenth century outlook. Asa Briggs (1968) quoted Joseph Chamberlain of Birmingham, whose words reflected the ethos of the times when he spoke of "new conceptions of public duty, new developments of social enterprise, new estimates of the natural obligations of the community to one another." Coinciding with the peak of Britain's economic and political hegemony collectivism was a response to a national agenda. From the point of view of this work there is the outlook of Lord Brabazon, who was struck by the French defeat by Germany in 1870 as an expression of German collective health and fitness (Brabazon, 1887). The 1906 school meals act was an early twentieth century expression of the welfare state; that is, it expressed the view that the nourishment of children was in the collective interest of all individuals. However, it should be noted that the Unionist government of the first decade wanted no increases in taxation. Their position was out of step with both public opinion and the new public philosophy or consensus. In 1889, the London School Board conducted the first of three studies, and on the basis of findings added in 1894 and 1898 formed a policy designed to feed poor children (Mac-Namara, 1904). However, it remained for the 1911 National Health Insurance Act to be the full expression of the new sensibilities as national policy on behalf of the poor recognizable to the modern mind.

Thus, the period ending in the brilliant summer of 1914 had reached the stage of recognizing that John Bull's health and existence elevated above the level of catastrophe was in the national interest. From a diverse, and irreconcilable range of points of view socialists and imperialists asserted that the health of the individual equaled the health of the nation. Little children in poor health would become unhealthy adults. Either because good health and a modicum of welfare were a political right or because emerging nationalism required a measured response delivered by fit young men reared, in turn, by healthy, educated mothers, the British nation achieved consensus. There was agreement that child health and family integrity should be strengthened. From threads of concern going back into the nineteenth century, an agenda of public welfare evolved in the twentieth century.

In offering this overview of signal occurrences and people we should view the course of events as far from inevitable. Goldthorpe (1962) pointed out that to view events and their sequence as requiring mere enumeration to be understood is to fall into the stance of what sociologists term *functionalism;* it is the assumption that a society perceives a problem and moves to correct it. This view slights the agendas of ideologues and the realities of political battles won and lost. Societies do not automatically respond to their needs; needs themselves are frequently post-dictive constructs whose obviousness lies in retrospection. Adjustments arrived at were not the alternative, and one perennial choice is to do nothing at all. Thus, we have traced social thought, but offer the caution that other figures, other solutions, might have prevailed; and no solutions might have evolved. To some extent, that tendency is overrun by events and by conditions reaching intolerable degrees of unpleasantness.

There is no teleology, or innate tendency for society to move towards a goal, and attainment of perfectionism in particular. That a degree of ameliorism had been reached by 1910 was fortuitous, in terms of the manpower needs of 1916 and the bottomless demands of trench warfare. In those terms, the conditions of the 1914–1918 war of attrition were set by the Prussian Law of 1828, which proscribed factory work and prescribed physical fitness (Jordan, 1987b) and by the revised British poor law of 1834 and the education and housing acts of later decades. They contributed to lessening the stress endured by the poor and working class in their formative years. Not until a second war, that of 1939–1945, would the comprehensive view of welfare and health be set forth in the Beveridge Report of 1944. By midcentury, however, an exhausted economy and drained treasury were no longer consonant with the value and necessity of comprehensive health, education, and welfare services. That such services were provided shows, as in the case of Sri Lanka (Ceylon) in later decades, that determination and being resolute in matters of child welfare are the more critical elements.

Discussion

Data and Ideology

*I*t is now appropriate to evaluate the evidence marshalled to address the question of whether health, especially that of the young, degenerated, and did so progressively, across the nineteenth century. In the ideal analysis of height we would have baseline data on a phenomenon, a treatment or experience ensues, and the subsequent state is compared with the baseline. Contemporary design allows us to incorporate several treatments and appraise the outcomes for subgroups of subjects. Clearly, there are no baseline data. Rather, I have emphasized nineteenth century data by indexing numerical data to that of the Galton committee in 1883. It has been possible to formulate subsets of people by gender and sociooccupational level. For public school boys studied by Galton in 1876, and for the factory boys and girls examined by Samuel Stanway in 1832, the sociooccupational level is clear; for some other groups it is probable that they should be viewed as heterogeneous, to say the least. Galton's subjects at the International Health Exhibition, who were probably middle class, with a mixture of working-class people, exemplify the idea.

An observation on the data sets employed is that they are longitudinal in terms of the period from George III to George V. However, in auxology, longitudinal generally refers to repeated measures on the same subjects, an approach not evident in the literature of the period until Boulton's fleeting reference in 1880 to ten-year, prospective group data. The data presented here are archival, and they are also cross

245

sectional. That is, they consist of measurements taken once from subjects of different ages in the same group. This inescapable fact lessens
the significance of the data, but does not invalidate it wholly. This
point is supported by the lack of empirical data in typical discussions
of the degeneracy question.

From the point of view of the person seeking to scan the nine-
teenth century broadly there is the problem of lacunae. Floud and
Wachter (1982) reconstructed data on boys in the Marine Society, and
I reconstructed data on juvenile and adult prisoners transported to
Australia in the 1820s, 1830s, and 1840s (Jordan, 1985; 1987a; 1990b).
In the first half of the nineteenth century data exist only sporadically,
and the first sixty years are best summarized at intervals of a decade.
In contrast, the years from 1870 to 1914 are full of data sets, some of
which are both national and large. An additional aspect in this latter
phase is the explicit connection to social policy. It is evident in the report of the physical deterioration interdepartmental report of 1904, for
example, in similar studies in Glasgow and Edinburgh and in the three
studies by the London Board of Education around the turn of the century (MacNamara, 1904).

Another aspect of archival data sets is that they frequently are
site specific. That is, they represent a given microhabitat. Examples
are the children growing up in Cock and Pie Fields in the slums of London. A rather different microhabitat is that of Quaker boys growing up
in York and described by R. Clark to Galton's 1883 committee. This
matter of clarifying the microhabitat or geographic origins for nineteenth century data sets is approached, but not managed completely,
in my formulation of convict boys' series by designating birth in
England, Scotland, Wales, or Ireland.

A policy statement or act is a statement based on conviction
propounded in an attempt to regulate human behavior or to relieve an
inequity. People arrive at firm and stable beliefs in many ways; for
some, revelation provides the necessary preparation, but for people
in public life, facts—or what are held to be the most valid generaliza-
tions from facts—provide a logical basis. From the time of the commentaries on the Bills of Mortality by John Graunt in the seventeenth
century and by William Petty in the eighteenth, the tradition has been,
increasingly, to derive policy from empiricism, rather than ideology.
After the Enlightenment, western Europe emphasized empiricism increasingly. In France, de Montbéliard provided data on the growth of a
single individual, his son; in early nineteenth century France, Benoiton de Chateauneuf and Villermé, together with Quetelet in Belgium,

extended the scope of inquiry from one subject to the epidemiology of health, sickness, and death.

In Britain, the Bashaws of Somerset House, as the commissioners were known, examined the operation of the Poor Laws (1834) and Dr. James Kay of Manchester wrote *The Moral and Physical Condition of the Working Classes Employed in the Cotton Manufacture in Manchester* (1832). Relatively unknown due to its obscure place of publication is Leonard Horner's 1837 report of the heights of 16,000 children in the factory districts of the North, primarily ("Practical Application of Physiological Facts," 1837). Chadwick's great study of the health of towns (1842), and the commissions inquiring into the employment of women and children piled fact upon fact. Shortly after, in 1845, Friedrich Engels wrote his polemic, *Condition of the Working Class in England*, drawing to no small degree on the 1832 work of another, former, Manchester resident, Dr. James Kay.

By midcentury two generations of people of conscience, and those without that encumbrance but interested in public affairs, had received a substantial body of facts concerning child and adult health. The debacle of the Crimea and the poor health of the troops revealed by Florence Nightingale and *The Times* raised the public's awareness of the health problems of the working class. In that same period a number of physicians in the tradition of Thomas Southwood Smith, especially William Farr and Charles Roberts, published studies of human growth emphasizing comparative heights.

A connection to public policy important for the question of how policy evolved was the practice of certifying children to work in factories. Youngsters adjudged to be thirteen were, on close inspection, frequently not that age, and only a birth certificate would suffice. The essential point of the issue was that the public good was served only by strict appraisal of the health and development of those seeking to enter the work force. In 1875, Dr. Steet reported on his study of would-be messengers for the telegraph service. This study resembles twentieth century studies of the work force because its tone is quite contemporary in outlook. In this period, the anthropologist John Beddoe was active, examining the somatypology of people in various regions of the British Isles. The great accomplishment of the period was the British Association study led by Francis Galton (1884) in its last five years. In that inquiry, 50,000 people in all walks of life were measured and their strength and sensory acuity assessed. A few years later, Galton acquired another large corpus of data from people visiting the Health Exhibition in South Kensington in 1885. In passing, it is interesting to note that much of the data set remained unanalyzed until the twentieth century (Johnson et al. 1985).

Significant in the evolution of ideology is the policy study of G. Udney Yule, published in 1899. In his study of changes in pauperism over two decades Yule laboriously calculated regression equations, and sophisticated analyses entered the policy scene. In Yule's 1899 study are copious amounts of data, rigorous analyses in an idiom acceptable today (Jordan, 1982; 1983) and conclusions buttressed by the combination of extensive information and careful study. Ideologically, 1890 saw the appearance of a major work in the welfare of poor families, Salvation Army-founder General William Booth's *In Darkest England, and the Way Out*. In this passionate volume, Booth set forth a minimum standard that was touched on in Chapter Five; there is Dr. William Aitken's (1862) citation of the value of a physical assessment of army recruits. Dr. Aitken made his case by the analogy of careful judgment in the care of a, "useful dog or valuable horse." Four decades later, General William Booth set a guide for welfare of the working man, "it is by standard of the London Cab Horse" (Booth, 1890, p. 19). By that analogy, which he traced back to Thomas Carlyle, Booth sought to set a minimum standard of "food, shelter and work . . . at present absolutely unattainable by millions." In 1859, the analogy had been cited by Mary Bayly in *Ragged Homes and How to Mend Them*; a brickmaker told her, "the horse employed in our brickyard is brought in at six o'clock in the morning, he has a proper time for rest in the day, and he is always taken off again at six in the evening; but the men must work fifteen and sixteen hour a day to get a living out of it."

By the time the new century began, expectations for the quality of major studies were high. The Interdepartmental Committee on Physical Degeneration of 1904 was a failure in some respects. It had little original data to offer beyond materials snatched from the Johanna Street School, although it assuaged public fears about inevitable progression of ill health from generation to generation. The Royal Commission on Physical Training (Scotland) had contributed to the same general sense of possible reversal of ill health. The Education Act of 1907 set the stage for meals and medical services in the schools. Although slightly beyond our period, the Carnegie report on the health of women and children in Scotland (Mackenzie, 1917) should be mentioned. That work documented how much more acute the problems were in Scotland. Smout (1986) has demonstrated how serious were the problems of housing and health in Scotland, and their correlates, child health and growth, remained a problem well into the twentieth century.

In tracing the accretion of knowledge about the health of the population it is important to avoid the error of overestimating the importance of an increasing pile of blue books, speeches to the National Association for the Promotion of Social Science, and reports in the *Journal of the Royal Statistical Society*. As James Douglas (1982) pointed out, facts are not inherently persuasive, and statistics may be received with groans and glassy stares. It will be recalled that Douglas cited the instance of an enlightened politician who referred to statistical information as the poison of human research that afflicts government commissions and departments.

Information formed people's sensibilities across the decades; however, those predispositions required the catalyst of an advocate in the form of an agent or an organization with an agenda to be expressed in public policy as law. We have listed several such individual reformers, and to our list of organizations we can add the nascent Labour Party and its emerging agenda. Two strands may be discerned; one was the search for economic security and a higher standard of living expressed in every workingmen's movement. The other was the ideological note caught by the Fabian socialists and expressed in its extreme form by the Marxists. Of the two, the Fabians were more influential co-opting christians pursuing the social gospel and middle-class intellectuals with high indignation quotients. Trade unionists tended to see the bread and butter issues and provided empirical validity for the ideology of the intelligentsia. Together, they pursued the agenda of fading Liberalism after our period had drawn to a close. Lloyd George's Liberal reforms in the first decade of the twentieth century can be viewed as successful, enlightened conservatism in the German style, or as proto-Marxism subject to delay, but eventually irresistible, in the long view. I incline to the former.

In Lloyd George's agenda of pensions and unemployment insurance we see the culmination of a century of evolving public philosophy. Decade by decade, concessions were extracted from the privileged. In 1868, W. R. Gregg had set forth the position of the favored quite squarely,

> democracy is every year advancing in power, and claiming the supreme
> right to govern and to guide:—and democracy means the management
> and control of social arrangements by the least educated classes,—by

those least trained to foresee or measure consequences,—least acquainted with the fearfully rigid laws of hereditary transmission,—least habituated to repress desires, or to forego immediate enjoyment for future and remote good.

But rising levels of education demonstrated to the common people that their powers of analysis were quite as good as their masters', and that it was time to render a bill of accounting long past due. Today, all nations place child health on the list of national resources. Despite its preindustrialized state and a rate of population growth at a very modern pace, Sri Lanka (Ceylon) found it possible to reduce infant mortality and raise levels of child health. Public policy in all countries now posits minimum expectations for children's growth that exceed the ambitions of our Victorian predecessors.

The earliest notations of degeneracy were based on observed deterioration of health and physique in the early decades of the nineteenth century. Overlying the clinical observations of public health experts and concerned middle-class people was the worry that the changes would be transmitted by heredity and that the status of the population was worsening generation by generation. With the passage of time, the corollaries of social disorganization, child labor, and poor parenting became apparent. However, the absence of a model of genetics left observers at the mercy of their observations compounded by their worst fears.

The arrival of Darwinian views on the mutation of organisms complicated the picture; social Darwinism was added to the biological picture, and the proliferating plebs was seen leading the way to a eugenical armageddon. If the fittest were surviving, for what were they fit, since they appeared more fecund and near feral to their social betters? That proposition, mutatis mutandis, survived the eugenics movement, and may still be heard today, occasionally.

A feature of the concept of degeneration as it changed across the decades was its vagueness. We have mentioned the continental theorists and the lack of a parallel in British thought (see Jordan, 1987a, for de Tocqueville's views). In Britain, *degeneracy* became a word useful for explaining mere changes. Thus, Professor E. R. Lankester (1880) used the term to explain changes in linguistics that we would see as inevitable, and neither good nor bad ("degeneracy"). Lankester also used the term to describe the condition of Australian peoples, Bushmen, and the inhabitants of Tierra del Fuego. Today, we regard their way of life as examples of ingenious adaptation to an appalling ecology for homo sapiens. The term *degeneracy* was also used to explain crime, especially in the writings of Cesare Lombroso. He insisted that he could discern stigmata of degeneracy into criminality and even found geniuses at risk for such primeval traits.

The Degeneracy Question

Consideration of the state of housing and its functional counterpart, accommodation, the high rate of child and adult mortality and the poor health of working people certainly indicates a nidus of sociomedical problems in the nineteenth century. Urbanization increased the problems and leads to the conclusion that no one exaggerated the poor state of individual and collective health. Commentators of the period formulated the observable, countable problems within their intellectual framework. Disease was understood largely in terms of its symptoms and their palliation. Genetics was a superficial combination of observed transmission of traits, but with little appreciation of what was transmitted directly as opposed to being evinced by interaction with particular environments.

Accordingly, to the best minds until the end of the century, there was a degeneracy crisis; that is, a state of society in which stature declined, disease expanded, and things were getting worse decade by decade. The absence of comprehensive data compounded the difficulties, and techniques of data analysis beyond counting were slow to develop. Had critical data been available, and had the zeitgeist encouraged mathematical-statistical techniques, the worriers might have been comforted, but only a little. But the times and fiscal conservatism ran against a comprehensive study of the health of the nation. And yet the outlines of such a study were clear, and observers could sketch the characteristics necessary to generate the requisite data. In 1903, the Royal College of Surgeons advised the Home Secretary that,

> Any investigation which does not take into account the condition of the labouring classes in the great industries of the country must necessarily give a very erroneous impression of the physique of these classes. The increase in the rate of wages in all forms of labour to that extent diminishes the attractions of a military career for those engaged in regular labour, and leads to a proportionally larger number of the "unemployed" offering themselves for service in the army. It is obvious that the casual labourers of the large towns represent the poorest portion of the population, amongst whom the lowest standard of physique would be found:

but the College is not in possession of any evidence which satisfies it that there is any physical degeneration of the urban population generally. Moreover, the fact that the urban death-rate has declined between 5 and 6 per thousand, and now more closely approximates that of the rural population makes it unlikely that such deterioration is taking place.

The question of what means are available for remedying existing defects in and improving the national health may, perhaps, be briefly summed up as those which tend to diminish poverty. At the same time, the College desires to point out that very great changes in the conditions of life have taken place during the last fifty years, the effects of some of which are not yet determined. Among these should be considered the alterations in character of the food, the compulsory education and confinement in schools of young children, and the altered conditions of female labour in towns. (*Report of the Royal College of Surgeons of England*, 1903)

Recalling the data of earlier chapters reminds us that the density of housing declined slowly, the mortality rate improved, tuberculosis and scarlet fever slowly subsided, and stature began to improve.

The fundamental and refractory element, of course, was not the observable degree of social discontinuity as national wealth exploded across the decades and slowly trickled into the lives of ordinary people. It was the haunting fear that the observably poor state of health would inevitably be transmitted. The question was complicated by the tendency to include morality, so that criminals—as created by the harsh codes of the time—seemed likely to breed criminal children by transmitting a moral defect through whatever mysterious process transmitted blue eyes or red hair. Today, we conclude that the degeneracy question was part fact—the bio-social data—and part imagination.

Health did not degenerate generation by generation through genetic mechanisms. On the other hand, it improved slightly and selectively in the period 1805–1914, but radical improvement came in later years (see Winter, 1979; 1982a; 1982b). The absence of an intellectual framework to separate health from morality, and genetics from descriptive statistics, did not exist. Only with adoption of a value-free approach to problems might amelioration have evolved as an autonomous theme; similarly, the subsequent development of mathematical models of genetics separated fact from fancy. However, even today it is hard for people to discuss AIDS and the HIV virus without the intrusion of censorious attitudes toward homosexuality. For the Victorians, the possibility of segregating the morality of the complex was slim and quite unnecessary. The widespread evidence of alcoholism and its social consequences led them to reduce the etiology to moral failure. Moral rejuvenation was the known way to end abuse of alcohol and its ramifications. Immorality was the perceived basis of disorganization within families, and so it was necessary to reclaim the drunkard from irresponsibility—itself a moral failure. Of course, moral reclamation of drunkards by Father Matthew of Cork and others led to rejuvenation, however temporary, of individuals' lives and those of their dependents. In the case of alcoholism, today's views concede that susceptibility to alcohol may well have a hereditary component.

However current the Victorians were on that score, they overestimated the progressive nature of the problems they observed. In the matter of stature, the data of Chapter Six suggest that heights were relatively stable within social groups, and that those of lowest stature registered slow improvement but not equality with the more favored. Even into the middle of the twentieth century and later (Rosenbaum et al, 1985), social class differences in adults' height were observable. In Fogel et al.'s (1983) view, the lowest heights of working class boys were probably reached in the period 1790–1810, and the drop at that time was relieved by 1820. Fogel and colleagues concluded that heights declined after 1838 for two decades. Based on the research of Floud, Wachter, and Gregory, Floud (1983) concluded that improvements in nutrition outweighed the deterioration in the Victorian environment.

Environmentalism has never quite been the dichotomous counterpart to nativism, since the uterus in which genes begin their awesome task of building a baby is an environment. The placenta grows ahead of the fetus in nutritive capacity so that the genetic code is matched, ideally, by a supply of building materials. A poor Victorian mother might have a small baby for reasons embedded in the uterine environment, not the chromosomes. Similarly, the familial instances of tuberculosis, in parents and children, can be explained parsimoniously by overcrowding and breathing the same air. Thus, environmentalism modestly formulated can explain cross-generational health without resource to genetics. Clearly, some conditions might be worse in one generation than in its predecessor. But that too can be formulated as an environment deteriorating across generations. The period of the French wars early in the nineteenth century created food problems. The end of hostilities created economic dislocation. The corn laws compounded the problems so that the poor became poorer. The Spitalfields weavers illustrate the case of a population whose economic experience led to increasing ill-health and reliance on charity.

Malignant, declining circumstances accounted for their wretched lot, with progressive decline across the generations in the social context being sufficient explanation; poverty, not moral failure or genetics, was the core of their problem.

The same environmentalism led to improvements across the nineteenth century, and the twentieth century consolidated the slow gains through constructive social policies. Poor children received school meals and health services and so grew into a stronger, taller generation than their forefathers. The genetic pool from which all drew their developmental blueprints did not change. Healthy environments at home, school, and in the community allowed genetic potentials to be more fully realized.

It is to the credit of succeeding generations of Victorians that people of conscience faced the correlates of rapid urbanization, overcrowding, malnourishment, disease, and death, with the limited intellectual and political tools at their disposal. Decade by decade, those tools and the formulation of the problems improved. The health of present-day Britons is excellent and their habitus is sound due to the courage and conscientiousness of their Victorian and Edwardian (Porter, 1991) ancestors. Their reforming zeal laid the foundation for twentieth century innovations in social policy and practice.

Stress

Finally, we return to the fundamental topic of this work, *stress* in the lives of the young. It is evident that the turmoil of the late eighteenth and early nineteenth centuries placed young people under stress. The most obvious form was factory work, followed by urbanization and its corollaries: overcrowding, infant mortality, and disease. Less obvious and ill-understood was the effect of socio-economic stress on the constitution of the collective population. It appeared that an acquired poor constitution would be transmitted as hereditary degeneracy. The worry was not ill-founded, although the problem was not genetic, but generations suffered until social reform redressed the circumstances of life. That process itself took several decades, and eventually created the present, generally satisfactory state in Britain.

As we have seen in Chapters One and Two, that process evolved by stages. It began with the insight, frequently disputed by articulate writers, that the problems were other than traditional. The Benthamites gathered their statistics and laid out their tables. Slowly, an analytic frame of mind evolved into a prescriptive approach.

However, the pace of evolution in policy could not proceed faster than the broader process of intellectual evolution in the formulation of problems, such as disease, and the nexus of biological change, such as evolution and genetics. The Victorian mind could generate the vague generalization of degeneracy; but the term was not empirical and analytic, since phenomena could not be explicated through mechanisms of biological change and diversification. Degeneracy retained a metaphoric quality illustrated with numbers from time to time, but there was no data-language of unambiguous terms or conventions in which views could be exchanged and in which testable hypotheses could emerge. More broadly put, some thoughts or concepts are unthinkable until the way of viewing the world permits, and until key concepts clarify ambiguities. At the same time, maturity of a nexus of thought probably prevents half-baked notions from seeing the light of day. Nineteenth century physics developed a complex around the nonexistent N-ray, a blind alley entered in the early, descriptive phase of studying X-rays. Current struggles with cosmology illustrate the problems in our generation.

The concept of stress illuminates to a degree the processes that make social change harmful at times. In the case of Victorian Britain and impact of two world wars in the twentieth century, economic stress was not eliminated, but has been prevented from evolving into social deterioration on a collective scale by enlightenment of public policy, generation by generation.

Appendix 1:
Data Sets of Heights

MALES

ID	WORK'G CLASS	YEAR COLLECTED	YEAR PUBLISHED	AUTHOR(S) OF PUBLICATION	DESCRIPTION OF SUBJECTS IN DATA SET
1	YES	1807	1982	WACHTER & TRUSELL	CHATHAM MARINES
2	YES	1816	1817	ARMY CONTRACTOR	LANARK HIGHLAND LOCAL MILITIA
3	YES	1817	1817	ARMY CONTRACTOR	EDINBURGH MILITIA
4	YES	1832	1833	STANWAY	FACTORY BOYS
5	YES	1832	1833	STANWAY	NON-FACTORY BOYS
6	YES	1833	1985	JORDAN	FRANCES CHARLOTTE BOYS A
7	YES	1837	1985	JORDAN	A & B BOYS
8	YES	1837	1837	HORNER-HARRISON	PRESTON WORKING CLASS
9	YES	1837	1837	HORNER-72 DOCTORS	YORKSHIRE & LANCASHIRE
10	YES	1838	1985	JORDAN	CONVICT BOYS ENGLAND-NON LONDON
11	YES	1838	1985	JORDAN	CONVICTS BOYS SCOTLAND
12	YES	1838	1985	JORDAN	CONVICTS BOYS IRELAND
13	YES	1838	1985	JORDAN	CONVICTS BOYS ALL
14	YES	1840	1977	GANDEVIA	CONVICT BOYS-LONDON
15	YES	1840	1977	GANDEVIA	CONVICT BOYS-NON LONDON
16	YES	1840	1977	GANDEVIA	CONVICT BOYS SCOTLAND
17	YES	1840	1977	GANDEVIA	CONVICT BOYS IRELAND
18	YES	1840	1977	GANDEVIA	CONVICTS: B. LONDON
19	YES	1841	1842	SYMONS	YORKSHIRE MINE BOYS
20	YES	1841	1982	FLOUD & WACHTER	MARINE SOCIETY BOYS
21	YES	1841	1985	JORDAN	LORD GODERICH BOYS B
22	YES	1841	1842	CHILDREN'S	DORSET FARMBOYS
23	YES	1841	1842	CHILDREN'S	POTTERIES-KILN BOYS
24	YES	1892	1892	ARCHDEACON WILSON	ROCHDALE BOYS
25	NO	1857	1884	R. CLARK (GALTON COMM)	YORK FRIENDS SCHOOL

MALES

ID	WORK'G CLASS	YEAR COLLECTED	YEAR PUBLISHED	AUTHOR(S) OF PUBLICATION	DESCRIPTION OF SUBJECTS IN DATA SET
26	YES	1861	1862	DANSON	LIVERPOOL FELONS
27	YES	1863	1864	YEATS	PECKHAM BOYS
28	YES	1869	1870	BEDDOE	BERWICKSHIRE FARMERS
29	YES	1869	1870	BEDDOE	AVERAGES
30	YES	1872	1873	BRIDGES & HOLMES (*)	MACCLESFIELD SILK FACTORY
31	YES	1872	1873	BRIDGES & HOLMES (A)	FACTORY SONS [FP]
32	YES	1872	1873	BRIDGES & HOLMES (B)	NON-FACTORY
33	YES	1872	1873	BRIDGES & HOLMES (C)	NON-FACTORY (NFP)
34	YES	1872	1873	BRIDGES & HOLMES (D)	URBAN FACTORY
35	YES	1872	1873	BRIDGES & HOLMES (E)	SUBURBAN FACTORY
36	NO	1873	1874	FERGUSON & RODWELL	GALTON'S DATA
37	YES	1875	1876	ROBERTS [J.R.S.S.]	ALL SUBJECTS
38	YES	1875	1876	ROBERTS [J.R.S.S.]	ROYAL MILITARY ASYLUM
39	YES	1875	1876	ROBERTS [J.R.S.S.]	FACTORY, COTTON
40	YES	1875	1876	ROBERTS [J.R.S.S.]	FACTORY, WOOL
41	YES	1875	1876	ROBERTS [J.R.S.S.]	NON-FACTORY, FACTORY TOWNS
42	YES	1875	1876	ROBERTS [J.R.S.S.]	NON-FACTORY, COUNTRY TOWNS
43	YES	1875	1876	ROBERTS [J.R.S.S.]	TOTAL URBAN
44	YES	1875	1876	ROBERTS [J.R.S.S.]	GREENWICH HOSPITAL SCHOOL
45	YES	1875	1876	ROBERTS [J.R.S.S.]	RURAL, FACTORY DISTRICTS
46	YES	1875	1876	ROBERTS [J.R.S.S.]	RURAL, AGRICULT. DISTRICTS
47	YES	1875	1876	ROBERTS [J.R.S.S.]	TOTAL, RURAL
48	YES	1875	1875	STEET	TELEGRAPH BOYS
49	YES	1875	1876	ROBERTS	LABOURING CLASS
50	NO	1875	1876	ROBERTS	NON-LABOURING CLASS
51	YES	1876	1877	LANE-FOX [PITT RIVERS]	2ND SURVEY SURREY MILITIA

MALES

ID	WORK'G CLASS	YEAR COLLECTED	YEAR PUBLISHED	AUTHOR(S) OF PUBLICATION	DESCRIPTION OF SUBJECTS IN DATA SET
52	NO	1878	1878	ROBERTS	COMMERICAL CLASS-COUNTRY
53	NO	1878	1878	ROBERTS	COMMERICAL CLASS-TOWN
54	YES	1878	1878	ROBERTS	LABOURING CLASS-III
55	YES	1878	1878	ROBERTS	LABOURING CLASS IV
56	YES	1878	1878	ROBERTS	LABOURING CLASS V
57	YES	1878	1878	ROBERTS	LABOURING CLASS VI
58	YES	1878	1878	ROBERTS	INDUSTRIAL CLASS VII
59	YES	1878	1878	ROBERTS	INDUSTRIAL CLASS VIII
60	YES	1878	1878	ROBERTS	ARTISAN CLASS
61	YES	1878	1878	ROBERTS	EARLSWOOD RETARDED
62	NO	1878	1878	ROBERTS	MOST FAVOURED CLASSES
63	NO	1883	1884	GALTON	BRITISH ASSOC-ALL
64	NO	1883	1884	GALTON	BRITISH PROFESSIONAL T & CO
65	NO	1883	1884	GALTON	BRITISH COMMERICAL T & CO
66	YES	1883	1884	GALTON	BRITISH LABOURING COUNTRY
67	YES	1883	1884	GALTON	BRITISH ARTISANS-TOWN
68	YES	1883	1884	GALTON	INDUSTRIAL SCHL. MANCHESTER
69	NO	1883	1884	LEVI [GALTON]	ENGLAND
70	NO	1883	1884	LEVI [GALTON]	WALES
71	NO	1883	1884	LEVI [GALTON]	SCOTLAND
72	NO	1883	1884	LEVI [GALTON]	IRELAND
73	NO	1884	1927	RUEGER & STOESSIGER	HEALTH EXHIBITION GALTON
74	NO	1884	1912	MUMFORD	MANCHESTER G.S. BOYS
75	NO	1884	1884	GALTON COMMITTEE	ARTISANS' SONS
76	NO	1888	1985	JOHNSON ET AL II	SCIENCE MUSEUM-GALTON
77	NO	1888	1889	VENN	CAMBRIDGE A GROUP

MALES

ID	WORK'G CLASS	YEAR COLLECTED	YEAR PUBLISHED	AUTHOR(S) OF PUBLICATION	DESCRIPTION OF SUBJECTS IN DATA SET
78	NO	1888	1889	VENN	CAMBRIDGE B GROUP
79	NO	1888	1889	VENN	CAMBRIDGE C GROUP
80	YES	1892	1904	THORNE	LCC SCHOLARSHIP BOYS
81	YES	1897	1899	MUFFANG	LIVPL. SCHOOL CHILDREN
82	YES	1902	1925	DUNSTAN	EAST SUSSEX RURAL
83	YES	1902	1903	ROY COMM PHYS TRAINING	EDINBURGH SCHOOL CHILDREN
84	YES	1902	1903	ROY COMM PHYS TRAINING	ABERDEEN SCHOOL CHILDREN
85	YES	1903	1904	WILSON (INTERDEPARTMENTAL)	DUNDEE JUTE MILL BOYS
86	YES	1903	1904	WILSON (INTERDEPARTMENTAL)	DUNDEE ELEM.SCHOOL BOYS
87	NO	1903	1904	BENNETT	PIMLICO MIDDLE CLASS
88	YES	1903	1904	BENNETT	SOUTHWARK WORK. CLASS
89	YES	1903	1903	CHALMERS	GLASGOW
90	NO	1903	1904	GLASGOW	
91	YES	1903	1905	DUNDEE SOCIAL UNION (WILSON)	DUNDEE SCHOOL CHILDREN
92	NO	1905	1906	CHARITY ORG. SOC. EDINBURGH	
93	YES	1905	1914	ELDERTON	GLASGOW A SCHOOL
94	YES	1905	1914	ELDERTON	GLASGOW B SCHOOL
95	YES	1905	1914	ELDERTON	GLASGOW C SCHOOL
96	NO	1905	1914	ELDERTON	GLASGOW D SCHOOL
97	NO	1905	1914	ELDERTON (JORDAN 87)	GRAND MEAN OF 4 MEANS
98	YES	1907	1918	MACKENZIE /ARKLE/(UNWIN)	LIVERPOOL

MALES

ID	WORK'G CLASS	YEAR COLLECTED	YEAR PUBLISHED	AUTHOR(S) OF PUBLICATION	DESCRIPTION OF SUBJECTS IN DATA SET
99	YES	1907	1918	MACKENZIE /ARKLE/(UNWIN)	PT SUNLIGHT
100	YES	1907	1913	GREENWOOD	LEED'S POOR CHILDREN
101	YES	1908	1909	ATTENDANCE COMMITTEE	BOLTON HALF-TIMERS
102	YES	1908	1909	ATTENDANCE COMMITTEE	BOLTON STUDENT FULL-TIME
103	YES	1908	1909	ATTENDANCE COMMITTEE	BLACKBURN HALF-TIMERS
104	NO	1908	1909	ATTENDANCE COMMITTEE (HALIFAX DATA)	BLACKBURN STUDENT FULL-TIME L GR. SCHL
105	NO	1908	1912	MUMFORD	ENGLAND
106	NO	1909	1911	TUXFORD & GLEGG	COUNTY ED AREA BOYS
107	NO	1909	1911	TUXFORD & GLEGG	URBAN ED AREA BOYS
108	NO	1909	1911	TUXFORD & GLEGG	NORTH OF ENGLAND BOYS
109	NO	1909	1911	TUXFORD & GLEGG	SOUTH OF ENGLAND
110	NO	1909	1911	TUXFORD & GLEGG	INSTITUTIONS CHILDREN
111	YES	1912	1913	POOR LAW COMMISSION	OUT-RELIEF CHILDREN
112	YES	1912	1913	POOR LAW COMMISSION	NATIONAL-ENGLAND
113	NO	1913	1914	GREENWOOD-SCHOOL. DRS	WORCS.BOYS
114	YES	1913	1914	WILLIAMS	
115	NO	1913	1914	WILLIAMS	CHARTERHOUSE BOYS
116	NO	1965	1966	TANNER ET AL	

FEMALES

ID	WORK'G CLASS	YEAR COLLECTED	YEAR PUBLISHED	AUTHOR(S) OF PUBLICATION	DESCRIPTION OF SUBJECTS IN DATA SET
1	YES	1829	1990	JORDAN	CONVICTS: SHIP HARMONY-LONDON
2	YES	1829	1990	JORDAN	CONVICTS: SHIP HARMONY-ENGLAND
					NONLONDON
3	YES	1829	1990	JORDAN	CONVICTS: SHIP HARMONY-WALES
4	YES	1829	1990	JORDAN	CONVICTS: SHIP HARMONY-SCOTLAND
5	YES	1829	1990	JORDAN	CONVICTS: SHIP HARMONY-IRELAND
6	YES	1829	1990	JORDAN	CONVICTS: SHIP HARMONY-ALL
7	YES	1832	1833	STANWAY	FACTORY GIRLS
8	YES	1832	1833	STANWAY	NON-FACTORY GIRLS
9	YES	1837	1837	HORNER-HARRISON	PRESTON WORKING CLASS
10	YES	1837	1837	HORNER-72 DOCTORS	YORKSHIRE & LANCASTER
11	YES	1841	1842	REPORT (S.S. SCRIVEN)	HALIFAX WORSTED MILL GIRLS
12	YES	1841	1842	SYMONS	COLLIER GIRLS-YORKS
13	YES	1841	1842	SYMONS	FARM GIRLS
14	NO	1897	1897	KERR	BRADFORD GIRLS–ALL CLASSES
15	YES	1872	1873	BRIDGES & HOLMES(*)	MACCLESFIELD SILK FACTORY
16	YES	1872	1873	BRIDGES & HOLMES(B)	FACTORY DAUGHTERS (FP)
17	YES	1872	1873	BRIDGES & HOLMES(C)	NON-FACTORY
18	YES	1872	1873	BRIDGES & HOLMES(D)	NON-FACTORY (NFP)
19	YES	1872	1873	BRIDGES & HOLMES(E)	URBAN FACTORY
20	YES	1872	1873	BRIDGES & HOLMES(F)	SUBURBAN FACTORY
21	YES	1873	1876	ROBERTS(J.R.S.S.) DR BRIDGES, MR HOLMES	FACTORY, COTTON
22	YES	1873	1876	ROBERTS(J.R.S.S.)	FACTORY, WOOL
23	YES	1873	1876	ROBERTS(J.R.S.S.)	NON-FACTORY, TOWNS
24	YES	1873	1876	ROBERTS(J.R.S.S.)	TOTAL, URBAN

FEMALES

ID	WORK'G CLASS	YEAR COLLECTED	YEAR PUBLISHED	AUTHOR(S) OF PUBLICATION	DESCRIPTION OF SUBJECTS IN DATA SET
25	YES	1873	1876	ROBERTS[I.R.S.S.]	RURAL, FACTORY DISTRICTS
26	YES	1873	1876	ROBERTS[I.R.S.S.]	RURAL, AGRICULTURAL DISTRICTS
27	YES	1875	1876	ROBERTS[I.R.S.S.]	ALL SUBJECTS
28	YES	1883	1884	GALTON COMMITTEE	MANCHESTER INDUSTRIAL SCHOOL-SWINTON
29	NO	1883	1884	GALTON COMMITTEE	BRITISH ASSOC-ALL
30	NO	1883	1884	GALTON COMMITTEE	BRIT. ASSOC. PROFESSIONAL-T & CO
31	NO	1883	1884	GALTON COMMITTEE	BRIT. ASSOC COMMERICAL T & CO
32	YES	1883	1884	GALTON COMMITTEE	BRIT. ASSOC LABOURING-COUNTRY
33	YES	1883	1884	GALTON COMMITTEE	BRIT. ASSOC ARTISANS-TOWN
34	NO	1884	1928	ELDERTON, MOUL & PAGE	
35	NO	1888	1987	JOHNSON ET AL II	SCIENCE MUSEUM-GALTON
36	YES	1897	1899	MUFFANG	LIVPL. SCHOOLS
37	YES	1902	1903	PHYS. TRNG. COMM	EDINBURGH
38	YES	1902	1903	PHYS. TRNG. COMM	ABERDEEN
39	YES	1902	1925	DUNSTAN	EAST SUSSEX-RURAL
40	YES	1903	1904	WILSON	DUNDEE JUTE MILL
41	YES	1903	1904	REPORT	GLASGOW
42	YES	1903	1904	BERRY	LCC SCHOLARSHIP GIRLS
43	YES	1904	1905	DUNDEE SOC UNION	DUNDEE
44	YES	1904	1906	CHARITY ORG SOC	EDINBURGH-SELECTED SCHL
45	YES	1904	1906	CHARITY ORG SOC	COUNTRY-POOR SCHOOL
46	NO	1904	1906	CHARITY ORG SOC	COUNTRY-PROSPEROUS SCHL
47	YES	1904	1906	CHARITY ORG SOC.	EDINBURGH-PUBLIC SCHOOL
48	NO	1904	1906	CHARITY ORG. SOC.	EDINBURGH HIGHER GR. SCHL
49	YES	1905	1914	ELDERTON	GLASGOW A SCHOOL

FEMALES

ID	WORK'G CLASS	YEAR COLLECTED	YEAR PUBLISHED	AUTHOR(S) OF PUBLICATION	DESCRIPTION OF SUBJECTS IN DATA SET
50	YES	1905	1914	ELDERTON	GLASGOW B SCHOOL
51	YES	1905	1914	ELDERTON	GLASGOW C SCHOOL
52	NO	1905	1914	ELDERTON	GLASGOW D SCHOOL
53	NO	1905		JORDAN, 1987	GRAND MEAN ALL
54	YES	1906	1926	HABAKUK	BARRY 02–09 COHORT
55	YES	1907	1913	GREENWOOD	LEEDS POOR CHILDREN
56	YES	1908	1918	UNWIN (DR. J. MACKENZIE)	PT. SUNLIGHT
57	YES	1908	1918	UNWIN (DR. J MACKENZIE)	LIVPL "B SCHOOL"
58	YES	1908	1909	SCHL ATTEND. COMM.	BLACKBURN–1/2 TIMERS
59	NO	1908	1909	SCHL ATTEND. COMM.	BLACKBURN–HIGH GRADE SCHL
60	YES	1909	1914	WILLIAMS	WORCS.
61	YES	1911	1914	ELDERTON (DR. PRIESTLY)	STAFFS.
62	YES	1912	1913	GREENWOOD	POOR LAW INSTITUTE
63	YES	1912	1913	GREENWOOD	POOR LAW INSTITUTE
64	NO	1914	1914	WILLIAMS B & P	ST. CATHERINE'S [PUBLIC] SCHOOL
65	YES	1914	1914	WILLIAMS B & P	ROY, SOLDIERS DGHTRS. HOME
66	NO	1965	1966	TANNER ET AL	

Appendix 2:
Kondratieff's Commodity Index and Heights

FIGURE A.1 KONDRATIEFF'S COMMODITY INDEX AND THE
HEIGHTS OF ALL MALES AND FEMALES

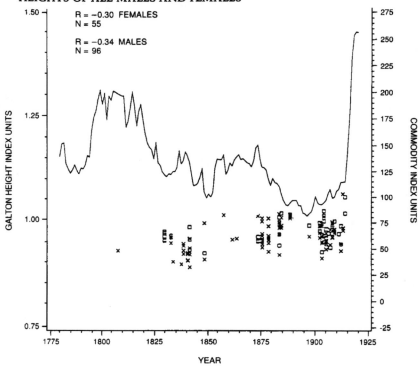

SEX ⌐⌐⌐⌐⌐ FEMALES   x x x MALES

FIGURE A.2 KONDRATIEFF'S COMMODITY INDEX AND THE HEIGHTS OF WORKING-CLASS MALES AND FEMALES

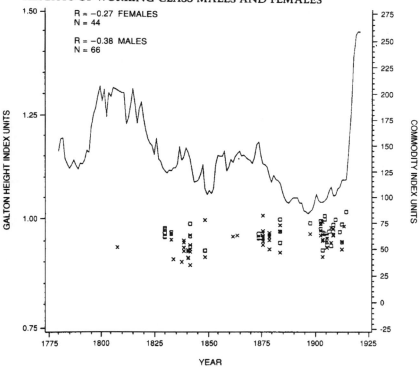

SEX ☐☐☐ FEMALES ✕✕✕ MALES

FIGURE   A.3   KONDRATIEFF'S   COMMODITY   INDEX   AND   THE
HEIGHTS OF NON-WORKING-CLASS MALES AND FEMALES

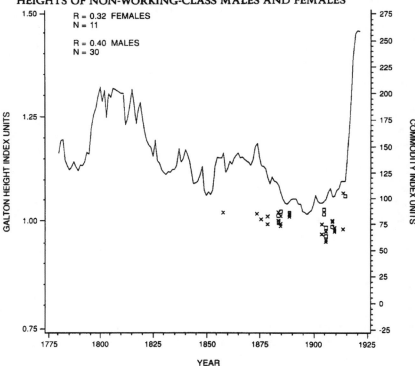

SEX   □□□ FEMALES   ×××MALES

FIGURE A.4 KONDRATIEFF'S COMMODITY INDEX AND THE HEIGHTS OF WORKING AND NON-WORKING-CLASS MALES

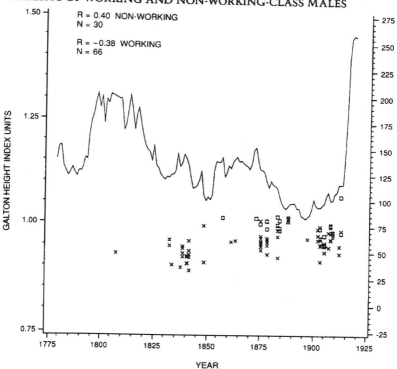

FIGURE A.5 KONDRATIEFF'S COMMODITY INDEX AND THE
HEIGHTS OF WORKING AND NON-WORKING-CLASS FEMALES

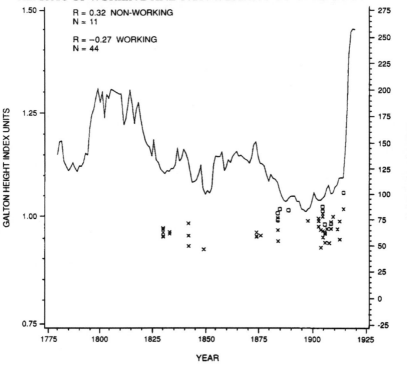

WORKING CLASS   □□□ NO   x x x YES

Bibliography

Acheson, D. (1991). Health and Housing. *Journal of the Royal Society of Health.* 111: 236–243.

Addison, P. (1983). "Winston Churchill and the Working Class, 1900–1914." In J. Winter, ed. *The Working Class in Modern British History: Essays in Honor of Henry Pelline.* Cambridge: Cambridge University Press.

Aitken, W. (1862). *On the Growth of the Recruit and Young Soldier.* London: Griffith, Bohn and Co.

Allday, J., ed. (1853). *True Account of the Proceedings Leading to, and a Full Report of the Searching Inquiry . . . Borough Gaol of Birmingham.* London: Pitman.

Altick, R. D. (1991). *The Presence of the Present.* Columbus: Ohio State University Press.

Altman, L. K. (1992). Deadly Strain of Tuberculosis is spreading Fast, U.S. Finds. *New York Times.* 24 January, A1, A10: 11 February.

Anderson, M. (1971). *Family Structure in Nineteenth Century Lancashire.* Cambridge: Cambridge University Press.

Antonov, A. N. (1947). "Children Born During the Siege of Leningrad in 1942." *Journal of Pediatrics* 30: 250–259.

Arkle, A. S. (1907). "Medical Examination of School Children." Reprinted in S. Unwin, ed., *The Six-Hour Day and Other Industrial*

Questions, by Lord Leverholme. London: George Allen and Unwin, 1918.

Armstrong, A. (1974). *Stability and Change in an English Country Town.* Cambridge: Cambridge University Press.

Armstrong, W. A. (1972). "The Use of Information About Occupation." In E. A. Wrigley, ed., *Nineteenth Century Society: Essays in the Use of Quantitative Methods for the Study of Social Data.* Cambridge: Cambridge University Press.

(Army Contractor). (1817). "Statement of the Sizes of Men in Different Counties of Scotland, Taken from the Local Militia." *Edinburgh Medical and Surgical Journal* 13: 260–264.

Asahina, K. (1975). Growth Acceleration in Japan. In K. Asahina and R. Shigiya, eds., *Physiological Adaptability and Nutritional Status of the Japanese.* Tokyo. University of Tokyo Press.

Ashmore, O. (1964). "Low Moor, Clitheroe: A Nineteenth Century Factory Community." *Transactions of the Lancashire and Cheshire Antiquarian Society* 73: 124–152.

Aspin, C., ed. (1972). *Manchester and the Textile Districts in 1849* (Reach, A. B.) Helmshore, England: Helmshore Local History Society.

Aspinall, A. and Smith, E. A. (1959). *English Historical Documents 1783–1832.* New York: Oxford University Press.

Bailey, V. (1984). "In Darkest England and the Way Out." The Salvation Army, Social Reform and the Labour Movement, 1885–1910. *International Review of Social History.* 29: 133–171.

Baines, T. (1873). *Yorkshire, Past and Present.* London: Mackenzie.

Bairagi, R. (1987). "A Comparison of Five Anthropometric Indices for Identifying Factors of Malnutrition." *American Journal of Epidemiology* 126: 258–267.

Baker, H. (1882). "On the Growth of the Manchester Population, Extension of the Commercial Centre of the City, and Provision for Habitation—Census Period, 1871–81." *Manchester Statistical Society: Transactions:* 1–27.

(Baker, R.) Statistical Committee on the Town Council. (1839). "Report upon the Condition of the Town of Leeds and of Its Inhabitants." *Journal of the Statistical Society* 2: 397–424.

Banning, C. (1946). "Food Shortage and Public Health, First Half of

1945." *Annals of the American Academy of Political Science* 245: 96–110.

Barron, G. B. (1888). "The Constitutional Characteristics of Those Who Dwell in Large Towns, as Relating to the Degeneracy of Race." *Proceedings of the Fifty Eighth Meeting of the British Association:* 836–837.

Bayly, M. (1859). *Ragged Homes, and How to Mend Them,* 2d ed. London: Nisbet.

Beard, G. W. (1879). "English and American Physique." *North American Review* 129: 588–603.

Beddoe, J. (1867). *On the Stature and Bulk of Man in the British Isles.* Bristol: Chillcott.

———. (1870). "The Stature of Bulk of Man in the British Isles. VII." *Journal of the Statistical Society* 33: 278–280.

———. (1904). "The Somatology of Eight Hundred Boys in Training for the Royal Navy." *Journal of the Anthropological Institute of Great Britain and Ireland* 34: 92–99.

———. (1911). *Memories of Eighty Years.* Bristol: J. W. Arrowsmith.

Behlmer, G. K. (1979). "Deadly Motherhood: Infanticide and Medical Opinion in Mid-Victorian England." *Journal of the History of Medicine and Allied Sciences* 43: 403–427.

Bell, Lady. (1907). *At the Works: A Study of a Manufacturing Town.* London: Nelson.

Bennett, J. H., ed. (1983). *Natural Selection, Heredity and Eugenics.* Oxford: Clarendon Press.

Bennett, L. W. (1904). (Letter) *Report of the Interdepartmental Committee on Physical Deterioration.* House of Commons, Sessional Papers, *32,* Appendix.

Bentley, B. B. (1954). "Sir John Eldon Gorst and the Children of the Nation." *Bulletin of the History of Medicine* 28: 243–251.

Beresford, M. W. (1967). "Prosperity Street and Others: An Essay in Visible Urban History." In M. W. Beresford and G. R. J. Jones, eds., *Leeds and Its Region.* Leeds, England: Arnold.

———. (1971). "The Back to Back House in Leeds, 1787–1937." In S. D. Chapman, *The History of Working Class Housing: A Symposium.* London: Rowman and Littlefield.

Bernstein, J. (1989). *The New Prosperity: Investment Opportunities in Long-Wave Economic Cycles.* New York: New York Institute of Finance.

Bielicki, T. and Charzewski, J. (1982) Growth Data as Indicators of Social Inequalities: The Case of Poland. *Yearbook of Physical Anthropology.* 25, 153–167.

Birch, R. C. (1974). *The Shaping of the Welfare State.* London: Longman.

Bishop, A. S. (1968). "Ralph Lingen, Secretary to the Education Department 1849–1870." *British Journal of Educational Studies* 16: 138–163.

Blishen, B. (1967). "A Socioeconomic Index for Canada." *Canadian Review of Sociology and Anthropology* 4: 41–53.

Boldsen, A. L. and Kronburg, D. (1984). "The Distribution of Stature Among Danish Conscripts in 1852–56." *Annals of Human Biology* 11: 555–566.

Bolitho, H. (1964). *Albert Prince Consort.* New York: Bobbs-Merrill.

Bond, B. (1962). "Recruiting the Victorian Army." *Victorian Studies* 5: 331–338.

Booth, W. (1890). *In Darkest England, and the Way Out.* London: Salvation Army.

Bosanquet, H. (1898). *Rich and Poor.* London: Macmillan.

———. (1904). "Physical Degeneration and the Poverty Line." *Contemporary Review* 147: 66–75.

Bottenberg, R. and Ward, J. (1963). *Applied Multiple Linear Regression.* United States Air Force, Aerospace Medical Division. San Antonio, Texas.

Boulton, P. (1876). "Some Anthropometrical Observations." *British Medical Journal* (March 4): 280–282.

———. (1880a). "On the Physical Development of Children." *Lancet* (October 16): 610–612.

———. (1880b). "On the Physical Development of Children; or, the Bearing of Anthropometry to Hygiene." *Lancet* 2: 502–504.

Bowditch, H. P. (1872). "Comparative Rates of Growth in the Two Sexes." *Boston Medical and Surgical Journal* 10: 434–435.

Bowler, P. J. (1991). "The Role of the History of Science in the Understanding of Social Darwinism and Eugenics." *Impact of Science on Society* 159: 273–278.

Bowley, A. L. (1895). "Changes in Average Wages (Nominal and Real) in the United Kingdom Between 1860 and 1891." *Journal of the Royal Statistical Society* 58: 223–285.

———. (1900). *Wages in the United Kingdom in the Nineteenth Century.* Cambridge: University Press.

———. (1910). "The Insufficiency of Official Statistics." *Nineteenth Century* 67: 931–945.

———. and Burnett-Hurst, A. R. (1915). *Livelihood and Poverty.* London: Bell.

———. (1937) *Wages and Income Since 1860.* Cambridge. Cambridge University Press.

Boyd, R. (1861). "Tables of the Weights of the Human Body and the Internal Organs in the Sane and the Insane of Both Sexes at Various Ages." *Philosophical Transactions of the Royal Society* (February 28): 124–126.

Boyne, A. W., Aitken, F. C., and Leitch, I. (1957). "Secular Change in Height and Weight of British Children, Including an Analysis of Measurements of English Children in Primary Schools: 1911–1953." *Nutrition Abstracts and Reviews* 27: 1–18.

———. and Leitch, I. (1954). "Secular Change in the Heights of British Adults." *Nutrition Abstracts and Reviews* 24: 255–269.

Brabazon, Lord. (1887). "Decay of Bodily Strength in Towns." *Nineteenth Century* 21: 673–676.

Bransby, E. R. and Gelling, J. W. (1946). "Variations in, and the Effects of Weather Conditions on, the Growth of Children." *Medical Officer* 75: 213–217.

Brent, W. B. (1844). "On the Stature and Relative Proportions of Man at Different Epochs and in Different Countries." *Report of the Annual Meeting of the British Association for the Advancement of Science.* Cambridge: British Association for the Advancement of Science.

———. (1845). "Tables Illustrative of the Height, Weight and Strength of Man." *Report of the Fifteenth Meeting of the British Associa-*

tion for the Advancement of Science. Cambridge: British Association for the Advancement of Science.

———— . (1848). "Comparative Heights of the Soldiers in the British and French Armies, in Proportions of 1,000." In T. C. Banfield and C. R. Weld, *The Statistical Companion.* London: Longman, Brown, Green, and Longmans.

Brickler, M. (1958). "The Classification of the Population by Social and Economic Characteristics." *Royal Statistical Society Journal* (A) 121: 161–195.

Bridges, J. H., and Holmes, T. (1873). *Report to the Local Government Board on Proposed Changes in Hours and Ages of Employment in Textile Factories.* London: HMSO.

Briggs, A. (1955). *Victorian People.* Chicago: University of Chicago Press.

———— . (1968). *Victorian Cities.* London: Pelican Books.

Brinkman, H. J., Drukker, J. W., and Slot, B. (1988). "Height and Income: A New Method for the Estimation of Historical National Income Series." *Explorations in Economic History* 25: 227–264.

The British Labourer's Protector and Factory Child's Friend. (1832). Bradford: J. Atkinson.

The Broad Street Pump. (1866). *The Times.* 28 July, and 4 August.

Brown, J. C. (1990). "The Condition of England and the Standard of Living: Cotton Textiles in the Northwest, 1806–1850." *Journal of Economic History* 50: 591–614.

Buchan, A., and Mitchell, A. (1875). "The Influence of Weather on Mortality from Different Diseases and At Different Ages." *Journal of the Scottish Meteorological Society* 4: 187–263.

Buchanan, I. (1985). "Infant Feeding, Sanitation and Diarrhoea in Colliery Communities, 1880–1911." In D. J. Oddy, and D. S. Miller, eds., *Diet and Health in Modern Britain.* London: Croom Helm.

Buck, W. E. (1886). "On 'Infantile Diarrhoea'." *Transactions of the Sanitary Institute of Great Britain* 7: 86–93.

Bulman, G. W. (1902). "Is Natural Selection Evolving a Sober Race?" *Westminister Review* 158: 497–505.

Bulwer, H. L. (1836). *The Monarchy of the Middle Classes*, 2 vols. London: Bentley.

Burke, G. (1971). *Towns in the Making.* London: Arnold.

Burnett, J. (1966). *Plenty and Want: A Social History of Diet in England from 1815 to the Present Day.* London: Nelson.

———. (1982). *Destiny Obscure: Autobiographies of Childhood, Education and Family from the 1820s to the 1920s.* London: Allen Lane.

Burns, J. (1906). *Presidential Address.* London: First National Conference on Infantile Mortality.

Buss, D. J. (1990). "The British Diet in the 1980s." *Journal of the Royal Society of Health* 110: 123–125, 129.

Butler, A. M., Ruffin, J. M., Sniffen, M. M., and Wickson, M. E. (1945). "The Nutritional Status of Civilians Rescued from Japanese Prison Camps." *New England Journal of Medicine* 233: 639–652.

Butt, J. (1971). "Working Class Housing in Glasgow, 1851–1914." In S. D. Chapman, ed., *The History of Working Class Housing.* Newton Abbot, England: David and Charles.

Caffyn, C. (1986). *Workers' Housing in West Yorkshire 1750–1920.* London: HMSO.

Cameron, N. (1979). "The Growth of London Schoolchildren 1904–1966: An Analysis of Secular Trend and Intra-County Variation." *Annals of Human Biology* 6: 505–526.

Campbell, M. J., Rodrigues, L., Macfarlane, A. J., and Murphy, M. F. G. (1991). "Sudden Infant Deaths and Cold Weather: Was the Rise in Infant Mortality in 1986 in England and Wales Due to the Weather?" *Paediatric and Perinatal Epidemiology* 5: 93–100.

Cantlie, J. (1885). *Degeneration Amongst Londoners.* London: Field and Tuer.

———. (1906). *Physical Efficiency: A Review of the Deleterious Effects of Town Life . . .* London: Putnam.

Carr-Hill, R. (1988). "Origins and Destinations of Disease." *Times Higher Education Supplement* (July 22).

Cattell, R. B. (1953). "A Quantitative Analysis of the Changes in Culture Pattern of Great Britain 1837–1937, by P-Technique." *Acta Psychologica* 9: 99–121.

Chadwick, E. (1842). "Report on the Sanitary Condition of the Labouring Population of Great Britain." *Parliamentary Papers* 3: 1–457.

Chaille, S. E. (1887). Infants, Their Chronological Progress. *New Orleans Medical and Surgical Journal:* 893–912.

Chalmers, Dr. (1903). *Report on the Physique of Glasgow School Children.* Edinburgh Charity Organization Society.

Chapin, A. (1836). "Recollections of the Sandwich Islands." *Youth's Companion* 10: 54–55.

Chateauneuf, Benoiton de, L. (1830). "De la Durée de la Vie." *Annales D'Hygiène Publique et de Médicine Légale* 3: 5–15.

Chatterton-Hill, G. (1907). *Heredity and Selection in Sociology.*

Children's Employment Commission. (1842a). "First Report of the Commissioners." *Parliamentary Papers.* London.

———. (1842b). "Appendix to First Report of Commissioners. Mines. Part II. Reports and Evidence from Sub-Commissioners." *Parliamentary Papers* 17: Appendix A.

———. (1843). "Second Report of the Commissioners." *Parliamentary Papers:* 100–102.

Christopher, W. S. (1900). "Measurements of Chicago Schoolchildren." *Journal of the American Medical Association* 35: 618–623, 683–687.

City of Edinburgh Charity Organisation Society. (1906). *Report on the Physical Condition of Fourteen Hundred School Children in the City Together with Some Account of their Homes and Surroundings.* London: King and Son.

"Cleanliness." (1834). *The Penny Magazine:* 157, 438.

Clements, E. M. B. (1953). "Changes in the Mean Stature and Weight of British Children over the Past Seventy Years." *British Medical Journal* (October 24): 897–902.

——— and Pickett, K. G. (1952). "Stature of Scotsmen Aged 18 to 40 Years in 1941." *British Journal of Social Medicine* 6: 245–252.

Coleman, B. I. (1973). *The Idea of the City in Nineteenth Century Britain.* London: Routledge and Kegan Paul.

"Condition of Labourers' Tenements in England." (1844). *Penny Magazine:* 437–438.

Cook, C., and Keith, B. (1975). *British Historical Facts 1830–1900.* New York: Macmillan.

Cook, L., and Stevenson, J. (1983). *The Longman Handbook of Modern British History 1714–1980.* London: Longman.

Corfield, P. J. (1987). "Class by Name and Number in Eighteenth Century Britain." *History:* 38–61.

"Correspondence." (1821). *The Kaleidoscope, or Literacy and Scientific Mirror.* 74, no. 168 (November 27).

Cowan, R. (1840). "Vital Statistics of Glasgow Illustrating the Sanatory Condition of the Population." *Journal of the Statistical Society* 3: 257–292.

Cowell, J. W. (1833) (evidence). First Report. Factories Inquiry Commission. *Parliamentary Papers.*

Cowlard, K. A. (1979). "The Identification of Social (Class) Areas and their Place in Nineteenth Century Urban Development." *Institute of British Geographers* 4: 239–257.

Crafts, N. R. F. (1983). "English Workers' Real Wages during the Industrial Revolution: Some Remaining Problems." *Journal of Economic History* 45: 139–144.

Crafts, N. F. R., Leybourne, S. J. and Mills, T. C. (1989). "Trends and Cycles in British Industrial Production, 1900–1913." *Journal of the Royal Statistical Society* (A) 153: 43–60.

Craig, J. (1963). "The Heights of Glasgow Boys: Secular and Social Influences." *Human Biology* 35: 524–539.

Crawford, T. (1887). "Devolution and Evolution." *British Medical Journal* 2: 337–338.

Crichton-Browne, J. (1902). "Physical Efficiency in Children." In W. Chance, ed., *Report of the Proceedings of the Third International Congress for the Welfare and Protection of Children.* London: P. S. King and Son.

Crocker, R. H. (1987). "The Victorian Poor Law in Crisis and Change: Southhampton, 1870–1895." *Albion* 19: 19–44.

Cronjé, G. (1984). "Tuberculosis and Mortality Decline in England and Wales, 1851–1910." In R. Woods and J. Woodward, *Urban Disease and Mortality in Nineteenth Century England.* New York: St. Martin's Press.

Crouzet, F. (1982). *The Victorian Economy.* New York. Columbia University Press.

Cruickshank, M. (1982). *Children and Industry: Child Health and Welfare in Northwest Textile Towns during the Nineteenth Century.* Manchester. Manchester University Press.

Cuff, T. (1989). "The Body-Mass Index of West Point Cadets in the Nineteenth Century." Paper presented to the Social Science History Association, Washington, D.C.

Cunningham, H. (1991). *Children of the Poor: Representations of Childhood Since the Seventeenth Century.* Oxford: Blackwell.

Dahrendorf, R. (1959). *Class and Conflict in an Industrial Society.* London:

———. (1982). *On Britain.* Chicago: University of Chicago Press.

Daley, A., and Benjamin, B. (1964). "London as a Case Study." *Population Studies* 17: 249–262.

Danson, J. T. (1862). "Statistical Observations Relative to the Growth of the Human Body (Males) in Height and Weight, from Eighteen to Thirty Years of Age as Illustrated by the Records of the Borough Gaol of Liverpool." *Journal of the Royal Statistical Society* 75: 20–26.

Darra Mair, L. W. (1910). *Report on Back-to-Back Houses: A Report on the Relative Mortality in Through and Back-to-Back Houses in Certain Towns in the West Riding of Yorkshire.* London: Local Government Board, H.M.S.O.

Davis, A. S. (1889). "Report on the Anthropometric Measurements." *Cheltonian:* 218–221.

Dawson, C. (1901). "The Housing of the People with Special Reference to Dublin." *Journal of the Statistical and Social Inquiry Society of Ireland* 11: 45–56.

Deane, P., and Cole, W. A. (1969). *British Economic Growth 1688–1959.* Cambridge: Cambridge University Press.

"Debates in the House of Commons on the Factory Bill, 19 and 23 February, and 27 April 1818." (1959). In A. Aspinall and E. A. Smith, eds., *English Historical Documents 1783–1832.* New York: Oxford University Press.

Defoe, D. (1726). *A Tour Through the Whole Island of Great Britain.* London.

Dennis, R. (1984). *English Industrial Cities of the Nineteenth Century: A Social Geography.* Cambridge: Cambridge University Press.

———. (1989). "The Geography of Victorian Values: Philanthropic

Housing in London, 1840–1900." *Journal of Historical Geography* 15: 40–54.

Desmond, A. (1991). *The Politics of Evolution: Morphology, Medicine, and Reform in Radical London*. Chicago: University of Chicago Press.

Dicey, A. (1905). *Law and Public Opinion*. London: Macmillan.

Dillon, T. (1974). "The Irish in Leeds, 1851–1861." *Thoresby Society Publications Miscellany* 54: 1–28.

Disraeli, B. (1845). *Sybil, or The Two Nations*. London.

Don, W. G. (1889). "Recruits and Recruiting." *Journal of the Royal United Services Institution* 33: 827–853.

Douglas, J. W. B. (1982). "Birth Cohort Studies and Policy Formation." In T. E. Jordan, et al., *Child Development, Information and the Formation of Public Policy: An International Perspective*. Springfield, Ill.: Charles C. Thomas.

Drapers' Company Research Memoirs: Studies in National Deterioration. (1906–1914). London: Dulau and Co.

Drescher, S. (1990). "The Ending of the Slave Trade and the Evolution of European Scientific Racism." *Social Science History* 14: 415–450.

Drummond, A. J. (1943). "Cold Winters at Kew Observatory, 1783–1942." *Quarterly Journal of the Royal Meteorological Society* 69: 17–32.

Ducpétiaux, E. (1855). *Budgets Économiques Des Ouvrières En Belgique*. Brussells. Commission Centrale de Statistique.

Dugdale, A. E. (1971). "An Age-Independent Anthropometric Index of Nutrition Status." *American Journal of Clinical Nutrition* 24: 174–176.

Duncan, O. D. (1961). "A Socio-Economic Index for All Occupations." In H. Reiss, et al., *Occupations and Social Status*. New York: Free Press.

Duncan, W. H. (1844). "On the Physical Causes of the High Rate of Mortality. Health of Towns Commission." *Parliamentary Papers*, Appendix.

El Shabrawy, M., et al. (1988). "Typhoid Carriers in Riyadh City, Saudi Arabia." *Journal of the Royal Society of Health* 108: 97–98, 101.

Elder, G. (1974). *Children of the Great Depression: Social Change in Life Experience.* Chicago: University of Chicago Press.

Elderton, E. (1914). "Height and Weight of School Children in Glasgow." *Biometrika* 10: 288–339.

Elderton, E. M., Moul, M., and Page, E. M. (1928). "On the Growth Curves of Certain Characteristics in Women and the Interrelationship of these Characteristics." *Annals of Eugenics* 3: 277–336.

Elley, W. B., and Irving, J. C. (1972). "A Socio-Economic Index for New Zealand Based on Levels of Education and Income from the 1966 Census." *New Zealand Journal of Educational Studies* 7: 153–167.

Elliott, D. (1982). "Municipal Government in Bradford in the Mid-Nineteenth Century." In D. Fraser, ed., *Municipal Reform and the Industrial City.* New York: St. Martin's Press.

Ellis, R. W. B. (1946). "Growth and Health of Belgian Children During and After the German Occupation." *Archives of Diseases of Childhood* 20: 92–109.

Emmison, F. G. (1944). "Essex Children Deported to a Lancashire Cotton Mill, 1799." *Essex Review* 53: 77–81.

"Employment of Children in Agriculture." (1869). *Lancet* 2: 712–713.

Engels, F. (1845). *The Condition of the Working Class in England.* Moscow: Progress Publishers.

Evans, J. (1987). *Death in Hamburg: Society and Politics in the Cholera Years 1830–1910.* Oxford: Clarendon Press.

Evans, R. J. (1988). "Cholera in Nineteenth Century Europe." *Past and Present* 120: 123–146.

Eveleth, P. B. and Tanner, J. M. (1976). *Worldwide Variation in Human Growth.* Cambridge: Cambridge University Press.

Eyler, J. M. (1979). *Victorian Social Medicine: The Ideas and Methods of William Farr.* Baltimore: Johns Hopkins University Press.

Farr, W. (1865). "The Mortality of Infants." *Journal of the Statistical Society* 28: 403–413.

———. (1878). "Report of the Anthropometric Committee." *Proceedings of the Forty Eighth Meeting of the British Association (Dublin),* pp. 153–56. London.

"The Fauna of the Streets." (1862). *Macmillan's Magazine* 5: 225–229.

Fergus, W. and Rodwell, G. F. (1874). "On School Statistics." *Journal of the Royal Anthropological Institute of Great Britain and Ireland* 4: 126–130.

Ferguson, F. (1987). "The Degeneracy of the Factory Population." *Sanitary Record* (September 15): 211–212.

Fildes, V. (1992) Breast-Feeding in London, 1905–1919. *Journal of Biosocial Science.* 24, 53–70.

Final Report of the Anthropological Committee. (1884). *Report of the Fifty Third Meeting of the British Association for the Advancement of Science.* London: John Murray. (Galton Committee)

Finnegan, F. (1982). *Poverty and Prejudice: Irish Immigrants in York, 1840–1875.* Cook, England: University Press.

Finnegan, J. and Sigsworth, E. (1978). *Poverty and Social Policy: An Historical Study of Batley.* York, England: York University.

"First Report of the Central Board of His Majesty's Commissioners Appointed to Collect Information in the Manufacturing Districts . . . with Minutes of Evidence." (1833). *Parliamentary Papers* 20: 88.

First Report of the Commissioners on the Health of Towns. (1844). *Parliamentary Papers.*

Fishman, W. B. (1988). *East End 1888: Life in a London Borough Among the Labouring Poor.* Philadelphia: Temple University Press.

Fitzroy, A. (1925). *Memoirs,* vol. 1. London: Hutchinson.

Fleischman, R. K. (1985). *Conditions of Life Among the Cotton Workers of Southeastern Lancashire During the Industrial Revolution.* New York: Garland Publishing Company.

Fletcher, J. (1842). "Abstract from a Register of Accidents in the Coal Mines of the Chambers and Werneth Company, at Oldham, during the Year Ended October, 1841." *Journal of the Statistical Society of London* 5: 222–225.

Flinn, M. W., ed. (1965). *Report on the Sanitary Condition of the Labouring Population of Gt. Britain, by Edwin Chadwick.* Edinburgh: Edinburgh University Press.

Florey, C. duV. (1970). "The Use and Interpretation of Ponderal Index and Other Weight-Height Ratios in Epidemiological Studies." *Journal of Chronic Diseases* 23: 93–103.

Floud, R. (1983). "A Tall Story? The Standard of Living Debate." *History Today* 33: 36–40.

——. (1989). Personal communication.

—— and Wachter, K. W. (1982). "Poverty and Physical Stature: Evidence on the Standard of Living of London Boys 1770–1870." *Social Science History* 6: 422–452.

——, Wachter, K., and Gregory, A. (1985). *The Physical State of the British Working Class 1870–1914: Evidence from Army Recruits.* Working Paper 1661. Cambridge, Mass.: National Bureau of Economic Research.

——, Wachter, K., and Gregory, A. (1990). *Height, Health and History: The Nutritional Status of the British, 1750–1980.* Cambridge: Cambridge University Press.

Flower, W. H., et al. (1893). "Anthropometric Laboratory—Report of the Committee." *Proceedings of the Sixty Third Meeting of the British Association,* pp. 654–663. London: John Murray.

Fogel, R. W. (1986). "Physical Growth as a Measure of the Economic Well-Being of Populations: The Eighteenth and Nineteenth Centuries." In F. Falkner and J. M. Tanner, *Human Growth: A Comprehensive Treatise,* vol. 3. New York: Plenum Press.

——, et al. (1983). "Secular Changes in American and British Stature and Nutrition." *Journal of Interdisciplinary History* 14: 445–481.

Forbes, J. D. (1836). "Experiments on the Weight, Height and Strength of Man at Different Ages." *British Association for the Advancement of Science London Reports* 5: 38–39.

——. (1837). "On the Results of Experiments on the Weight, Height and Strength of Above 800 Individuals." *Proceedings of the Royal Society of Edinburgh* 1: 160–161.

Forbes, T. (1986). "Deadly Parents: Child Homicide in Eighteenth- and Nineteenth-Century England." *Journal of the History of Medicine and Allied Services* 41: 175–199.

——. (1988). "Coroners' Inquisitions from London Parishes of the Duchy of Lancaster: The Strand, Clapham, Enfield and Edmonton, 1831–1883." *Journal of the History of Medicine and Allied Sciences* 43: 191–203.

Forrester, J. W. (1985). "Economic Conditions Ahead: Understanding the Kondratieff Wave." *Futurist* 19: 16–20.

Forsdahl, A. (1977). "Are Poor Living Conditions in Childhood and Adolescence an Important Risk Factor for Arteriosclerotic Heart Disease?" *British Journal of Preventive and Social Medicine* 31: 91–95.

Fraser, D. (1973). "Areas of Urban Politics. Leeds, 1830–1880." In H. J. Dyos and M. Wolff, eds., *The Victorian City: Images and Realities*, vol. 2. London: Kegan Paul.

Fried, A. and Elman, R., eds. (1969). *Charles Booth's London*. London: Pelican.

Frisch, R. E. (1978). Population, Food Intake and Fertility. *Science*. 199: 22–30.

"Further Papers Relative to Convict Discipline and Transportation. Van Diemen's Land." (1845–1850). *Parliamentary Papers* 8: 41–42.

Fussell, G. E. (1929). "The Change in Farm Labourers' Diet During Two Centuries." *Economic History* 1: 268–274.

Galton, F. (1874). "Notes on the Marlborough School Statistics." *Journal of the Royal Anthropological Institute of Great Britain and Ireland* 4: 130–135.

———. (1876). "On the Height and Weight of Boys Aged 14, in Town and Country Public Schools." *Journal of the Anthropological Institute of Great Britain and Ireland* 5: 174–181.

———. (1885). "On the Anthropometric Laboratory at the Late International Health Exhibition." *Journal of the Anthropological Institute of Great Britain and Ireland* 14: 205–219.

———. (1886). "Regression Towards Mediocrity in Hereditary Stature." *Journal of the Anthropological Institute of Great Britain and Ireland* 15: 246–263.

———. (1962). *Hereditary Genius (1892 ed.)*. Cleveland: World Publishing Co.

———. (1906). "Anthropometry at Schools." *Journal of Preventive Medicine* 14: 93–98.

————, et al. (1894). "Physical and Mental Deviations from the Normal Among Children in Public and Other Elementary Schools." *Proceedings of the Sixty Second Meeting of the British Association*, pp. 434–437. London: John Murray.

Gandevia, B. (1976). "Some Physical Characteristics, Including Pock Marks, Tattoos and Disabilities, of Convict Boys Transported to Australia from Britain." *Australian Pediatric Journal* 12: 6–13.

————. (1977). "A Comparison of the Heights of Boys Transported to Australia from England, Scotland, and Ireland c. 1840, with Later British and Australian Developments." *Australian Pediatric Journal* 13: 91–97.

————. (1978). *Tears Often Shed: Child Health and Welfare in Australia from 1778.* Sydney: Pergamon Press.

Garrow, J. S. (1981). *Treat Obesity Seriously: A Clinical Manual.* Edinburgh: Churchill Livingstone.

Garvey, G. (1968). "Kondratieff, N. D." *International Encyclopedia of the Social Sciences*, vol. 8, pp. 443–444. New York: Macmillan.

Gaskell, P. (1833). *The Manufacturing Population of England.* London: Baldwin and Craddock.

Gaskoin, G. (1882). "The Range of Hereditary Tendencies in Health and Disease." *Transactions of the Sanitary Institutes of Great Britain* 3: 100–108.

Gattie, W. M. (1890). "The Physique of European Armies." *Fortnightly Review* 1: 566–585.

Gayer, A. D., Rostow, W. W., and Schwartz, A. D. (1953). *The Growth and Fluctuation of the British Economy, 1790–1850.* Hassocks, England: Harvester Press.

Gazely, I. (1989). "The Cost of Living for Workers in Late Victorian and Edwardian Britain." *Economic History Review* 42: 207–221.

Geddes, P. (1915). *Cities in Evolution: An Introduction to the Town Planning Movement and to the Study of Civics.* Reprinted: New York: Fertig, 1968.

Gelb, S. A. (1989). " 'Not Simply Bad and Incorrigible': Science, Mortality, and Intellectual Deficiency." *History of Education Quarterly* 29: 359–379.

Gilbert, B. (1965). "Health and Politics: The British Physical Deterioration Report of 1904." *Bulletin of the History of Medicine* 39: 143–153.

Gilbert, E. W. (1958). "Pioneer Maps of Health and Disease in England." *Geographical Journal* 124: 172–183.

Gillingham, J. (1982). "How Belgium Survived: The Food Supply Problem of an Occupied Nation." Center for International Studies, University of Missouri—St. Louis.

———. (1985). *Ideology, and Politics in the Third Reich: Ruhr Coal, Hitler and Europe.* New York: Columbia University Press.

Godwin, G. (1859). *Town Swamps and Social Bridges.* London: Routledge, Warner and Routledge.

Goffman, I. (1962). *Asylums: Essays on the Social Situation of Mental Patients and Other Inmates.* Chicago: Aldine.

Golding, J., Haslum, M., and Morris, H. C. (1984). "What Do Our Ten Year-Old Children Eat?" *Health Visitor* 57: 178–179.

Goldthorpe, J. (1962). "The Development of Social Policy in England 1800–1914." *Transactions of the Fifth World Congress of Sociology* 4.

Gorst, J. E. (1905a). "Physical Deterioration in Great Britain." *North American Review* 181: 1–10.

———. (1905b). "Governments and Social Reform." *Fortnightly Review* 83: 843–885.

Gould, B. A. (1869). *Investigations in the Military and Anthropological Statistics of American Soldiers.* New York: Hurd and Houghton.

Granville, J. M. (1880). "A Note on Intention in the Determination of Sex, and the Mental and Physical Inheritance of Children." *Lancet* 2: 524–526.

Granville, P. B. (1874). *Autobiography of A. B. Granville, M.D., F. R. S.—Being Eighty Eight Years of the Life of Physician,* 2 vols. London: H. S. King.

Graunt, J. (1662). *Natural and Political Observations Mentioned in a Following Index and Made upon the Bills of Mortality.* London.

Gray, J. (1908). "The Importance of School Anthropometrics in the Study and Control of National Evolution." In J. Kerr and E. W. White-Wallace, eds., *Second International Congress on School Hygiene: Transactions,* vol. 2, pp. 574–579. London.

——— and Tocher, J. F. (1900). "The Physical Characteristics of Adults and School Children in East Aberdeenshire." *Transactions of the Anthropological Institute of Great Britain and Ireland* 30: 104–124.

Gray, R. Q. (1976). *The Labour Aristocracy in Victorian Edinburgh.* Oxford: Clarendon Press.

Greasley, D. (1989). "British Wages and Income, 1856–1913: A Revision." *Explorations in Economic History* 26: 248–259.

Greene, L. (1970). "Manual for Scoring Socio-Economic Status for Research on Health Behavior." *Public Health Reports* 85: 815–827.

Greenhow, Dr. (1972). "Privy Council Medical Reports 1861, No. 4." In E. R. Pike, *Golden Times: Human Documents of the Victorian Age.* New York: Schocken Books.

Greenwood, A. (1913). *The Health and Physique of Schoolchildren.* London: P. S. King.

Greenwood, J. (1881). *Low-Life Deeps: An Account of the Strange Fish to Be Found There.* London: Chatto and Windus.

Greg, P. (1861). "Homes of the London Workmen." *Macmillan's Magazine* 5: 63–70.

Gregg, W. R. (1868). "On the Failure of 'Natural Selection' in the Case of Men." *Fraser's Magazine* 78: 353–362.

Gregory, G. (1840). "Statistics of Mortality and Disease in London." *Lancet:* 79–90.

Grimshaw, P. (1989). *Paths of Duty: American Missionary Wives in Nineteenth Century Hawaii.* Honolulu: University of Hawaii Press.

Guy, W. A. (1881). "On Temperature and Its Relation to Mortality: An Illustration of the Application of the Numerical Method to Its Discovery of Truth." *Journal of the Royal Statistical Society* 44: 235–262.

Hall, J. C. (1853). "The Health of Towns—Prevention of Cholera." *The Times* (September 17).

Hall, J. C. (1867). Diseases of Artisans. I. The Sheffield File Cutter's Disease. *St. George's Hospital Reports.* 2: 35–46.

Hamlin, C. (1988). "Muddling in Bumbledom: On the Enormity of Large Sanitary Improvements in Four British Towns, 1855–1885." *Victorian Studies* 32: 55–83.

Hammond, B. (1928). "Urban Death Rates in the Early Nineteenth Century." *Economic History* 1: 419–428.

Hammond, J. L., and Hammond, B. (1930). *The Age of the Chartists 1832–1854: A Study of Discontent.* London: Longmans, Green.

Hardy, A. (1988). "Diagnosis, Death, and Diet: The Case of London, 1750–1909." *Journal of Interdisciplinary History* 18: 387–401.

Hare, S. (1839). "Abstract of Outline of Subjects for Statistical Enquiries." *Journal of the Statistical Society of London* 1: 426–427.

Harling, P. (1992) The Power of Persuasion: Central Authority, Local Bureaucracy and the New Poor Law. *English Historical Review.* *107*, 30–53.

Harris, B. (1989). "Medical Inspection and the Nutrition of School-Children in Britain, 1900–1950." Ph.D. dissertation, University of London.

Harrison, B. (1981). "Women's Health and the Women's Movement in Britain: 1840–1940." In C. Webster, ed., *Biology, Medicine and Society 1840–1940.* London: Cambridge University Press.

Harrison, G. A., Weiner, J. S., Tanner, J. M., and Barnicot, N. A. (1964). *Human Biology.* Oxford: Oxford University Press.

Harrison, J. (1835). "Extracts from the Reports of the Inspectors of Factories, Illustrating the State of Health in the Different Factories." *Edinburgh Medical and Surgical Journal* 44: 425–432.

Hartwell, R. M. (1959). "Interpretations of the Industrial Revolution in England: A Methodological Inquiry." *Journal of Economic History* 19: 229–249.

Harvey, A. C. (1981). *Time Series Models.* New York: John Wiley and Sons.

Hawkins, C. (1895). "Memorandum on the Anthropometric Effects of Gymnastics at Haileybury College." *Parliamentary Papers* 44: 345–351.

Hearle, T. (1983). "Fighting Fit: Military Influences on Boys' Physical Education in the Early Nineteenth Century." In N. Parry and D. McNeal, eds., *Fitness of the Nation—Physical and Health Education in the Nineteenth and Twentieth Centuries.* Leicester, England: History of Education Society.

Heath, R. (1893). *The English Peasant. Studies: Historic, Local, and Biographic.* London: Unwin; reprinted: Wakefield, England: E. P. Publishing, 1978.

Hennock, E. P. (1976). "Poverty and Social Theory in England: The Experience of the Eighteen-Eighties." *Social History:* 67–91.

Heywood, C. (1988). *Childhood in Nineteenth Century France.* Cambridge: Cambridge University Press.

Hiernaux, J. (1964). "Weight/Height Relationship During Growth in Africans and Europeans." *Human Biology* 36: 273–293.

Hill, H. (1854). "Tabular Return of the Stature and Weight of Children in Tasmania . . . " *Royal Society of Tasmania: Papers and Proceedings* 2: 172.

Himmelfarb, M. G. (1968). *Victorian Minds.* New York: Alfred A. Knopf.

———. (1971). "Mayhew's Poor: A Problem of Identity." *Victorian Studies* 14: 308–320.

———. (1991). *Poverty and Compassion: The Moral Imagination of the Late Victorians.* New York: Alfred A. Knopf.

Hird, F. (1898). *The Cry of the Children. An Exposure of Certain British Industries in Which Children are Iniquitously Employed.* London: Bowden.

Hirst, J. D. (1991). "Public Health and the Public Elementary Schools, 1870–1907." *History of Education* 20: 107–118.

Hohenberg, P. (1968). *A Primer on the Economic History of Europe.* New York: Random House.

"The History of a Hospital." (1862). *Macmillan's Magazine* 5: 252–260.

Hole, J. (1866). *The Homes of the Working Classes.* London: Longmans, Green.

Hollingshead, A. B. (1957). *Two Factor Index of Social Position.* New Haven, Conn.: Yale University Press.

Hollingshead, J. (1861). *Ragged London in 1861,* Introduction by A. S. Wohl. Reprinted: London: Dent, 1986.

Hoppit, J. (1990). "Counting the Industrial Revolution." *Economic History Review* 43: 173–193.

Horn, P. (1974). *The Victorian Country Child.* Kineton: Hornwood Press.

Horn, P. (1989). *The Victorian and Edwardian Schoolchild.* London: Alan Sutton.

Horner, L. (1837). "Practical Application of Physiological Facts." *Penny Magazine* 6: 270–272.

———— . [1841]. "Factory Inspector's Special Reports on the Practicability of Legislation for the Prevention of Accidents" In G. M. Young and W. D. Handcock, eds., *English Historical Documents 1833–1874*. Oxford: Oxford University Press. 1956.

Horsfall, T. C. (1904). *The Example of Germany: The Improvement of the Dwellings and Surroundings of the People*. Manchester, England.

Hull, H. (1854). "Tabular Return of the Structure and Weight of Children in Tasmania." *Royal Society of Tasmania: Papers and Proceedings* 2: 172.

Humphries, S., Mark, J., and Perks, R. (1988). *A Century of Childhood*. London: Sidgwick and Jackson.

Hunt, A. R. (1903). "The Physique of the Present and the Evolution of the Future." *Westminister Review* 160: 563–568.

Husband, W. D. (1863). "Infant Mortality." *Transactions of the National Society for the Promotion of Social Science* 4: 498–508.

Hutchison, R. (1868). "Report on the Dietaries of Scotch Agricultural Labourers." *Transactions of the Highland and Agricultural Society of Scotland* 2: 1–29.

Ikin, J. I. (1864). "On the Prevalent Causes of Rejection of Recruits Enlisted in the West Riding, and Northern District." *Transactions of the National Association for the Promotion of Social Science* 8: 525–531.

Irwin, D. A. (1991). "Was Britain Immiserized During the Industrial Revolution?" *Explorations in Economic History* 28: 121–124.

Johnson, J. H., and Pooley, C. G. (1982). *The Structure of Nineteenth Century Cities*. London: Croom Helm.

Johnson, R. C., et al. (1985). "Galton's Data a Century Later." *American Psychologist* 40: 875–892.

Jordan, T. E. (1966). *Perspectives in Mental Retardation*. Carbondale: Southern Illinois University Press.

———— . (1976). *The Mentally Retarded*, 4th ed. Columbus, Ohio: Charles E. Merrill.

———— . (1980). *Development in the Preschool Years*. New York: Academic Press.

————. (1982). "Lancashire Lasses and Yorkshire Lads: Childhood in the Early Nineteenth Century." *Journal of the Royal Society of Health* 102: 14–20.

————. (1983). "Developing an International Index of Quality of Life for Children: The NICQL Index." *Journal of the Royal Society of Health* 103: 127–130.

————. (1984). "The St. Louis Baby Study: Theory, Practice and Findings." In S. A. Mednick, M. Harway, and K. M. Finello, eds., *Handbook of Longitudinal Research. Volume One. Birth and Childhood Cohorts.* New York: Praeger.

————. (1985). "Transported to Van Diemen's Land: The Boys of the *Frances Charlotte* (1832) and *Lord Goderich* (1841)." *Child Development* 56: 493–516.

————. (1987a). "The Keys of Paradise: Godfrey's Cordial and Children in Victorian Britain." *Journal of the Royal Society of Health* 107: 19–22.

————. (1987b). *Victorian Childhood: Themes and Variations.* Albany: State University of New York Press.

————. (1988). "British Data Sets on Height 1805–1913." Unpublished paper.

————. (1990a). "The Trend of Heights and Body Mass in Victorian Youth, 1805–1914." Unpublished paper.

————. (1990b). " 'For Their Country's Good.' The Convict Women of the Ship *Harmony*—1829." *International Review of Comparative and Applied Criminal Justice* 14: 83–95.

————. (1991a). "Social Change, Height and Body Mass in Victorian Youth, 1805–1914." *Annals of Human Biology.* (in press).

————. (1991b). "An Index of the Quality of Life for Victorian Children and Youth: The VICY Index." *Social Indicators Research* (in press).

————. (1991c). "Children of the Mobility: A Street-Level View of Early Victorian Children." *Journal of the Royal Society of Health* 112, 25–30.

————. (1991d). "Linearity, Gender and Social Class in Economic Influences on Nineteenth Century Heights in Britain." *Historical Methods* 24: 116–123.

————— . (1991e). " 'A Ship of Clever Lads': Origins, Occupations and Heights of Male Convicts on the Transports, John Brewer (1842) and John Renwick (1843)." *International Journal of Comparative and Applied Criminal Justice.* 16, (in press).

————— . (1991f). "The Trend of Estimated Body Mass of Working Class Youth (Quetelet's w/h^2) in Great Britain, 1832–1911." Unpublished paper.

————— . (1991g). "The St. Louis Baby Study." In C. H. Young, K. L. Savola, and E. Phelps, eds., *Inventory of Longitudinal Studies in the Social Sciences.* Newbury Park, Calif.: Sage Publications.

————— . (1992a). "An Index of the Quality of Life for Victorian Children and Youth, the VICY Index." *Social Indicators Research* 28: 109—129.

————— . (1992b). " 'L'Homme Moyen' and the Quality of Life for British Adults, 1815–1914: An Index." Unpublished paper.

————— . (1992c). "Quality of Life in Victorian Britain, 1815–1914: An Empirical Consideration." Unpublished paper.

————— and Silva, P. A. (1988). "Height and Weight Comparison of Children in New Zealand and America." *Journal of the Royal Society of Health* 108: 166–172.

Journeyman Engineer (Thomas Wright) (1867). *Some Habits and Customs of the Working Class.* London.

Journeyman Engineer (Thomas Wright) (1868). *The Great Unwashed.* London: Tinsley Brothers.

Judd, D. (1977). *The Boer War.* London: Hart-Davis, MacGibbon.

Karn, M. N. (1937). "Summary of Results of Investigations into the Height and Weight of the British Working Classes During the Last Hundred Years." *Annals of Eugenics* 7: 376–398 (Xerox).

Kay, J. P. (1832). *The Moral and Physical Condition of the Working Classes Employed in the Cotton Manufacture in Manchester.* Manchester, England.

Kelly, J. L., Stanton, W. R., Silva, P. A., and Jordan, T. E. (1991). "Comparison of United States and New Zealand Children's Body Mass." *Journal of the Royal Society of Health* 111: 51–53.

Kerr, J. (1897). "School Hygiene, Its Mental, Moral and Physical Aspects." *Journal of the Royal Statisical Society* 60: 613–680.

————— and Wallis, E. W. (1908). *Second International Congress on School Hygiene. Volume II. Transactions.* London: Royal Sanitary Institute.

Killeen, J., Vanderburg, D., and Harlan, W. R. (1978). "Application of Weight-Height Ratios and Body Indexes to Juvenile Populations—The National Health Examination Survey Data." *Journal of Chronic Diseases* 31: 529–537.

Kingsland, S. (1987). "Evolution and Debates over Human Progress from Darwin to Sociobiology." In M. S. Teitelbaum and J. M. Winter, eds., *Population and Resources in Western Intellectual Traditions.* New York: Cambridge University Press.

Kirby, R. G. and Musson, A. E. (1975). *The Voice of the People. John Doherty, 1798–1854.* Manchester, England: Manchester University Press.

Knight, J. (1984). *The Heights and Weights of Adults in Great Britain.* London: Office of Population Censuses and Surveys.

Koditschek, T. (1990). *Class-Formation and Urban Industrial Society: Bradford, 1750–1850.* New York: Cambridge University Press.

Komlos, J. (1985). "Stature and Nutrition in the Habsburg Monarchy: The Standard of Living and Economic Development in the Eighteenth Century." *American Historical Review* 90: 1149–1160.

————— . (1986). "Patterns of Children's Growth for East-Central Europe in the Eighteenth Century." *Annals of Human Biology* 13: 33–48.

————— . (1987). "The Height and Weight of West Point Cadets: Dietary Change in Antebellum America." *Journal of Economic History* 47: 897–928.

————— . (1989). *Nutrition and Economic Development in the Eighteenth Century Habsburg Monarchy: An Anthropometric History.* Princeton, N.J.: Princeton University Press.

————— . (1990). "Height and Social Status in Eighteenth-Century Germany." *Journal of Interdisciplinary History* 4: 607–621.

Kondratieff, N. D. (1926). "Die Langen Wellen der Konjunktur." *Archiv fur Sozialwissenschaft und Sozialpolitik* 56: 573–609.

Lambert, R. (1963). *Sir John Simon 1816–1904 and English Social Administration.* London: MacGibbon and Kee.

Landauer, T. K. (1973). "Infantile Vaccination and the Secular Trend in Stature." *Ethos* 1: 499–503.

Lane-Fox, A. (Pitt Rivers) (1875). "Note on the Chest Measurements of Recruits." *Journal of the Anthropological Institute of Great Britain and Ireland* 5: 101–106.

————. (1877). "Measurements Taken of the Officers and Men of the Second Royal Survey Militia According to the General Instructions Drawn up by the Anthropometric Committee of the British Association." *Journal of the Anthropological Institute of Great Britain and Ireland* 6: 443–457.

Langdon-Down, J. H. (1866). "Observations on an Ethnic Classification of Idiots." In T. E. Jordan, *Perspectives in Mental Retardation.* Carbondale: Southern Illinois University Press, 1966.

Lankester, E. R. (1880). *Degeneration, A Chapter in Darwinism.* London: Macmillan.

LaPorte, M. (1946). "Effect of War-Imposed Dietary Limitations on Growth of Paris School Children." *American Journal of Diseases of Children* 71: 244–247.

Latta, T. A. (1832). "Malignant Cholera. Documents Communicated by the Central Board of Health, London, Relative to the Treatment of Cholera by the Copious Injection of Aqueous and Saline Fluids in the Veins." *Lancet* 2: 274–277.

Livingstone, D. (1991). "The Moral Discourse of Climate: Historical Considerations on Race, Place and Virtue." *Journal of Historical Geography* 17: 413–434.

Lee, R. (1981). "Short-Term Variation. Vital Rates, Prices and Weather." In E. A. Wrigley and R. S. Schofield, eds., *The Population History of England, 1541–1871.* Cambridge, Mass.: Harvard University Press.

Leech, J. (1841). *Portraits of Children of the Mobility.* London: Richard Bentley.

Leith-Adams, A. (1875). "On the Physical Requirements of the Soldier." *British and Foreign Medico-Chirurgical Review* 55: 202–217.

Levi, L. (1884). "What Is the Social Condition of the Working Classes in 1884 as Compared with 1857 . . . " *Transactions of the National Association for the Promotion of Social Science* 28: 588–606.

Lewis, L. F. (1942). "Secular Trend of Temperature at Oxford." *Quarterly Journal of the Royal Meteorological Society* 68: 61–62.

Liardet, F. (1839). *The State of the Peasantry in the County of Kent.* Central Society of Education. London: Taylor and Walton.

Lindert, P. and Williamson, J. G. (1982). "Revising England's Social Tables 1688–1812." *Explorations in Economic History* 19: 385–408.

——— and Williamson, J. G. (1983). "English Workers' Living Standards During the Industrial Revolution." *Economic History Review* 36: 1–25.

Lindsay, S. M. (1906). "Child Labor A National Problem." *Annals of the American Academy of Political and Social Science* 27: 331–336.

Little, W. J. (1862). "On the Influence of Abnormal Parturition, Difficult Labours, Premature Birth, and Asphyxia Neonatorum, on the Mental and Physical Condition of the Child, Especially in Relation to Deformities." *Transactions of the Obstetrical Society of London.*

Livi, R. (1892). "Essai D'Anthropométrie Militaire: Resultats Obtenus du Dépouillement des Feuilles Sanitaires des Militaires des Classes 1859 à 1863, Fait par l'Inspection de Santé Militaire de l'Armée Italienne . . . " *Bulletin de l'Institut Internationale de Statistique* 7: 273–285.

Lloyd-Jones, R. (1990). "The First Kondratieff: The Long Wave and the British Industrial Revolution." *Journal of Interdisciplinary History* 4: 581–605.

Logan, W. P. D. (1950). "Mortality in England and Wales from 1848 to 1947." *Population Studies* 4: 132–178.

Lomax, E. (1979). "Infantile Syphilis as an Example of Nineteenth Century Belief in the Inheritance of Acquired Characteristics." *Journal of History of Medicine and Allied Sciences* 34: 23–39.

Lombroso, C. (1891). *The Man of Genius.* London: Scott.

London, J. (1903). *People of the Abyss.* London: Macmillan.

Lorimer, D. A. (1978). *Colour, Class and the Victorians.* New York: Holmes and Weier.

Lowe, R. (1983). "The Early Twentieth Century Open Air Movement: Origins and Implications." In N. Parr and D. McNeal, eds., *Fit-*

ness of the Nation—Physical and Health Education in the Nineteenth and Twentieth Centuries. Leicester, England: History of Education Society.

Luckin, B. (1977). "The Final Catastrophe—Cholera in London, 1866." *Medical History* 21: 32–43.

———. (1984). "Evaluating the Sanitary Revolution: Typhus and Typhoid in London, 1851–1900." In R. Woods and J. Woodward, *Urban Disease and Mortality in Nineteenth Century England*. New York: St. Martin's Press.

Lyell, C. (1839). *Elements of Geology*. Philadelphia: Kay.

Macaulay, T. B. (1846). "The Ten Hours Bill." In J. Clive and T. Pinney, eds., *Thomas Babington Macaulay: Selected Writings*. Chicago: University of Chicago Press. 1972.

MacDonagh, O. (1955). "Emigration and the State, 1833–55: An Essay in Administrative History." *Transactions of the Royal Historical Society* 5: 133–159.

———. (1958). "The Nineteenth Century Revolution in Government: A Reappraisal." *Historical Journal:* 52–67.

———. (1961). *A Pattern of Government Growth 1800–1860. The Passenger Acts and Their Enforcement*. London: MacGibbon and Kee.

MacGrigor. (1857). "On Recruiting Statistics." *Lancet* 1 (February 7): 146–147.

Mackenzie, W. L. (1917). *Scottish Mothers and Children: Being Report on the Physical Welfare of Mothers and Children*. Dunfermline: Carnegie United Kingdom Trust.

MacLeod, R. M. (1966). "Social Policy and the Floating Population." *Past and Present* 35: 101–132.

McMaster, A. B. (1911). "Notes on Schoolchildren." *Transactions of the Rochdale Literary and Scientific Society* 10–12 (1909–1916): 69–79.

Macmillan, M. (1896). "The Half-Time System." *The Clarion* (September 12), p. 293.

MacNamara, T. J. (1904). "Physical Condition of Working Class Children." *Nineteenth Century* 66: 307–311.

Malthus, T. (1798). *An Essay on the Principle of Population*. London: Anonymous.

Mangan, J. A. (1986a). *Athleticism in the Victorian and Edwardian Public School.* London and Philadelphia: Falmer Press.

———. (1986b). *The Games Ethic and Imperialism.* London: Viking Books.

Marchand, J. (n.d.). "Aids to Purity," London. Quoted in S. Hynes, *The Edwardian Turn of Mind.* Princeton, N.J.: Princeton University Press, 1968.

Marcus, S. (1974). *Engels, Manchester, and the Working Class.* New York: Random House.

Marshall, H. (1839). *On the Enlisting, Discharging and Pensioning of Soldiers.* London.

Marshall, W. A. (1975). "The Relationships of Variations in Children's Growth Rates to Seasonal Climate Variations." *Annals of Human Biology* 2: 243–250.

Masterman, C. F. G. (1901). *The Heart of the Empire: Discussions of Problems of Modern City Life in England.* London: Unwin.

Matheson, R. E. (1903). "The Housing of the People of Ireland During the Period 1841–1901." *Journal of the Statistical and Social Inquiry Society of Ireland* 11: 83, 196–212.

Maurice, F. (1903). "National Health: A Soldier's Study." *Contemporary Review* 83: 41–56.

Mazumdar, P. M. H. (1980). "The Eugenists and the Residuum: The Problem of the Urban Poor." *Bulletin of the History of Medicine* 54: 204–215.

McGuire, C. M. and White, G. (1955). *The Measurement of Social Status: Research Paper in Human Development No. 3.* Austin: University of Texas Press.

McKelway, A. J. (1906). "Child Labor in the Southern Cotton Mills." *Annals of the American Academy of Political and Social Science* 27: 5–11.

McKeown, T. (1979). *The Role of Medicine: Dream, Mirage or Nemesis?* Oxford: Basil Blackwell.

——— and Record, R. G. (1963). "Reasons for the Decline of Mortality in England and Wales During the Nineteenth Century." *Population Studies* 16: 94–122.

————, Record, R. G., and Turner, R. D. (1975). "An Interpretation of the Decline of Mortality in England and Wales During the Twentieth Century." *Population Studies* 29: 391–422.

McKenzie, J. C. (1962). "The Composition and Nutritional Value of Diets in Manchester and Dukinfield 136 and 1841." *Transactions of the Lancashire and Cheshire Antiquarian Society.* 1962, 72: 123–140.

McMillan, M. (1906). "Building Up the British Race." *Labour Leader* (July 6), p. 100.

MacNeil, K. (1991). "The Case Against Interpreting Regression Weights." *Multiple Linear Regression Viewpoints* 17: 40–47.

————, Kelly, F. J., and MacNeil, J. (1975). *Testing Research Hypotheses Using Multiple Linear Regression.* Carbondale: Southern Illinois University Press.

Mearns, A. (1883). *The Bitter Cry of Outcast London.* London.

Meath, Earl of. (1904). "The Deterioration of British Health and Physique." *Public Health* 16: 387–392.

Meckel, R. (1990). *Save the Babies: American Public Health Reform and the Prevention of Infant Mortality 1850–1929.* Baltimore: Johns Hopkins University Press.

Medical Gentleman. (1851). *An Enquiry into Destitution, Prostitution and Crime in Edinburgh.* Reprinted as *Lowlife in Victorian Edinburgh, by a Medical Gentleman* Edinburgh: Harris, 1980.

Memorandum by the Director General, Army Medical Service, on the Physical Unfitness of Men Offering Themselves for Enlistment in the Army. (1903). London.

Memorandum in Regard to the Condition of the Teeth of School Children, and Report of the Inter-Departmental Committee on Physical Deterioration. (1906). London: British Dental Association.

Mercer, A. (1990). *Disease, Mortality and Population in Transition: Epidemiological-Demographic Change in England Since the Eighteenth Century as Part of a Global Phenomenon.* New York: Columbia University Press.

Mercer, J. E. (1897). "The Conditions of Life in Angel Meadow." *Transactions of the Manchester Statistical Society* 41: 159–180.

Meredith, H. V., Spurgeon, J. H., and Meredith, E. M. (1981). "Early Seriatim Research on Human Somatic Growth." *Growth* 45: 151–167.

Miles, (1902). "Where to Get Men?" *Contemporary Review* 81: 78–86.

Military Asylum. (1823). *The Times* (February 22).

Mills, D. R. (1978). "The Quality of Life in Melbourn, Cambridgeshire, in the Period 1800–1850." *International Review of Social History* 23: 382–404.

Mills, N. (1933). "Child Growth Under the Half-Time Factory System." *Transactions of the Rochdale Literary and Scientific Society* 17–18 (1932–1934): 69–79.

Mitchell, B. (1962). *Abstract of British Historical Statistics.* Cambridge: The University Press.

Mitchell, B. R. (1975). *European Historical Statistics 1750–1970.* New York: Columbia University Press.

Mokyr, J. (1988). Personal communication.

——— and O'Grada, C. (1992). "The Heights of the British and Irish c. 1800–1815: Evidence from Recruits of the East India Company's Army." In J. Komlos, ed., *Essays in Anthropometric History.* (forthcoming).

——— and O'Grada, C. (1988). "Poor and Getting Poorer? Living Standards in Ireland Before the Famine." *Economic History Review* 61: 209–235.

Morant, G. M. (1950). "Secular Changes in the Heights of British People." *Royal Society of London Proceedings* 137: 443–452.

Morel, B. (1857). *Traité des Dégénérescences Physiques, Intellectuelles et Morales De L'Espèce Humaines.* Paris: Baillères.

Morgan, J. E. (1865). "The Danger of Deterioration of Race from the Too Rapid Increase of Great Cities." *Transactions of the National Association for the Promotion of Social Science* 9: 427–449.

Morgan, N. J. (1988). "People or Property? The Objectives of Housing Management Policies in the United Kingdom, 1880–1939." Paper presented to the Social Science History Association.

Morrison, W. D. (1896). *Juvenile Offenders.* London.

Mowat, C. L. (1957). "Charity and Casework in Late Victorian London: The Work of the Charity Organization Society." *Social Service Review* 31: 258–270.

———. (1961). *The Charity Organization Society 1869–1913: Its Ideas and its Work.* London: Methuen.

Muffang, M. H. (1899). "Ecoliers et Etudiants de Liverpool." *L'Anthropologie* 10: 21–41.

Mumford, A. A. (1912). "The Physique of the Modern Boy." *Transactions of the Manchester Statistical Society:* 127–168.

Nardinelli, C. (1980). "Child Labor and the Factory Acts." *Journal of Economic History* 40: 739–755.

———. (1990). *Child Labor and the Industrial Revolution.* Bloomington: Indiana University Press.

National Health and Military Service. (1903). *British Medical Journal* 2: 202–203.

Neale, R. S. (1972). *Class and Ideology in the Nineteenth Century.* London: Routledge and Kegan Paul.

———. (1981). *Class in English History 1680–1850.* Oxford: Basil Blackwell.

Neild, W. (1841). "Comparative Statement of the Income and Expenditure of Certain Families of the Working Classes in Manchester and Dukinfield, in the Years 1836 and 1841." *Journal of the Royal Statistical Society* 4: 320–324.

Neison, F. G. P. (1858). "On Phthisis in the Army." *Proceedings of the Twenty Eighth Meeting of the British Association,* pp. 189–194. London: John Murray.

Newbold, P. and Agiakloglou, C. (1991). "Looking for Evolving Growth Rates and Cycles in British Industrial Production, 1700–1913." *Journal of the Royal Statistical Society* (A) 154: 341–348.

Newens, E. M. and Goldstein, H. (1972). "Height, Weight and the Assessment of Obesity in Children." *British Journal of Preventive and Social Medicine* 26: 33–39.

Newsholme, A. (1905). "Alleged Physical Deterioration in Towns." *Public Health* 17: 293–300.

Nicholas, S., ed. (1988). *Convict Workers: Reinterpreting Australia's Past.* Sydney: Cambridge University Press.

————— and Shergold, P. R. (1988). "Convicts as Workers." In S. Nicholas, ed., *Convict Workers: Reinterpreting Australia's Past.* Sydney: Cambridge University Press.

————— and Steckel, R. H. (1991). "Heights and Living Standards of English Workers During the Early Years of Industrialization, 1770–1815." *Journal of Economic History.* 51: 937–957.

Noble, D. (1843). *Facts and Observations Relative to the Influence of Manufacturers Upon Health and Life.* London: Churchill.

Norton, B. (1981). "Psychologists and Class." In C. Webster, ed., *Biology, Medicine and Society 1840–1940.* London: Cambridge University Press.

"Noxious Effects of Improper Habitations." (1844). *Penny Magazine:* 397–398.

Nylin, J. (1929). *Acta Medica Scandinavica,* Supplementum 31.

Nukada, A. (1975). "Industrialization as a Factor for Secular Increase in Physiques of School Children in Japan." In K. Asahina and A. Shigiya, eds., *Phusiological Adaptability and Nutritional Status of Japanese. B. Growth, Work Capacity and Nutrition of Japanese.* Tokyo: University of Tokyo Press.

O'Brien, P. and Keyder, C. (1978). *Economic Growth in Britain and France 1780–1914.* London: Allen and Unwin.

Oddy, D. J. and Yudkin, J. (1969). An Evaluation of English Diets of the 1860's. *Proceedings of the Nutrition Society.* 28: 13A–14A.

Oddy, D. J. (1982). "The Health of the People." In T. Barker and M. Drake, eds., *Population and Society in Britain 1850–1980.* New York: New York University Press.

Office of Population Censuses and Surveys. (1985). *Mortality Statistics: Serial Tables. Review of the Registrar General on Deaths in England and Wales 1841–1980. Series DH1 No. 15.* London: Her Majesty's Stationery Office.

Olmsted, F. L. (1859). *Walks and Talks of an American Farmer in England.* Reprinted: Ann Arbor: University of Michigan Press, 1967.

"On the Choice of a Labouring Man's Dwelling." (1832). *The Penny Magazine* 2: 15–16.

Oppenheim, J. (1991). *Shattered Nerves: Doctors, Patients, and Depression in Victorian England.* Oxford: Oxford University Press.

Osborn, A. F. (1987). "Assessing the Socio-economic Status of Families." *Sociology* 21: 429–448.

Osborn, A. F. and Morris, T. C. (1979). "The Rationale for a Composite Index of Social Class and Its Evaluation." *British Journal of Sociology* 30: 39–60.

Ostrom, C. W. (1978). *Time Series Analysis: Regression Techniques.* Beverly Hills, Calif.: Sage Publications.

P. J. H. (1960). "Andrew Ure." *Dictionary of National Biography,* vol. 20. Oxford: Oxford University Press.

Palgrave, R. H. I. (1869). "On the House Accommodation of England and Wales, with Reference to the Census of 1871." *Journal of the Royal Statistical Society* 22: 411–427.

Parry, N. A., and McNair, D., eds. (1984). *The Fitness of the Nation— Physical and Health Education in the Nineteenth and Twentieth Centuries.* Leicester, England: History of Education Society.

Pearson, K. (1894). "Growth of St. Louis Children." *Nature* 51: 145–146.

———. (1900). "Data for the Problem of Evolution in Man. III. On the Magnitude of Certain Coefficients of Correlation in Man and Etc." *Proceedings of the Royal Society* 66: 23–37.

———. (1903). "On the Inheritance of the Mental and Moral Characteristics in Man, and its Comparison with the Inheritance of Physical Characters." *Journal of the Anthropological Institute of Great Britain and Ireland* 33: 179–237.

———. (1905). "National Deterioration." *The Times* (August 25).

———. (1907). *National Life from the Standpoint of Science,* 2d ed. London: Black.

Pember Reeves, M. S. R. (1913). *Round About a Pound a Week.* London: Bell.

Phillips, B. (1846). "The Prevalence and Alleged Increase of Scrofula." *Journal of the Statistical Society* 8: 152–157.

"The Physical Condition of Rochdale Children. School Board Return." (1892). *Rochdale Observer* (May 7).

"Physical Degeneration. The Case for Inquiry. I. Origin of the Belief in the Existence of Degeneration in the National Physique." (1903). *British Medical Journal* (November 21): 1338–1339.

Pick, D. (1989). *Faces of Degeneration: Aspects of a European Disorder c. 1848–1914.* Cambridge: Cambridge University Press.

Pickering, H. J. (1901). "The Condition of the Teeth of Schoolchildren." *Public Health* 13: 280–285.

Pinchbeck, I. and Hewitt, M. (1973). *Children in English Society. II. From the Eighteenth Century to the Childrens Act 1848.* London: Routledge and Kegan Paul.

Pineo, P. C., Porter, J., and McRoberts, H. A. (1979). "The 1971 Census and the Socio-economic Classification of Occupations." *Canadian Review of Sociology and Anthropology* 14: 91–102.

Plackett, R. L. (1986). "The Old Statistical Account." *Journal of the Royal Statistical Society* (A) 149: 247–251.

Pooley, C. G., and Irish, S. (1987). "Access to Housing on Merseyside, 1919–39." *Institute of British Geographers: Transactions* 12: 177–190.

Porter, D. (1991). "Enemies of the Race": Biologism, Environmentalism, and Public Health in Victorian England. *Victorian Studies* 34: 159–178.

Porter, W. T. (1894). "The Growth of St. Louis Children." *Transactions of the Academy of Science of St. Louis* 6: 263–380.

"Practical Application of Physiological Facts." (1837). *Penny Magazine* (July 15): 270–273.

Price. (1774). "Observations on the State of the Population in Manchester, and Other Adjacent Places. By Dr. Perceval." *Philosophical Transactions* 64: 54–66.

Price, R. (1972). *An Imperial War and the British Working Class.* London: Routledge and Kegan Paul.

Prochaska, F. K. (1980). *Women and Philanthropy in Nineteenth Century England.* Oxford: Clarendon Press.

———. (1988). *The Voluntary Impulse: Philanthropy in Modern Britain.* London: Faber and Faber.

———. (1990). "Philanthropy." In F. M. C. Thompson, ed., *Cambridge Social History of Britain,* vol. 3. *Social Agencies and Institutions.* Cambridge: Cambridge University Press.

Quennell, P. (1969). *Mayhew's London.* London: Hamlyn Publishing Group.

Quetelet, L.-A. (1835). *A Treatise on Man, And the Development of His Faculties.* Edinburgh: 1842; reprinted: New York: Franklin, 1968.

——. (1871). *Anthropométrie: ou Mésure des Différentes Facultes de l'Homme.* Brussells: G. Muquardt.

Rafter, N. H. (1988). *White Trash: The Eugenic Family Studies 1877– 1919.* Boston: Northeastern University Press.

Ransome, A. (1887). "Pthisis Centers in Manchester and Salford." *Report of the 57th Meeting of the British Association for the Advancement of Science,* p. 852. London: John Murray.

Reed, R. B. and Berkey, C. S. (1989). "Linear Statistical Model for Growth in Stature from Birth to Maturity." *Journal of Human Biology* 1: 257–262.

Reichart, P. A. (1984). "Toothpastes Containing Betel Nut (Areca Catechu L.) from England of the Nineteenth Century." *Journal of the History of Medicine and Allied Sciences* 39: 65–68.

"Relationship of Nutrition, Disease and Social Conditions: A Graphical Presentation." (1983). *Journal of Interdisciplinary History* 14: 503–506.

"Report from the Commissioners on Employment of Children." (1842). *Parliamentary Papers* 14: 5–61.

"Report from the Committee of the House of Commons on the Petitions Against the Employment of Boys in Sweeping Chimneys." (1817). *Parliamentary Papers* 6: 171.

Report of the Fifty Third Meeting of the British Association for the Advancement of Science. (1833). London: John Murray, 1884.

Report of the Interdepartmental Committee on Physical Deterioration. (1903). House of Commons. Sessional Papers, no. 32, appendix.

Report of the Interdepartmental Committee on Partial Exemption from School Attendance, vol. 2, (1909).

The Report of the Poor Law Commissioner, Reprinted from the Times. (1909). London: The Times.

"The Report of the Privy Council upon Physical Deterioration." (1904). *Lancet* 2: 390–392.

Report of the Royal College of Surgeons of England on the Physical Disability of Recruits for the Army. (1903). London.

Report of the Royal Commission on Physical Training (Scotland). (1903). London.

Reports from the Assistant Hand-Loom Weavers' Commissioners. (1839). *Parliamentary Papers* 23.

Richardson, B. W. (1887). *The Health of Nations. A Review of the Works of Edwin Chadwick, with a Biographical Dissertation.* London: Dawson.

Rippon-Seymour, H. (1903). "The Royal Commission on Physical Training (Scotland, 1902)." *Westminister Review* 160: 306–312.

Roberts, C. (1876). "The Physical Requirements of Factory Children." *Journal of the Royal Statistical Society* 39: 681–733.

———. (1878). *Manual of Anthropometry.* London.

———. (1895). "Memorandum on the Medical Inspection of, and Physical Education in, Secondary Schools." Reports from Commissioners, Inspectors, and Others: Secondary Education, *Parliamentary Papers,* 44: 352–374.

———. (1900). "Anthropometry as Applied to Social and Economic Questions." *Humanitarian* 3: 422–429.

Roberts, R. (1971). *The Classic Slum: Salford Life in the First Quarter of the Century.* Manchester, England: Manchester University Press.

Rodger, R. (1965). "Political Economy, Ideology and the Persistence of Working Class Housing Problems in Britain, 1850–1914." *International Review of Social History* 32: 109–143.

Rodgers, B. (1952). "The Social Science Association, 1857–1886." *Manchester School of Economic and Social Studies* 20: 283–310.

Rolt, L. T. C. (1957). *Isambard Kingdom Brunel.* London: Longmans Green.

Rona, R. J., Swan, D. A., and Altman, D. G. (1978). "Social Factors and Height of Primary Schoolchildren in England and Scotland." *Journal of Epidemiology and Community Health* 32: 147–154.

Rona, R. J., and Chinn, S. (1987). "National Study of Health and Growth: Social and Biological Factors Associated with Weight-for-Height and Triceps Skinfold of Children from Ethnic Groups in England." *Annals of Human Biology* 14: 231–248.

Rose, J. (1986). *The Edwardian Temperament, 1895–1919.* Athens: Ohio University Press.

Rosen, G. (1973). "Disease, Debility and Death." In J. H. Dyos and M. Wolff, eds., *The Victorian City: Images and Realities,* vol. 2. London: Kegan Paul.

Rosenbaum, S. (1988). "100 Years of Heights and Weights." *Journal of the Royal Statistical Society* (A) 151: 276–309.

———. (1990). "More Than a Century of Army Medical Statistics." *Journal of the Royal Society of Medicine* 83: 456–463.

———, Skinner, R. K., Knight, I. B., and Garrow, J. S. (1985). "A Survey of Heights and Weights of Adults in Great Britain, 1980." *Annals of Human Biology* 12: 115–127.

Rostow, W. W. (1948). *British Economy of the Nineteenth Century.* Oxford: Clarendon Press.

Rowntree, R. S. (1901). *Poverty: A Study of Town Life.* London: Macmillan.

———. (1904). "Physical Deterioration and the Poverty Line." *Contemporary Review.*

———. (1941). *Poverty and Progress: A Second Social Survey of York.* London: Longmans, Green.

Royal Commission on Physical Training (Scotland): Report. (1903). London.

Ruger, H. A. and Stoessiger, B. (1927). "On the Growth Curves of Certain Characteristics of Man." *Annals of Eugenics* 2: 76–110.

Rumsey, H. (1871). "On a Progressive Physical Degeneracy of Race in the Town Populations of Great Britain." *Transactions of the National Association for the Promotion of Social Science* 15: 466–472.

Rushton, P. (1977). *Housing Conditions and the Family Economy in the Victorian Slum: A Study of a Manchester District, 1790–1871.* Manchester University. Unpublished Ph.D. dissertation.

Russell, J. B. (1888). *Life in One Room.* Glasgow: Maclehose.

Ruskin, J. (1896). *Fors Clavigera,* vol. 3. London: George Allen.

Rutter, M. (1988). *Studies of Social Risk: The Power of Longitudinal Data.* Cambridge: Cambridge University Press.

Sala, G. A. (1857). "Fishers of Men or Recruiting for Her Majesty's Forces in London." *Illustrated Times* 5: 379–381.

Sandberg, L. and Steckel, R. H. (1980). "Soldier, Soldier, Soldier, What Makes You Grow So Tall? A Study of Height, Weight and Nutrition in Sweden 1720–1821." *Economy and History* 23: 91–105.

———. (1987). "Heights and Economic History: The Swedish Case." *Annals of Human Biology* 14: 101–110.

Sargant, G. H. (1887). "Food as an Aid to Elementary Education." *Report of the 57th Meeting of the British Association for the Advancement of Science*, pp. 881–882. London: John Murray.

Schmieken, J. A. (1988). "The Victorians, The Historians, and the Idea of Modernism." *American Historical Review* 93: 287–316.

Schofield, R. (1983). "The Impact of Scarcity and Plenty on Population Change in England, 1541–1871." *Journal of Interdisciplinary History* 14: 265–291.

Schultz, S. K. (1989). *Constructing Urban Culture: American Cities and City Planning, 1800–1920.* Philadelphia, Pennsylvania: Temple University Press.

Scrope, G. P. (1833). *Principles of Political Economy.* London. Cited in W. L. Mitchell, *The Making and Using of Index Numbers.* Washington, D.C.: Bureau of Labor, 1915.

Shaftesbury. (1965). "Children in Mines and Collieries." In W. Kessen, ed., *The Child.* New York: John Wiley and Sons.

Shapiro, E. (1991). "The Nanny Says Yes, but the F.D.A. Says No." *New York Times* (September 7).

Sharpey, Dr. and Boyd, R. (1861). "XI. Tables of the Weights of the Human Body and Internal Organs in the Sane and Insane of Both Sexes at Various Ages, Arranged from 2614 Post-Mortem Examinations." *Philosophical Transactions* (February 2): 241–262.

Shaw, M. E. (1975). "The Children of the Working Class in the Leeds Area, 1830–1871." Unpublished M. Philosophy thesis, London University.

Shee, G. F. (1903). "The Deterioration in the National Physique." *Nineteenth Century* 52: 798–805.

Shepard, R. J. (1991). *Body Composition in Biological Anthropology.* Cambridge: Cambridge University Press.

Shortt, J. (1863). "Notes on Differences in Weight and Stature of Europeans and Some Natives of India." *Transactions of the Ethnological Society* 2: 213–216.

Silva, P. A. (1991). *List of Publications and Reports As At 1 September, 1991*. Dunedin, New Zealand: University of Otago.

Sims, G. R. (1889). *How the Poor Live*. London: Chatto and Windus.

Silver, H. (1977). *The Concept of Popular Education: A Study of Ideas and Social Movements in the Early Nineteenth Century*. London: Methuen.

Simpson, S., ed. (1988). "A Trade Union Solitary: Memoir of a Mid-Nineteenth Century Miner." *History Workshop* 25: 148–165.

Skelley, A. R. (1977). *The Victorian Army at Home. The Recruitment and Terms and Conditions of the British Regulars, 1859–1899*. Montreal: McGill-Queen's University Press.

Slater, G. (1930). *Poverty and the State*. London: Constable.

Smith, A. E. (1904). *Physical Deterioration: Its Causes and Remedy*. New York: E. P. Dutton.

Smith, A. M., Chinn, S., and Rona, R. J. (1980). "Social Factors and Height Gain of Primary Schoolchildren in England and Scotland." *Annals of Human Biology* 7: 115–124.

Smith, E. (1862). "A Statistical Inquiry into the Prevalence of Numerous Conditions Affecting the Constitution in 1000 Consumptive Persons." *Proceedings of the Thirty Second Meeting of the British Association*, pp. 174–175. London: John Murray.

Smith, E. (1864). *Practical Dietary for Families, Schools, and the Labouring Classes*. London.

Smith, F. B. (1988). *The Retreat of Tuberculosis, 1850–1950*. London: Routledge, and Chapman and Hall.

Smith, G. (1870). "The Employment of Children in Brick and Tile Making Considered in Relation to the Factory and Workshop Acts." *Transactions of the National Association for the Promotion of Social Science* 14: 537–540.

———. (1878). *Our Canal Population: A Cry From the Boat Cabins, With Remedy*. London: Haughton.

Smith, W. D. (1974). *Stretching their Bodies: The History of Physical Education*. London: David and Charles.

Smout, T. C. (1986). *A Century of the Scottish People 1830–1950*. London: Collins.

Smyth, A. E. (1904). *Physical Deterioration: Its Causes and the Cure*. London: Murray.

Soloway, R. (1982). "Counting the Degenerates." *Journal of Contemporary History* 17: 137–164.

———. (1990). *Demography and Degeneration: Eugenics and the Declining Birthrate in Twentieth Century Britain*. Chapel Hill: University of North Carolina.

Southall, H. R. (1988). "The Origins of the Depressed Areas:Unemployment, Growth, and Regional Economic Structure in Britain Before 1914." *Economic History Review* 61: 236–258.

Springall, L. M. (1936). *Labouring Life in Norfolk Villages, 1834–1914*. London: Allen and Unwin.

Springhall, J. O. (1971). "The Boy Scouts, Class and Militarism in Relation to British Youth Movements 1908–1930." *International Review of Social History* 16: 125–158.

Stanway, S. (1833). "First Report of the Central Board of His Majesty's Commissioners for Inquiry into the Employment of Children in Factories." *Parliamentary Papers* 20.

"Statement of the Sizes of Men in Different Countries of Scotland, Taken from the Local Militia." (1817). *Edinburgh Medical and Surgical Journal* 13: 260–264.

Steckel, R. (1983). "Height and per Capita Income." *Historical Methods* 16: 1–7.

———. (1979). "Slave Height Profiles from Coastwise Manifests." *Explorations in Economic History.* 16: 363–380.

Steedman, C. (1990). *Childhood, Culture and Class in Britain: Margaret McMillan, 1860–1931*. New Brunswick, New Jersey. Rutgers University Press.

Steet, G. C. (1874–1876). "Notes on the Development and Growth of Boys Between Thirteen and Twenty Years of Age." *St. George's Hospital Reports* 8: 49–56.

Stein, Z., Susser, M., Saenger, G., and Marolla, F. (1975). *Famine and Human Development*. New York: Oxford University Press.

Stephenson, W. (1888). "On the Relation of Weight to Height and the Rate of Growth in Man." *Lancet* 2: 560–564.

Stevens, G. and Cho, J. H. (1985). "Socio-Economic Indexes and the New 1980 Census Occupational Classification Scheme." *Social Science Research* 14: 142–168.

Stewart, W. (1885). "On the Effect that the Trade and Mode of Living Have Upon the Health and Physique of the Lancashire Working People." Unpublished M.D. thesis, Edinburgh University.

Sutter, J., Izac, R. E., and Toan, T. N. (1958). "L'Evolution de la Taille des Polytechniciens, 1801–1954." *Population* 13: 373–406.

Sykes, J. F. J. (1901). *Public Health and Housing. The Influence of the Dwelling upon Health in Relation to the Changing Style of Habitation.* London.

Sykes, W. H., Guy, W. R., and Neison, F. G. P. (1848). "Report of a Committee of the Council of the Statistical Society of London . . . to Investigate the State of the Inhabitants and Their Dwellings in Church Lane, St. Giles." *Quarterly Journal of the Statistical Society of London.* 11: 1–24.

Sylvester, D. W. (1974). *Robert Lowe and Education.* Cambridge: Cambridge University Press.

Symons, J. C. (1842). "Yorkshire Coalfield. Appendix C. Measurement of Collier Boys." *Appendix to the First Report of the Commissioners, Children's Employment Commission.* London: House of Commons.

Szreter, S. R. S. (1986). "The First Scientific Social Structure of Modern Britain 1875–1883." In L. Bonfield, R. M. Smith, and K. Wrightson, eds., *The World We Have Gained.* London: Basil Blackwell.

———. (1988). "The Importance of Social Intervention in Britain's Mortality Decline c. 1890–1914: A Reinterpretation of the Role of Public Health." *Society for the Social History of Medicine* 1: 1–37.

Tanner, J. M. (1981). *A History of the Study of Human Growth.* Cambridge: Cambridge University Press.

———. (1982). The Potential of Auxological Data for Monitoring Economic and Social Well-Being. *Social Science History* 6: 571–581.

———, Whitehouse, R. H., and Takaishi, M. (1966). Standards from Birth to Maturity for Height, Weight, Height Velocity, and Weight Velocity: British Children, 1965. Part II. *Archives of Diseases of Childhood.* 41: 613–635.

————— . (1986) Growth as a Mirror of the Condition of Society: Secular Trends and Class Distinctions. In A. Demirjian and M. Brault Dubuc, eds., *Human Growth: A Multidisciplinary Review.* London. Taylor and Francis.

Taylor, A. J. (1975). *The Standard of Living in Britain in the Industrial Revolution.* London: Methuen.

Taylor, W. (1903). Memorandum on the Physique of Recruits by the Director General, Army Medical Service. *Journal of the Royal Army Medical Corps.* 1: 224–230.

The Broad Street Pump. (1866). *The Times* (July 28 and August 4).

Thompson, E. P. (1980). *The Making of the English Working Class.* London: Pelican Books.

Thompson, F. (1939). *Lark Rise.* Oxford: Oxford University Press.

Thompson, F. M. L. (1988). *The Rise of Respectable Society: A Social History of Victorian Britain, 1830–1900.* London: Fontana.

Thomson, J., and Smith, A. (1877). *Street Life in London.* London: Low, Marston, Searle and Rivington.

Thorne, L. T. (1904). "The Physical Development of the London Schoolboy." *British Medical Journal* (April 9): 829–831.

Tranter, N. L. (1973). *Population Since the Industrial Revolution: The Case of England and Wales.* London: Croom Helm.

Trolloppe, F. (1840). *The Life and Adventures of Michael Armstrong, the Factory Boy.* London: Colburn.

Tucker, R. (1936). "Real Wages of Artisans in London, 1729–1935." *Journal of the American Statistical Association* 31: 78–79.

Tufnell, F. C. (1862). "The Education of Pauper Children." *Transactions of the National Association for the Promotion of Social Science* 6: 278–286.

Tully, A. M. T. (1924). "The Physique of Glasgow Schoolchildren (1921–22)." *Journal of Hygiene* 23: 186–197.

Tuxford, A. W. and Glegg, R. A. (1911). "The Average Height and Weight of English School Children." *British Medical Journal* (June 17): 1423–1424.

"Twenty-Third Annual Report of the Poor Law Board." (1871). *Parliamentary Papers* 27: 207.

Unwin, S., ed. (1918). "Leverholme." *The Six-Hour Day and Other Industrial Questions. by Lord Leverholme.* London: George Allen and Unwin.

Unwin, T. F., ed. (1906). *The Hungry Forties.* London: Unwin.

Ure, A. (1835). *The Philosophy of Manufactures.* London: Charles Knight.

Urwick, E. J., ed. (1904). *Studies of Boy Life in Our Cities.* London: Dent.

Valoaras, V. G. (1946). "Some Effects of Famine on the Population of Greece." *Milbank Memorial Fund Quarterly* 24: 215–234.

van Wieringen, J. C. (1979). "Secular Growth Changes and Environment—An Analysis of Developments in the Netherlands, 1850–1978." *Collegium Antropologicum* 3: 35–48.

Venn, J. (1889). "Cambridge Anthropometry." *Journal of the Anthropological Institute of Great Britain and Ireland* 18: 140–154.

Verhulst, P. F. (1838). "Notice Sur La Loi que la Population Suit dans son Accroissement." *Correspondence Mathematique et Physique* 3, no. 2: 113–121.

Villermé, L.-R. (1829). "Memoire sur LaTaille de l'homme en France." *Annales D'Hygiène Publicque et de Médicine Légale* 1: 351–399.

———. (1840). *Tableau de L'etat Physique et Moral des Ouvriers,* 2 vols. Paris: Renouard.

Vines, J. H. (1903). "The Physique of Scottish Children." *Westminister Review* 160: 319–322.

von Thyszka, C. (1914). *Lohne und Lebenskosten in Westeuropa im 19 Jahrhundert.* Leipzig: vonDunder and Humblot (sic).

Wachter, K. W., and Trussell, J. (1982a). "Estimating Historical Heights." *Journal of the American Statistical Association* 77: 279–293.

———. (1982b). "Rejoinder." *Journal of the American Statistical Association* 77: 301–303.

Wall, R. (1974). *Slum Conditions in London and Dublin.* London: Gregg International Publishing.

———. (1989). *Some Inequalities in the Raising of Boys and Girls in Nineteenth- and Twentieth-Century England and Wales.* Minneapolis: University of Minnesota Press.

Wallace, A. R. (1892). "Human Progress: Past and Future." *Arena* 26: 145–159.

——— . (1893). "Are Individually Acquired Characters Inherited?" *Fortnightly Review* 59: 490–498, 655–658.

Walton, J. K. (1989). "Fish and Chips and the British Working Class, 1870–1930." *Journal of Social History* 23: 243–263.

——— and Wilcox, A. (1991). *Low Life and Moral Improvement in Mid-Victorian England: Liverpool through the Journalism of Hugh Shimmin.* Leicester, England: Leicester University Press.

Walvin, J. (1987). *Victorian Values.* Athens: University of Georgia Press.

Ward, D. (1962). "The Pre-Urban Cadastre and the Urban Pattern of Leeds." *Annals of the American Association of Geographers* 52: 150–166.

Ward, D. A. (1980). "Environs and Neighbours in the 'Two Nations.' Residential Differentiation in Mid-Nineteenth Century Leeds." *Journal of Historical Geography* 6: 133–162.

Ward, W. P., and Ward, P. C. (1984). "Infant Birth Weight and Nutrition in Industrializing Montreal." *American Historical Review* 89: 324–345.

Warner, F. (1892). "Distributions as to Physical Deviations from the Normal as Seen Among 5,000 Children." *Proceedings of the Sixty Second Meeting of the British Association,* pp. 910–911. London: John Murray.

——— . (1893). "Results of an Inquiry as to the Physical and Mental Condition of Fifty Thousand Children Seen in One Hundred and Six Schools." *Journal of the Royal Statistical Society* 56: 71–95.

——— . (1896). "Mental and Physical Conditions among Fifty Thousand Children Seen 1892–94, and the Methods of Studying Recorded Observations, with Special Reference to the Determination of the Causes of Mental Dulness and Other Defects." *Journal of the Royal Statistical Society* 59: 125–162.

Warwick. (1906). *A Nation's Youth. Physical Deterioration: Its Causes and Some Remedies.* London: Cassell.

Watterson, P. A. (1988). "Infant Mortality by Father's Occupation from the 1911 Census of England and Wales." *Demography* 25: 289–306.

Webb, S. (1906). "Physical Degeneracy or Race Suicide?" *The Times* (October 11).

Wenlock, R. W. (1990). "The Diets of British School Children." *Journal of the Royal Society of Health* 110: 50–53.

Werner, E., Bierman, J. M., and French, F. E. (1971). *The Children of Kauai.* Honolulu: University of Hawaii Press.

Werner, E. and Smith, R. S. (1971). *Kauai's Children Come of Age.* Honolulu: University of Hawaii Press.

Werner, E. and Smith, R. S. (1982). *Vulnerable but Invincible: A Longitudinal Study of Resilient Children and Youth.* New York: McGraw Hill.

Werts, C. and Linn, R. L. (1970). "A General Linear Model for Studying Growth." *Psychological Bulletin* 73: 17–22.

Whetham, W. C. D. and Whetham, C. D. (1909). *The Family and The Nation: A Study in Natural Inheritance and Social Responsibility.* London: Longmans, Green.

White, A. (1901). *Efficiency and Empire.* London: Methuen.

Wigglesworth, . (1846). "On the Mortality of Children." *Proceedings of the Sixteenth Meeting of the British Association,* p. 100. London.

Williams, M. H., Bell, J., and Pearson, K. (1914). "A Statistical Study of Oral Temperatures in School Children with Special Reference to Parental, Environmental and Class Differences." *Drapers' Company Research Memoirs: Studies in National Deterioration.* London: Dulau and Co.

Williams, W. M. J. (1894). "A Poor Man's Budget." *Fortnightly Review* 61: 306–326.

Williamson, J. G. (1982). "Was the Industrial Revolution Worth It? Disamenities and Death in Nineteenth-Century British Towns." *Explorations in Economic History* 19: 221–245.

———. (1985). *Did British Capitalism Breed Inequality?* London: Allen and Unwin.

———. (1989). Personal communication.

——— (1990). *Coping With City Growth During the British Industrial Revolution.* Cambridge: Cambridge University Press.

Wilson, A., and Ashplant, T. F. (1988). "Whig History and Present-Centered History." *Historical Journal* 31: 1–16.

Wilson, H. (1905). "Deaths from Overlying of Children." *The Times*. 3 January.

Windle, B. C. A. (1894). "Anthropometric Work in Schools." *Medical Magazine* 2: 631–649.

Winter, J. M. (1979). "Infant Mortality, Maternal Mortality, and Public Health in Britain in the 1930's." *Journal of European Economic History* 8: 439–462.

———. (1982a). "Aspects of the Impact of the First World War on Infant Mortality in Britain." *Journal of European Economic History* 11: 713–738.

———. (1982b). "The Decline of Mortality in Britain 1870–1950." In T. Barker and M. Drake, eds., *Population and Society in Britain 1850–1980*. New York: New York University Press.

Wise, D. (1962). *Diary of William Tayler Footman, 1837*. London: St. Marylebone Society.

Withers, C. W. J. (1988). "Destitution and Migration: Labour Mobility and Relief from Famine in Highland Scotland 1836–1850." *Journal of Historical Geography* 14: 128–150.

Wohl, A. D., ed. (1978). *The Victorian Family: Structure and Stress*. New York: St. Martin's Press.

Wolff, G. (1935). "Increased Bodily Growth of Children Since the War." *Lancet* 1: 1006–1011.

Woods, R. (1978). "Mortality and Sanitary Conditions in the 'Best Governed City in the World'—Birmingham, 1870–1910." *Journal of Historical Geography* 4: 25–36.

——— and Hinde, P. R. A. (1987). "Mortality in Victorian England: Models and Patterns." *Journal of Interdisciplinary History* 18: 27–54.

——— and Woodward, J. (1984). *Urban Disease and Mortality in Nineteenth Century England*. New York: St. Martin's Press.

———, Watterson, P. A., and Woodward, J. H. (1988). "The Causes of Rapid Infant Mortality Decline in England and Wales, 1861–1921, Part I." *Population Studies* 42: 343–366; "Part II." 43: 113–132.

Wrigley, E. A. and Schofield, R. S. (1981). *The Population History of England, 1541–1871*. Cambridge, Mass.: Harvard University Press.

Yasumoto, M. (1973). "Urbanization and Population in an English Town: Leeds During the Industrial Revolution." *Keio Economic Studies* 10: 61–94.

Yeats, J. (1864). "On Human Growth in Towns." *Transactions of the National Society for the Promotion of Social Science* 7: 536–547.

Young, J. A. (1979). "Height, Weight and Health: Anthropometric Study of Human Growth in Nineteenth Century American Medicine." *Bulletin of the History of Medicine* 53: 214–243.

Yule, G. U. (1899). "An Investigation into the Causes of a Change in Pauperism in England, Chiefly During the Last Two Intercensal Decades (Part I)." *Journal of the Royal Statistical Society* 63: 249–268.

Name Index

321

London, J., 32
Lowe, R., 231-232
Luckin, B., 32, 81, 96
Lyell, C., 60, 66

M

MacDonagh, O., 240, 241
MacGrigor, -., 129, 163, 164
Mackenzie, W. L., 42, 249
MacMaster, A. B., 94
Macmillan, M., 55, 220-221
MacNamara, T. J., 243, 246
MacNeil, K., 102
MacNeil, K., Kelly, F. J. and Mac-Neil, J., 102, 105
Malthus, T., 187
Marcus, S., 55
Marshall, H., 155, 160, 161
Marshall, W. A., 98
Martyr, M., 229
Marx, K., 11, 14, 23, 209
Masterman, C. F. G., 20, 44
Matheson, R. E., 35
Mathew, Fr., 254
Maurice, F., ("Miles"), 171, 236
Mayhew, H., 20, 32, 127
McGuire, C. M. and White, G., 126
McKelway, A. J., 156
McKeown, T., 76, 77
McKeown, T. and Record, R. G., 82, 90
McKeown, T., Record, R. G. and Turner, R. D., 81, 90
McKenzie, J. C., 42, 43
McMillan, M., 220-221
MacNeil, K., Kelly, F, J. and McNeil, J., 102
Mearns, A., 31, 228
Meath, Earl of, 236
Meckel, R., 80
Mendel, G., 14, 16, 24
Medical Gentleman, 20, 35, 42
Memorandum in Regard to the Condition of the Teeth of School Children, and Report of the Inter-

Departmental Committee on Physical Deterioration, 93
Mercer, A., 76, 81, 90, 92
Micawber, W., 73
Miles, (see Maurice, F.)
Mill, J. S., 126
Mills, N., 45, 57, 58
"A. Miner", 54
Mitchell, J., 10, 37, 45, 192, 197
Mitchell, B. R., 191
Mokyr, J., 185, 187
Mokyr, J. and O'Grada, C., 118, 155
Morant, G. M., 142, 155, 205
Morel, B., 6, 18, 19
Morgan, J. E., 171
Mowat, C. L., 225
Mumford, A. A., 15, 144

N

Nardinelli, C., 53
Neale, R. S., 126, 150
Neild, W., 67, 69
Neison, F. G. P., 158, 162
Newbold, P. and Agiakloglou, C., 180
Newens, E. M. and Goldstein, H., 149
Newsholme, A., 16, 69
Nicholas, S. and Shergold, P. R., 118, 127
Nicholas, S. and Steckel, R. H., 118
Nicholls, Dr., 118
Nightingale, F., 161, 248
Noble, D., 21, 56
Nylin, J., 99

O

O'Brien, P. and Keyder, C., 184
Oddy, D. J. and Yudkin, J., 67
Oddy, D. J., 2
Olmstead, F. L., 9
Oppenheim, J., 76
Osborn, A. F., 126

Subject Index

W

Printed in Great Britain
by Amazon.co.uk, Ltd.,
Marston Gate.